Blind to Sameness

Blind Oracles

Blind to Sameness

*Sexpectations and the Social
Construction of Male and Female Bodies*

ASIA FRIEDMAN

The University of Chicago Press   Chicago and London

ASIA FRIEDMAN is assistant professor of sociology and criminal justice at University of Delaware.

The University of Chicago Press, Chicago 60637
The University of Chicago Press, Ltd., London
© 2013 by The University of Chicago
All rights reserved. Published 2013.
Printed in the United States of America

22 21 20 19 18 17 16 15 14 13   1 2 3 4 5

ISBN-13: 978-0-226-02346-5 (cloth)
ISBN-13: 978-0-226-02363-2 (paper)
ISBN-13: 978-0-226-02377-9 (e-book)

Library of Congress Cataloging-in-Publication Data

Friedman, Asia.
    Blind to sameness : sexpectations and the social construction of
male and female bodies / Asia Friedman.
        pages cm
    Includes bibliographical references and index.
    ISBN 978-0-226-02346-5 (cloth : alkaline paper) —
ISBN 978-0-226-02363-2 (pbk. : alkaline paper) —
ISBN 978-0-226-02377-9 (e-book)   1. Sex differences (Psychology)—
Social aspects.   2. Sex differences—Social aspects.   3. Sex
recognition (Zoology)—Social aspects.   4. Body image—Social
aspects.   5. Perception—Social aspects.   6. Social perception.
7. Transgender people—Interviews.   8. Blind—Interviews.   I. Title.
    BF692.2.F75 2013
        305.3—dc23
                                                            2012044071

Contents

The body is what it is perceived to be; it could be otherwise if perception were different.

DAVID ARMSTRONG, "BODIES OF KNOWLEDGE"

Above all the other senses, sight makes us know and brings to light the many differences between things.

ARISTOTLE, *METAPHYSICS*

herding this manuscript through the critical final stages. My husband, Jeremy Olshan, entered my life just as these ideas were taking form. He has been a sounding board, an editor, a therapist, and a welcome distraction. I particularly want to acknowledge the many predawn hours he spent proofreading the manuscript before the final submission. I also thank the rest of my family and friends—particularly my sons, Finn and Sawyer—for sustaining me outside of work. Finally, I wish to thank all the blind people and transgender people who gave their valuable time to a young researcher with a lot of strange questions about male and female bodies.

Introduction

In July 1976 the first class of women arrived at West Point for cadet basic training. As with all first-year students, the women were issued uniforms on their first day and required to visit the campus barber if they were not in compliance with "hair regulations." The rules for female cadets stated that hair had to end above the collar and could not stick out more than an inch and a half from any point. Several months later, in early September, the cadets—now uniformly dressed and coiffed—attended an annual dance called the Plebe Hop. To the academy's administrators something immediately seemed amiss. With all the major differences in dress and grooming eliminated, the students looked so much the same that the administrators were unable to visually distinguish the males from the females. As one observer described it, the sight of "mirror-image couples dancing in short hair and dress gray trousers" was so unsettling that the officials swiftly changed the rules: if the female students wanted to dance in the future, they would have to wear skirts.[1]

Suppose we all stopped participating in gendered grooming practices—foregoing gender-specific haircuts, makeup, and clothing, just as a start. Would there still be bodily differences between males and females? The short answer is yes, unquestionably. Some men would still have pronounced hair loss, most men would still have more facial hair, many more women than men would have prominent breasts, and the genitals would of course still exist. Taking the existence of certain biological sex differences as a given, however, there remains another equally important question that is often overlooked in accounts of the social construction of sex: What *else* exists along with sex differences? For instance, are eyes, ears, noses, arms, legs, hands, and toes "male" and "female"? Further, if a significant proportion of the body is *not* sex dimorphic, what happens cognitively to ensure that we almost always visually perceive male and female bodies as more different than similar, and even experience this perception as unproblematic and self-evident? Framed in this way, the key question before scholars of the social construction of sex is, not whether sex differences exist, but what else exists amid sex differences, and why do we not focus on those things in equal measure?

Although it has been well established by gender theorists that the creation and display of difference on (and through) the body is an important aspect of the social construction of gender, highlighting the ways that cultural norms shape how we present our physical differences as the *objects* of perception, the role of the perceiver in sex attribution is much less understood. In light of this, this book explores the question of how—by what kinds of cognitive and sensory processes—perception contributes to the social construction of male and female bodies. That is to say, I highlight the elevation of sex differences not only through gender normative practices of self-presentation and display but through social norms of selective perception. This includes both selective attention to sex differences and selective *inattention* to sex similarities. Previously discussed almost entirely in the context of display, the amplification of sex differences is a well-known feature of the social construction of gender. The corresponding diminishment of sex similarities, however, has essentially been ignored.

My central argument is that when we see sex, some parts of the body are noticed, and others are ignored. In fact, the proportion that is relevant for sex attribution is probably smaller than the proportion that is disregarded. As I will demonstrate, this is especially evident when we consider that dominant conceptions of sex are based only, or mostly, on visual data and therefore exclude all the information available through the other senses, much of which conveys a great deal of ambiguity. The sexes, in short, are not nearly as physically different as they typically seem, yet we are socialized to be blind to their sameness.

Some gender scholars have claimed there are actually between five and twenty biological sexes,[2] while others have suggested that, in an ideal world, there would be only one gender.[3] My approach is not to argue that there is "really" only one sex but to show that there may be one sex or there may be twenty, depending on the particular lens one uses to perceive the human body, what details one considers relevant, and why. That said, I cannot deny the number two has unique—and uniquely distorting—cognitive properties. Binaries invite oppositional logic, rigid thinking, and disproportionate attention to differences (and therefore disproportionate inattention to similarities). Any number beyond two, on the other hand, is inherently multidimensional, does not lend itself as easily to bifurcation, and forces us to contend with more ambiguity, making the cognitive and perceptual work of categorization much more apparent. In light of this, I am committed to unsettling the binary opposition between male and female, not to make the point that sex sameness is the more empirically correct view but to promote a more complex, flexible-minded understanding of sex.

For the most part, in this book, I use the term *gender* when referring to normative cultural discourses about maleness/masculinity and femaleness/femininity, and the term *sex* when discussing bodily differences. Ultimately, however, one of the key implications of my argument is that the sex/gender distinction is a false dichotomy, based on the mistaken idea that what separates sex from gender is that sex is purely biological. Sex is also a sociocultural product. Looked at one way, the sex/gender distinction was meant to capture that fact—to acknowledge the cultural dimension of maleness and femaleness—but because of its conceptual structure, it partitions off a terrain of "sex proper" that is defined as purely biological. Vital to our understanding as they may be, biological contributions to the study of sex are certainly not the entire story.

Further, while sex attribution is my case, I also have a broader agenda, which is to present a general sociological theory of sensory perception. Just as Simone de Beauvoir analyzed gender as a case study in phenomenology, I propose that gender, particularly as it manifests as a cognitive schema for seeing human bodies, is a powerful case study in social perception. The fact that our perceived reality is constructed is pretty well-worn territory. I am much more interested in what I see as the next question, which is to examine the *mechanisms* of social construction. As a result, I mostly restrict my focus to the *how* questions of the social construction of reality. Building on perceptions of sex, I argue that the social construction of visual perception is a key mechanism of the social construction of reality in general, and that attention and disattention are among the primary sociocognitive processes involved. I make this argument in part by showing that some notion of selective sensory attention underlies five of the major concepts scholars have previously developed to describe the social construction of reality (frame, schema, habitus, perspective, and thought style).

Distilled to a generic sociological principle, the point is that we always see things through one or more lenses, or filters, that shape and package the world around us. More specifically, there is always "excess" visual information that, while equally real and technically perceptible, remains unnoticed because we are primed—whether by language, social expectations, prior experience, or social norms—to focus on other details. In short, we visually attend to what we have learned is salient, sometimes even to the point that social forms of salience totally obscure the logic of the biological information.

Consider the familiar concept of the "opposite" sex, which implies the sexes are not just different but different to the greatest degree possible. While some amount of biological difference—which we might think of as complementarity—is required for sexual reproduction, Raymond Birdwhistell's research analyzing sex differences in nonverbal communication proposes that humans are actually one of a number of "weakly dimorphic" species.[4] Genetically speaking, males and females are in fact 98 percent identical.[5] Yet the cultural notion of "opposite" sexes expands that 2 percent difference to 100 percent. Indeed, when we pointedly attend to the specificity and complexity of human bodies, it becomes immediately evident that it is social, not biological, logic that leads us to see male and female bodies as "opposites." Only by social measures are we more different than similar.

Following Erving Goffman, I conceptualize perception as an active social process. However passive the role of the audience may seem, the perceiver constantly makes "inferences" and interprets the information provided by the performer, since these signs are never sufficient in and of themselves to define the situation.[6] As human beings, in Phillip Vannini, Dennis Waskul, and Simon Gottschalk's words, we simultaneously *sense* and *make sense of* what we perceive. "To see, for example, entails more than opening our eyes to allow light passively to bounce off our retinas. We must actively perceive that which is seen and thus *make sense* of somatic experiences. . . . In this way, sensing and sense-making are necessarily conjoined, codetermined, and mutually emergent in active and reflexive practices in which we are both the subject and object of the sensations we perceive or, for that matter, fail to recognize."[7] The concept of *perceptual work*[8] both foregrounds those aspects of sensory perception that make it an active cultural process and connects the sociology of perception to conceptual models in other sociological subfields that highlight the interplay of cultural constraint and agency in seemingly personal processes, as exemplified by the concepts of *identity work, body work, memory work, autobiographical work,* and *emotional labor.*[9] More broadly, what underlies the concept of perceptual work is the idea that sensory "objects" are never self-evident and require interpretation and meaning construction by the perceiver. This insight has a long history in symbolic interactionism and ethnomethodology, perhaps most famously illustrated in Howard Becker's study on marijuana use, in which he argues that perceiving and interpreting the effects of marijuana are far from purely physiological, since socially learned reflexive work is required to understand how the otherwise "vague impulses and desires" should be experienced and interpreted.[10]

Indeed, a key theme of the epistemology of the past few decades has been the discrediting of the idea of a raw perceptual "given," completely unmediated by concepts.[11] This growing agreement that perceptions are always at some level conceptions is also becoming visible within cognitive science; for instance, the new field of social cognitive neuroscience aims to relate brain mechanisms to the typical concerns of social psychologists, challenging the presumption that scientists are not interested in culture or the social world.[12] One common critique of brain mapping is that it is reductionist, looking only at brain matter and wiring. Yet at the same time, the field is becoming quite inclusive of things like culture and nurture—particularly when they show up as visible differences in the brain.[13] However, recent social scientific research on imaging technologies (which is how neuroscientists typically study perception) shows that brain scientists are often not very self-reflexive about the interpretive work involved in visual perception—the complexities of "seeing" and "not seeing" when reading brain images, as well as how the cultural contexts of visuality and disciplinary boundaries influence how interpretations circulate and are received.[14] This research points out that a comprehensive understanding of magnetic resonance imaging (MRI) and positron emission tomography (PET) images requires an account of the environment of production and reception of such images, and more generally that social scientists offer a sophisticated understanding of the norms, patterns, and conventions involved in perception—what Vannini, Waskul, and Gottschalk refer to as the "sensory or somatic order."[15]

For example, there is an emerging collection of research beginning to coalesce around a sociology of the invisible.[16] This includes work on social norms and patterns of ignorance, denial, erasure, and disattention. When analyzing visual perception, it is essential to study what goes unseen, not because of particular properties of the stimulus itself, which brain scientists do explore,[17] but because it is "irrelevant" to the perceiver. These spaces of invisibility have their own patterns and shapes, and complement what is seen to create social order as we know it.[18] More broadly, cultural sociologists and cognitive sociologists are interested in the ways that norms of attention and relevance, as well as norms of inattention and irrelevance, cause us to see and not see certain social realities. A sociology of the senses therefore offers an understanding of perception that is important and distinct from traditions of research on perception in other disciplines, such as psychology, philosophy, and neuroscience; yet there is currently no coherent, codified subfield of sociology devoted to perception.

While cognitive and cultural sociology can provide a rich conceptual vocabulary to address perceptual norms, perceptual patterns, and processes of perceptual enculturation, sociologists are traditionally less sure-footed when it comes to accounting for the role of materiality in social processes, though this has changed significantly in the last several decades with the rapid growth of the sociology of the body and embodiment. Although I do not focus on the neuronal aspects of visual processing, a key thread of my argument in chapter 2 and throughout the book is that social scientists need to develop better metaphors and conceptual systems to capture the interaction of biology and culture, and I propose *filter analysis* as one promising possibility.

When using the term *filter* I specifically have in mind a mental "strainer," or "sieve," through which visual stimuli pass before they are consciously perceived, letting in culturally approved details while sifting out the culturally irrelevant. This approach, which directly engages with the body's fleshy materiality by seeking out this "perceptual residue" or "bodily excess," avoids lapsing into overly textual and disembodied accounts of the social construction of the body. This has been correctly identified as a limitation of many theories of the social construction of the body (and sex in particular), especially those rooted in queer theory and poststructuralist philosophy—for instance, Judith Butler's argument that sex is always already gender.[19] The filter metaphor provides a more grounded approach to analyzing the social construction of the body by highlighting those features of the materiality of bodies that are normatively disattended.

In trying to capture the process of sex attribution, I faced a methodological challenge shared by anyone who studies these taken-for-granted processes informing social life: How to examine a perceptual process that is largely automatic and subconscious, and that most people believe is self-evident? My solution to this problem was to bring together two groups who represent extreme cases in relation to the visual perception of male and female bodies. I adopt the perspective of "outsiders," people who either do not participate in visual sex attribution or do it very differently, and "experts," people who are unusually self-conscious and deliberate about sex attribution.

I chose to interview blind people because, given the centrality of visual information to sex attribution among the sighted, their narratives provide access to a perceptual experience of sexed bodies that is totally different in sensory content from the typical sighted experience. Drawing on twenty-seven in-depth interviews, I highlight the primary cues blind people use to attribute sex, as well as several distinctive features of the nonvisual *process* of sex attribution (including salience, speed, and diachronicity). What I found, in brief, is that while blind people are unable to perceive certain sex differences that seem visually obvious, the sighted are equally unaware of many sensory aspects of sex that are obvious to blind people. Their rarely foregrounded nonvisual modes of perceiving bodies thus bring to light aspects of the process of visual sex attribution that we may otherwise take for granted as sighted people, and clarify the extent to which our dominant understanding of sex is specifically "sex seen," as opposed to "sex sensed" more broadly. In a way, then, I studied blind people to show that the sighted are actually "blind" too. More generally, in light of the exceptional social prominence of visual perception, sociologists can gain great insight into the social construction of reality by bracketing the visual and exploring other modes of sensory perception.

I describe these respondents as *blind* rather than using other terms such as *visually impaired*, because almost without exception, this is the word they use and prefer. As with any term, however, there are complexities obscured by the category *blind*. Some of the respondents never had any visual perception, while others were born with varying degrees of sight that later disappeared or significantly worsened: just over half the participants were born blind or lost their vision in the first year of life; three participants became blind between ages 1 and 10; the remaining ten became blind at age 11 or older. Further, even within each of those groups, blindness manifests in different ways. Some respondents see absolutely nothing—one person described this as trying to see through your elbow. At the other end of the spectrum are those respondents who have a very limited amount of useable visual perception (only in one area of their field of vision, for example, or only when holding something very close to their eyes). I did not predefine who would qualify as blind for the purposes of this study, allowing anyone to participate if they understood themselves as blind. I initially thought there might be interesting differences between those respondents who never had vision or lost their vision at a very early age (and thus were never exposed to visual sex differences) and those who were sighted into late childhood or adulthood. Despite looking across these groups for patterns of variation, I did not observe significant systematic differences in their descriptions of how they currently attribute sex. None of the respondents currently had enough visual acuity to use visual information to assign people as "male" or "female" in everyday interactions.

While blind people made interesting informants primarily because they do *not* participate in visual sex attribution, transgender people possess varying degrees of "expert knowledge" about seeing sex. Many transgender people actively and consciously present themselves as female (if they were assigned "male" at birth) or male (if originally assigned a "female" sex). As a result, they are deeply aware of the differences between male and female bodies—as well as their underlying similarities. This is not to say that transpeople are more deliberately "doing gender"[20] than the rest of us (with the attendant implication of falsehood or fabrication). At least in part, their elevated awareness arises because non-transgender (*cisgender*) people look so hard at *them*, and then in turn they look hard at themselves as they try to avoid drawing the focus of that disciplining gaze. This perspective gives them different sensitivities to how they attribute bodies as male or female, as well as to how, when, and why they are—or are not—"read" as male and female by others.

I use *transgender* as an umbrella term to capture a continuum of "differently" sexed and gendered identities that encompasses transsexuals, cross-dressers, and anyone else who self-identifies as transgender or whose gender identity does not correspond normatively with his or her birth sex.[21] When referring to specific respondents, I use whatever terminology they used to describe themselves to me. These terms included *transsexual* (twenty-seven respondents), *transgender/transgenderist* (seven respondents), *cross-dresser* (four respondents), and *intersexual* (four respondents). I offer the following definitions with the understanding that these are rapidly changing identity terms and always contested: *Cross-dressers* present as their gender "opposite," although they usually do not do so full-time, and for the most part they rely on clothing, wigs, and cosmetics, and do not wish to physically alter their bodies (although there is variation on this point, as many male-to-female cross-dressers, for instance, do have electrolysis to remove their facial hair, and some take hormones). *Transsexuals* generally have an overwhelming desire to surgically alter their sex, but the degree to which they have or will act on this desire can vary. While some have already had sexual reassignment surgery (SRS), many are *preoperative*, meaning they plan to have chest reconstruction and/or SRS in the future. In other cases, transsexuals have no plans for surgery and intend to remain *nonoperative*. When people refer to themselves as *transgender*, either this can be intended to invoke the whole spectrum of categories I am describing, or it can mean that they wish to present as androgynous or divide their time living in two different gender roles (another more recent term for this is *genderqueer*, although none of my respondents referred to themselves this way). Many transgenderists take hormones and undergo electrolysis, and some plan to have, or have had, facial or chest surgery. For the most part, they do not wish to have SRS. *Intersexuals* are people born with both male and female sexual characteristics (genitals or gonads). Cross-dressers, transsexuals, and transgenderists can each be either male-to-female (MTF, or *transwomen*) or female-to-male (FTM, or *transmen*), which refers to the direction of their transition—from their sex assignment at birth to the sex or gender with which they currently identify. My sample includes thirty-six transwomen and five transmen. It is unclear why more transwomen than transmen responded to my study announcement. When I asked my respondents about this, several suggested that with the use of testosterone transmen can often develop an appearance indistinguishable from non-transgender men, allowing them significant leeway in making decisions about whether to publicly identify as transsexual. As a result they are more likely to "go stealth" or "woodwork" and thus would no longer be "out" as transpeople, an option not as many transwomen have.[22]

There is clearly much variability within the umbrella category *transgender*. While not perfectly distributed, my sample includes a fairly broad representation of that spectrum of lived experience. Despite this variation, what all these different identities have in common is that they do not take sex attribution for granted in the same way cisgender people do.

I did not include a "control" group to represent the typical visual process of sex attribution. My reasoning is that, by nature, the taken-for-granted is impossible to ask about directly, as ethnomethodologists and symbolic interactionists have long pointed out. This of course was the reason for Harold Garfinkel's "breaching experiments"—to help identify the taken-for-granted by serving as "aids to a sluggish imagination."[23] Although it is not an experiment, this study is designed around two populations that, for reasons of circumstance, speak from unique perspectives that magnify the social construction of dominant visual perceptions of sex. Kristen Schilt similarly argued that the experiences of transgender people can provide theoretical and empirical leverage on broader social processes; in her case, those processes that uphold workplace gender inequality.[24] Here I continue her empirical illustration of transgender people's unique perspective on gender, while also including a second group whose experiences provide a very different, but similarly unique, perspective on visual sex attribution. This approach also reflects the distinction Susan Stryker makes between "transgender studies" and "the study of transgender phenomena." In "transgender studies," she argues, "it is not just transgender phenomena per se that are of interest, but rather the manner in which these phenomena reveal the operations of systems and institutions that simultaneously produce various possibilities of viable personhood, and eliminate others. Thus the field of transgender studies, far from being an inconsequentially narrow specialization . . . represents a significant and ongoing critical engagement with some of the most trenchant issues in contemporary humanities, social sciences, and biomedical research."[25] Generally speaking, then, although both transgender people and blind people are in an exceptional position with regard to visual perceptions of sex, I use their narratives not only to highlight their differences but also to shed light on more commonplace practices of sex attribution.

Most fundamentally, I aim to challenge the visual self-evidence of sex differences—to tell a story that helps the reader see the body differently. One way I do that is by examining the ways the respondents' narratives reveal our taken-for-granted cognitive and perceptual map of the body, bringing some of what is normally backgrounded into the foreground. I also use their descriptions to dismantle the usual visual gestalt for seeing sex, breaking the body down into parts in order to assess their sex specificity individually.

The research took the form of semistructured life-history interviews. While I had a number of different questions in mind based on my interest in capturing the perceptual processes behind sex attribution, I also allowed the respondents to direct the discussion in order to learn what was most salient to them about bodily sex and sex attribution. Before starting the interviews, I was unsure how I would be received as a cisgender woman researching transgender people and as a sighted person studying the blind. While I do not believe it is necessary to be an "insider" to establish good rapport or to gain acceptance as a researcher, I was careful to be open about my interests, and I made clear that I was willing to answer questions about myself as well as the study. Some respondents did ask me why I was interested in this subject, and I responded honestly that my choices were mostly driven by theoretical questions in the sociology of cognition and perception, the sociology of the body, and gender studies, but that a close friend also came out as a transman and transitioned just prior to my deciding on the design of the empirical portion of the study, which was probably not coincidental.

During the interviews it became evident that some of the blind respondents in particular had agreed to speak with me despite reservations about the value of social research, especially when studies emphasize the ways blind people are different. These respondents were concerned about whether such a focus on differences hinders societal acceptance for blind people. This suspicion of dwelling on differences underlies one of the fundamental analytic strategies of critical disability studies, which is to highlight the continuum between "able" and "disabled" bodies—for instance, reconceptualizing variations in sensory perception as normal and fundamental to human experience, rather than "impairments," a strategy Lennard Davis refers to as defamiliarizing disability.[26] Stephen Kuusisto's description of the "planet of the blind" as a place where "no one needs to be cured" is another example of this perspective, as is Rod Michalko's argument that blindness is not exceptional but can actually teach us about sight.[27] When it seemed necessary and appropriate, I explained to these respondents that I am at least as interested in the ways that they are similar to sighted people as I am in their differences, and that my primary aim is to increase awareness of the multiplicity of perceptual possibilities. This seemed to satisfy at least some of their concerns, and my sense is that they usually felt more positive about the research by the end of the interview. Most of the transgender people I spoke with seemed very comfortable being interviewed, and some in fact made comments about the potential value of social research.

In addition to participating in the interviews, I asked most of the transgender respondents I met in person and a few of those I interviewed over e-mail or Internet chat to complete a one-page survey that asked them to rate twenty-three different body parts on a scale of 1 to 10 in terms of their importance for sex attribution, and I refer to these results occasionally to add support or complexity to a theme from the interview material. To broaden the evidence for my claims, I also incorporate a number of compelling fragments of popular culture that capture aspects of the hegemonic cultural narrative about sexed bodies. My data allow me to discuss only contemporary US norms, though I briefly present evidence that other cultures participate in at least some comparable sex-differentiating practices. (For more detailed information about my samples and research methods, see the methodological appendix.)

When analyzing the interviews, I approached them from a perspective that combines the sociology of culture, cognition, and perception, the sociology of the body, and gender theory (including certain aspects of queer theory and transgender studies), and in turn this research brings new insights and conceptual tools to each of these fields. In relation to gender theory, I join those who argue that sex is as much a product of social norms and conditioning as it is a product of nature.[28] There are various ways scholars have previously argued that sex is socially constructed, including highlighting the exceptions to binary sex,[29] identifying historical differences in conceptualizations of sex,[30] and analyzing the ways gender norms influence the science on sex differences.[31] The particular way that I have chosen to illustrate that sex is a social product is to treat the concepts of *gender* and *sex difference* as categories of the mind that construct our visual experience of bodily sex. Stated differently, I argue that *sex difference is a mental filter through which we construct visually distinct things called "male" and "female" bodies.* This is quite similar to Suzanne Kessler and Wendy McKenna's view of gender as an a priori cognitive schema that structures the phenomenal world. As Mary Hawkesworth argues, however, the notion of a cognitive schema that underlies Kessler and McKenna's work is undertheorized.[32] I go further than they did in specifying the mechanics of the cognitive and perceptual dimension of gender, and propose that using the metaphor of a social filter to analyze visual perception allows for more precise descriptions of what goes on interpretively when we see sex.

The notion of a *sociocognitive filter* is the conceptual tool I bring to cognitive and cultural sociology. Although the cognitive psychologist Donald Broadbent proposed a filter model of attention in 1958 to explain how certain sensory data are passed over with very little processing, the filter metaphor has not had much influence in cognitive and cultural sociology. This is despite the fact that selective attention is a central concern of the sociology of the mind.[33] Further, as I demonstrate in chapter 1, some notion of selective visual attention actually underlies many of the most prominent theories of the social construction of reality.

One of the benefits of filter analysis is that it allows for a sustained focus on these visual foundations of the social construction of reality. While sociologists have long claimed reality is socially constructed, they have not sufficiently attended to the role of sensory perception in the construction process. In particular, given its unique social prominence, we must take visual perception much more seriously as a central mechanism of the social construction of reality. At the same time, however, we want to avoid overlooking the nonvisual. Sociologists can gain great insight by bracketing the visual and attending instead to other rarely foregrounded modes of sensory perception.

The metaphor of filtration also offers a new way to think about the relationship between social constructionist perspectives and material reality, one that highlights the interaction of biology and culture without denying either one. In bringing equal focus to what we perceive and what we ignore, the filter metaphor encourages respectful acknowledgment of both biology and culture in forming our perceptions of male and female bodies, thus facilitating a "material social constructionism." Monica Casper and Lisa Jean Moore describe this perspective as follows:

We work in a tradition of material social constructionism and thus ground our analysis in the historical and sociocultural forces that have shaped and created bodies. We consider these bodies as shifting and plural, alive with multiple potentials. . . . Although corporeality must be acknowledged and integrated into social theory, corporeality itself is not static. . . . Social scientists must resist the temptation to see corporeality as sui generis, even though bodies might appear to have obdurate and consistent physical characteristics. For at the same moment that actual physical bodies exist, our understanding of these bodies, our interpretations and explanations of bodily processes, give meaning to their materiality.[34]

While biology certainly structures our perceptions, it cannot fully account for the patterns of attention and disattention that lead us to group human beings into visually distinct things called "male" and "female." Some of what we see when we see sex is real biological differences. But there is also tremendous cultural pressure to ignore sex similarities. This cultural blindness to sex sameness is a hegemonic perceptual norm that is hard to resist—a "social fact."[35] To account for these important patterns of inattention, we must specifically examine what we *cannot* see in order to see sex differences.

Like "silence breakers," who defy social conventions of what should be noticed by discussing the undiscussable, one of my main objectives in this work is to highlight the many physical similarities between the sexes that are there, ready to be acknowledged, but are normally relegated to the background of our perceptions.[36] The observation that the shape of background regions is often not registered perceptually (even though it is technically equally available to the senses) dates back to the Gestalt psychologist Edgar Rubin, whose famous figure/ground vase demonstrates the cognitive practice of selective attention (see fig. 1).[37] While some amount of backgrounding is necessary to see any meaningful "figure," when norms of disattention become reified, sex differences begin to seem as though they are *actually* more salient than sex similarities, when they are only more *socially* salient. What silence breakers do generically is to unsettle these norms of attention, bringing the background into the foreground.[38] Indeed, when the background is pointed out, one begins to see both the vase and the faces in Rubin's

FIGURE 1   The Rubin vase.

example, suggesting that acknowledging the background promotes mental flexibility.

This is my approach to demonstrating the social construction of sex. Using the metaphor of a social filter to guide my analysis, I examine the mental and perceptual act of sex attribution, highlighting both what we are socially expected to notice and what we are socially expected to ignore. By increasing the visibility of the background of "male" and "female" bodies, I foreground the proverbial elephant in the room, sex sameness, illustrating the powerful role selective perception plays in the social construction of "male" and "female" bodies. This more proportionate attention to sex similarities and sex differences, I argue, cultivates the mental flexibility necessary to see both possibilities.

I organized this book thematically, rather than treating blind and transgender people as two separate "case studies." In broad strokes, the progression of my argument is as follows: In chapter 1 I explore socio-optical construction, the visual dimension of the social construction of reality, and present filter analysis as a conceptual system for the development of a more comprehensive sociology of perception. In chapter 2, I bring this focus on perception to the sexed body, introducing the mental filter of sex difference and the concept of *sexpectations*, the belief that "everyone is always either male or female" that organizes our visual perceptions of bodies. I also highlight the overwhelming number of social norms and institutions that emphasize sex differences while ignoring sex similarities. Chapter 3 considers in much greater detail the socio-optical construction of sex difference, focusing specifically on social norms of attention and relevance. I present lists of the most common visual and nonvisual sex cues, breaking the usual gestalt-like, holistic impression of sex into its component parts. In chapter 4 my primary target is what is typically *not* seen—those bodily details that are cognitively filtered out of our perceptions or eliminated through polarizing display practices. Here I present evidence that "male" and "female" bodies are proportionately more similar than different, but that we are socialized to be blind to sex sameness. Chapter 5 extends this exploration of sex sameness beyond my respondents' narratives, bringing in evidence from anatomy textbooks, drawing textbooks, and body measurements, among other things. I conclude by considering the broader intellectual implications of *bodily excess* and *perceptual residue*, two of the key conceptual insights of filter analysis, specifically highlighting their potential as analytical devices to promote mental flexibility.

Toward a Sociology of Perception

There is always more than one way to see something. This was the fundamental insight of Bronislaw Malinowski's observation that the Trobriand Islanders usually perceived children as resembling their father, even when he saw stronger resemblances to the mother.[1] It is also supported by experimental research on cultural differences in sensory perception spanning at least half a century. For instance, James Bagby's 1957 study found that when presented with two different images simultaneously, one depicting a scene from US culture (such as a baseball game) and one depicting a comparable scene from Mexican culture (such as a bullfight), Mexicans and Americans selectively perceive the scene from their own culture.[2] Similar research demonstrated that people from India and people from the United States tend to recall different details of wedding ceremonies, and that East Asians are more likely to attend to a broad perceptual field, while Westerners tend to center their attention on a focal object.[3]

Such optical diversity, however, is not just cross-cultural. Different historical periods can also constitute distinct "optical communities."[4] This is the enduring conclusion of Ludwik Fleck's argument that historically distinct "thought styles" resulted in different interpretations of the same bacterial cultures,[5] as well as Thomas Kuhn's observation that scientists perceive the exact same instruments and experimental materials differently under different historical "paradigms." As Kuhn describes: "After the assimilation of Franklin's paradigm, the electrician looking at a Leyden jar saw something different from what he had seen before. The device had become a condenser, for which neither the jar shape nor glass was required. . . . Lavoisier . . . saw oxygen where Priestly had seen desophlostated air and where others had seen nothing at all."[6]

Visual perception of the same sensory information also varies *within* the same culture and the same historical period. Gender, race, class, occupations, and even hobbies can all entail distinct perceptual conventions and forms of perceptual expertise. Studies of eyewitness accounts, for instance, have found that males and females tend to notice different aspects of a scene and thereby remember somewhat different details.[7] An extensive array of research also demonstrates that people are much better at recognizing faces of their own race or ethnic group.[8] In the case of occupations, Charles Goodwin writes about the development and use of "professional vision,"[9] adding support to Fleck's prior argument that scientific training includes visual socialization through which scientists gain a "readiness for directed perception."[10] As N. R. Hanson put it, "The infant and the layman can see: they are not blind. But they cannot see what the physicist sees; they are blind to what he sees."[11] Consider in this context the perceptual expertise of radiologists described by Jerome Groopman: "The flux of white specks across a black background makes the discrete outlines of organs difficult, if not impossible, for me to make out. Of course, for . . . radiologists who use this technology daily, the images are as familiar as the palms of their hands, and the contrasts of black, white, and gray full of meaning."[12] The same is true of other professions, which is why C. Wright Mills argues that "different technical elites possess different perceptual capacities."[13] Scholars have offered similar observations about the optical socialization involved in pursuing different hobbies. Gary Fine, for instance, found that mushroom hunters perceive amazing amounts of sensory detail invisible to the uninitiated, who lack the relevant "template for looking."[14] Finally, Pierre Bourdieu has argued that class position is attended by "perceptual schemes" that structure aesthetic judgments about art, among other things.[15]

Despite these accounts of diverse optical communities at almost every level of analysis, very few sustained sociological examinations of perception have emerged. Each of the optical communities alluded to above gives rise to perceptual patterns that are neither individual nor universally human. Rather, these patterns are the result of "optical socialization," constituting a characteristically sociological dimension of visual perception.[16] The distinct scope and focus of the sociology of perception is the intermediate level of analysis between "perceptual individualism" and "perceptual universalism," which consists of the many *perceptual norms, perceptual traditions,* and *processes of perceptual enculturation* associated with membership in different social groups. In other words, the sociology of perception ignores perceptual idiosyncrasies but does not assume everyone perceives in a universal way. Given what we already know, the most interesting questions to be addressed by the sociology of perception do not have to do with *whether* culture influences perception, which has been at least preliminarily established, but with *how*—through what kinds of sociocognitive and perceptual *processes*—this optical diversity is created.

Among the most important reasons to develop a more comprehensive sociology of perception is that it challenges the taken-for-granted epistemology of sight—the assumption that our visual perceptions are a complete, unaltered reflection of the sensory stimuli provided by the empirical world, which largely endures despite growing acknowledgment in both the social and cognitive sciences that sensory perceptions are never unmediated by concepts. Before going further, then, it may be helpful to more fully define this "commonsense" view. It is typically assumed that seeing is a passive input process in which sensory stimuli are the only influence. In this understanding, seeing does not involve thinking or interpretation but is a matter of direct sensory perception.[17] The metaphor that best captures this folk theory of sight is the mirror, which suggests that what is seen is a mirror image of empirical reality without distortion or selection.[18]

This constellation of beliefs also leads us to trust sight uniquely among the senses. Many sayings reflect this faith in vision: "I saw it with my own eyes"; "sight unseen"; "seeing is believing"; "a picture is worth a thousand words." In this way, sight is elevated over the other senses in terms of its ability to provide accurate information about a perceptual object. Sayings that capture this association between vision and truth are to "have vision," to "see the light," and to "see things as they really are."[19]

Despite the many examples of different optical communities, then, people are often unaware of sociocultural influences on visual perception. A sociology of perception challenges the taken-for-granted folk theories of sight that do not acknowledge socio-optical diversity or its epistemological implications.

Another important reason to examine sensory perception sociologically is that perception is a powerful but understudied dimension of the social construction of reality. For instance, in *The Social Construction of Reality*, Peter Berger and Thomas Luckmann make the claim that conversation is the *most important* vehicle of reality maintenance;[20] perception, on the other hand, does not receive any explicit acknowledgment as playing a role in the social construction process. There is no entry in the index under *perception, vision, visual, sensory,* or *senses.* Yet many passages, such as the one that follows, seem to demand an analysis of the social construction of perception: "The reality of everyday life is taken for granted *as* reality. It does not require additional verification over and beyond its simple presence. It is simply *there,* as self-evident and compelling facticity. I *know* that it is real."[21] Yet how do we gain this "knowledge" that reality is "simply *there*" without needing additional verification? *How* do we come to experience it as "real"? It is through perception that information enters our minds in the first place. As such, subconscious cultural influences at the level of perception undergird this broadly shared analytic perspective, as well as a number of related sociological subfields such as the sociology of knowledge. As Eviatar Zerubavel says in relation to cognitive sociology, "A good way to begin exploring the mind would be to examine the actual process by which the world 'enters' it in the first place. The first step toward establishing a comprehensive sociology of the mind, therefore, would be to develop a *sociology of perception.*"[22] Yet there is currently no coherent sociological subfield devoted to perception.

Despite the very limited number of works specifically sailing under the banner of "the sociology of perception"[23]—taking the social construction of perception as their central object of analysis—one can find references to sensory perception throughout classical and contemporary sociology. Georg Simmel offers one of the more extended discussions of the sociological importance of the senses, arguing that vision plays a unique sociological role because "the union and interaction of individuals is based upon mutual glances."[24] Perception also plays an important role in much of Erving Goffman's thinking (e.g., the concept of *civil inattention*)[25] and in Harold Garfinkel's work on "background" knowledge.[26] Other sociologists who have explicitly argued for the centrality of perception to sociological inquiry include Arthur Child, who claims that perception buttresses the sociology of knowledge;[27] Donald Lowe, who offers that perception is the link between the content of thought and the structure of society;[28] and, more recently, Phillip Vannini, Dennis Waskul, and Simon Gottschalk, who argue that the senses and sensations are "the key form of humans' active construction of the world."[29] There are also traces of a sociology of perception in the classical sociological concepts of *collective conscience*,[30] *class consciousness*,[31] and *collective attention*.[32] Given this long history of nods to the role of perception in social life—not to mention the outright statements of its sociological significance—the topic is ripe for a more extended treatment.

A sociological analysis of sensory perception can be approached in a number of different ways. One strategy is to systematically capture and catalog varying perceptions of the same object, analyzing the structures of attention involved in alternate ways of seeing (or hearing, smelling, tasting, or touching) the same thing. Another approach is to document historical shifts in perceptual conventions and the primacy of different senses.[33] A third important area of inquiry is to investigate the ways perception gets enlisted in other processes of social construction (of reality, of race, of gender, of aesthetic judgment, and so on). These projects do not exhaust the concerns of a sociology of perception, which can include any work examining perception as a social process, as well as those using "sensuous" research methods attentive to the researcher's embodied perceptual experience.[34]

Here I employ a cognitive sociological approach, emphasizing the link between perception and cognition and highlighting the sociocultural organization of both. Although there is some debate surrounding the timing and the extent to which the different senses are penetrated by cognition and culture, there is broad agreement that cognition shapes perception at some level prior to consciously experienced sensations.[35] As Harry Lawless put it in relation to olfactory perception, it is not just a matter of "how well the nose is working" but also "how well the brain that is hooked to the nose is working."[36] Strictly speaking, what human beings see, feel, taste, touch, and smell is not the world per se but a version of the world their minds have created.[37] In light of this, in this book I explore the ways social patterns of thought create mental templates for the perceptual construction of reality.

Expectations, Selective Attention, and Social Construction

Scholars have used a variety of concepts to describe the social construction of reality, including *paradigms*,[38] *perspectives*,[39] *styles*,[40] *models*,[41] *schemas*,[42] *mental maps*,[43] *habitus*,[44] *frames*,[45] and *filters*.[46] Deborah Tannen suggested that the notion of expectations unifies several of these seemingly very different theories.[47] Although she mostly focused her analysis on frames and schemas, I want to be much more inclusive and demonstrate an underlying similarity among most, if not all, of these concepts that specifically addresses the role of social expectations in creating patterns of thought and sensory perception.

One way to begin to examine exactly how social structures of expectation influence perception is to turn to findings in social psychology about cognitive-processing biases, such as "expectation effects" and "confirmatory hypothesis testing," which lead us to unconsciously reject or ignore sensory information challenging our expectations.[48] This point is captured well by Jerome S. Bruner and Leo Postman's playing card experiment in which participants were shown ordinary cards mixed with anomalous cards (such as a red two of clubs). People saw only the types of cards they expected to see until learning through prolonged exposure that there were additional categories for which previous experience had not equipped them.[49] As Maurice Merleau-Ponty so pithily put it: "We need to know what we are looking for, otherwise we would not be looking for it."[50] Mental preparation also played a role in the discovery of asteroids, which Thomas Kuhn ties to William Herschel's discovery of Uranus, the first sighting of a "new" planet in several millennia. "The minor paradigm change forced by Herschel helped to prepare astronomers for the rapid discovery, after 1801, of the numerous minor planets or asteroids. Because of their small size, these did not display the anomalous magnification that had alerted Herschel. Nevertheless, astronomers prepared to find additional planets were able, with standard instruments, to identify twenty of them in the first fifty years of the nineteenth century."[51] The same is true of the microscope. What we now call "germs" were always technically visible through this technology, but it was only once microscopists grew cognitively sensitized into a "myopic style of focusing" that these microorganisms could be seen in any meaningful way.[52]

It is important to emphasize that the expectations that I am concerned with here are specifically *social* expectations. Those based on individual experience also produce expectation effects, but it is the influence of social expectations on perception that is most relevant to the sociology of perception and an analysis of the role of the senses in the social construction of reality.[53] The perceptual effects produced by social expectations reflect an unmistakably social logic; they are organized to produce particular socially shared and socially anticipated meanings. More specifically, social expectations create a state of "perceptual readiness"[54] to quickly recognize particular socially relevant cues by sensitizing us to some kinds of information—and thereby also collectively desensitizing us to others. Stated another way, social expectations *prime* members of a social collective to perceive things the same way. Priming is part of "implicit cognition"; that is, evaluations and decisions that are automatically activated without the person's awareness.[55] Part of the basis for this subconscious "evaluation" is increased sensitivity to certain stimuli due to prior experience.

Cognitive sociologists capture these socially calibrated fluctuations in focus with the concept of *attention*. Following Goffman's ideas in *Frame Analysis*, as well as his concepts of *rules of irrelevance* and *civil inattention*, the cognitive sociological use of *attention* and *disattention* highlights the mental fences with which we typically frame social reality, regarding most things as "out of frame" and unworthy of our attention.[56] Defined in this way, attention can refer to the mental act of selectively focusing our awareness, but it can also refer to selective *sensory* attention—registering only selected details among the technically available stimuli while disattending the rest.

Selective attention is sometimes defined as the result of an individual actor's conscious intentions—that is, the conscious focusing of attention involved in the purposeful execution of visually guided action.[57] What cognitive sociologists highlight is the *normative* character of our attention. In his recent work on the sociology of denial, for instance, Zerubavel describes this socially conventional exclusion of details that are technically within our field of vision as follows: "Ignoring something is more than simply failing to notice it. Indeed, it is quite often the result of some pressure to actively disregard it. Such pressure is usually a product of social norms of attention designed to separate what we conventionally consider 'noteworthy' from what we come to disregard as mere background 'noise.'"[58] Attention is not simply a reflection of what we as individuals *choose* to look at. While it can be a tool we direct and control, attention is also a form of social constraint, reflecting what we *must* look at (as well as what we must not see) as members of social groups. One powerful illustration of the normative dimension of visual attention is the influence of language.

Benjamin Whorf famously argued that we perceive the world in the "types" dictated by our linguistic system: "The categories and types that we isolate from the world of phenomena we do not find there because they stare every observer in the face; on the contrary, the world is presented in a kaleidoscopic flux of impressions which has to be organized by our minds—and this means largely by the linguistic systems in our minds."[59] Alfred Schutz and Thomas Luckmann similarly describe language as "filtering" and "consolidating" reality, essentially determining "the typical meaning-structures of the normal adult's experience."[60] For instance, since Navajo grammar necessitates recognition of shape, when Navajo speakers are presented with objects that could be grouped by color or by shape, they tend to ignore color and privilege shape. Since *empirically* color and shape are equally salient, this illustrates the decidedly normative organization of our practices of visual attention and disattention.[61]

The essential point is that we are "perceptually readied"—whether by language, social expectations, or social norms—to seek out and register those details that reflect our collective expectations, while overlooking other details that are equally perceptible and "real." Put another way, the social world primes us to allow certain sensory information to disappear into the *background* of our perceptions. Ruth Hubbard, Mary Henifin, and Barbara Fried highlight this connection between social norms and backgrounding when they describe scientific "facts" as "generated within a fabric of societal norms" that "pushes certain realizations into the foreground, while others readily merge with the background of the unnoticed and hence remain undescribed."[62] The distinction between figure and ground originated with Edgar Rubin, whose vase/face optical illusion demonstrates that seeing something in the "foreground" always involves *not* perceptually registering the surrounding background region. What cognitive sociologists emphasize are the ways that figure and ground can be created by social norms and expectations. The background does not consist only of what is *empirically* less salient or even less *personally* salient; it is also a reflection of what is less *socially* salient. These practices of backgrounding and foregrounding selected details of our visual field play a central role in the social construction of our perceptual realities.

Indeed, some concept of selective perception underlies at least five of the major concepts scholars previously developed to describe the social construction of reality: frame, schema, habitus, perspective, and thought style. Although not necessarily central to his or her analysis, in each case the author makes some reference to social norms of attention and disattention. In drawing out this common conceptual thread, my point is to demonstrate, first of all, that a shared sociocognitive and perceptual process underlies each of these apparently very different theories of the social construction of reality, and second, that the social organization of visual attention is an important process underlying the social construction of reality that merits a fuller and more focused analysis.

I already alluded to the centrality of selective attention in Goffman's work on reality maintenance—for instance, in the practice of "face-work," in which we ignore other actors' potentially face-threatening behavior. More generally, the concept of *framing* basically boils down to a process of selective attention. To *frame* something is to determine which details are "in frame" and which can be disregarded as "out of frame," which is in essence a process of selective attention.[63]

Definitions of *schemata* also frequently include references to attention and disattention—for instance, describing schemas as "cognitive structures" that selectively represent "relevant attributes,"[64] or as "knowledge structures" that determine "what aspects of the social environment are taken into account, how they are interpreted, and how we react."[65] Another definition that specifically highlights selective *inattention* states that "schemata . . . allow the brain to exclude the specific details of a new experience and retain only the generalities that liken the event to other experiences in one's past. . . . Discrepant features . . . are adjusted or omitted so that the information conforms to the schema in use."[66]

Bourdieu's descriptions of *habitus* similarly highlight socially normative practices of selective attention and disattention. Functioning as a "pertinence principle" or "principle of selection," he explains, habitus allows for an "unconscious deciphering of the countless signs which at every moment say what is to be loved and what is not, what *is* or *is not* to be seen."[67] In other instances, Bourdieu relies on the concept of a schema (his exact wording is "schemes of perception and appreciation") when describing perception, and he specifically mentions selective attention as one way habitus operates.[68]

The concepts of *perspective* and *thought style* also fundamentally describe processes of selective attention that allow people to, in Tamotsu Shibutani's words, "define identical situations differently, responding *selectively* to diverse aspects of their environment."[69] Fleck similarly refers to thought styles as a "readiness for directed perception," and explicitly makes the point that this includes collective forms of disattention, which he refers to as "restricted" attention. For instance, he recounts that the expectations of their particular "thought style" led bacteriologists to disattend bacterial cultures that were either very fresh or very old as "not even worth examining." "As a result," he explains, "all secondary changes in the cultures . . . escaped attention. . . . The thought style, developed in this particular way, made possible the perception of many forms as well as the establishment of many applicable facts. But it also rendered the recognition of other forms and other facts impossible."[70]

In many of these examples, the authors not only highlight the role of selective attention in the social construction of reality, but they explicitly emphasize the role of selective *sensory*—specifically visual—attention and disattention. To further underscore this point, I would like to introduce two more examples that directly address the role of selective visual perception in the social construction of reality. First, in Kuhn's theory of scientific revolutions, paradigm shifts are fundamentally about the reorganization of visual stimuli; where earlier scientists saw one thing, adherents of a new paradigm literally see something else. In his words, "Led by a new paradigm, scientists adopt new instruments and look in new places. Even more important, during revolutions scientists see new and different things when looking with familiar instruments in places they have looked before."[71] Likewise, Goffman refers to our "very considerable capacity for perceptual discrimination in regards to matters of frame," and directly mentions the uniquely powerful role of *visual* perception (over other forms of sensory perception) in framing in the following passage: "What is heard, felt or smelled attracts the eye, and it is the seeing of the source of these stimuli that allows for a quick identification and definition—a quick framing of what has occurred."[72]

Generally speaking, what each of these examples suggests is that sensory perception is not passive, but is a key mechanism through which we actively create social reality. That is, some form of *perceptual work* underlies the process of reality construction as described by a number of the most prominent social theorists, including Goffman, Bourdieu, Fleck, and Kuhn. More specifically, in each case the author refers to the role of socially coordinated practices of visual attention and inattention in the construction of taken-for-granted social realities.

Having established that selective visual attention is one answer to the question of *how* reality is socially constructed, I would like to turn briefly to another equally important question: *Why* do we do this? What is achieved by collectively ignoring so much of the sensory information that confronts us in the course of our daily lives? One answer is that social norms of selective attention are among the primary ways we cognitively coordinate social life. Without ongoing normative practices of disattention—"rules of irrelevance"—we could not maintain the shared, ever-fragile "definition of the situation."[73] The relatively extreme example of the gynecological examination effectively illustrates the necessity of collective and coordinated practices of disattention to maintain a shared medical reality against competing sexual meanings.[74] While the reality of a gynecological exam is particularly "precarious," competing meanings must be kept at bay through disattention in any situation, lest they threaten definitions of reality.

What this example highlights generically, then, is the prevalence of ambiguity in social life and our efforts to manage it cognitively. Any time we maintain the definition of the situation against competing meanings, or disambiguate a figure from its surrounding ground, we are using attention and disattention to cognitively create boundaries out of an underlying continuousness. The ambiguity inherent in this continuousness is a source of great anxiety. Ambiguity is anxiety evoking because, as Mary Douglas explains, "the yearning for rigidity is in us all. It is part of our human condition to long for hard lines and clear concepts."[75] William James similarly remarks that "we carve out order by leaving the disorderly parts out."[76] However, there is some evidence that this aversion to ambiguity is a distinctly modern phenomenon. As Yi-Fu Tuan observes in his analysis of historical differences in perception, "To a modern thinker the tolerance of the premodern mind for incoherence is baffling."[77] In his view, this modern yearning for segregation is one reason we are so "infatuated with sight," which is the sense most associated with differentiation and distancing, and therefore what allows us to perceptually create a world of discrete objects.[78] To achieve this neatly classified visual reality, however, we must disattend not only any ambiguous visual information but also the information coming in through the other senses, which is often significantly more ambiguous.

Another way to understand the practice of disattending ambiguity is to view it as a form of denial. The characteristic feature of denial is that, faced with a fact that is too uncomfortable to acknowledge, one simply behaves as though it does not exist. This is not to say that a person in denial is aware of the threat and puts on a show; he or she literally cannot perceive or acknowledge it. In a parallel fashion one may say that ambiguity is often so cognitively and affectively uncomfortable that it induces a collective form of denial; that is, our cultural defense mechanisms compel us to collectively *disattend* ambiguity, forcing the world into the expected mental niches. In Edmund Leach's words, "It is . . . by refusing to admit that there is any ambiguity that we manage to perceive the world as we do."[79] In short, then, ambiguity leads to anxiety, which leads us to disattend certain aspects of experience to restore the comfort of a cleanly classified world.[80] Given that these collective practices of selective disattention are so fundamental to creating and maintaining social reality, it seems important to identify a conceptual system that can effectively serve us in analyzing them.

Filter Analysis

One of my central claims in the previous section was that—although not always directly acknowledged as such—normative practices of selective attention and inattention actually form a common theme connecting many of the most prominent theories of the social construction of reality. On a conceptual level, however, most of the associated metaphors for social construction fail to fully capture these social processes of attending and ignoring.

For one thing, several of the available concepts (including schema, habitus, and paradigm) are not based on a concrete spatial image that provides a specific, useful guide for an analysis of attention and disattention. While these concepts all describe the broad idea of a shared perception, they do not provide a model to understand *how* particular perceptions are cognitively structured. In light of this, one of the virtues of the metaphor of a frame is that it is based on a very evocative spatial image that effectively illustrates that we focus on some details while ignoring others. However, due to its structure, the frame metaphor suffers from two important analytic limitations. First, although frame offers a clear depiction of "in" and "out," it is a binary representation in which the attended and disattended are fully separated and spatially contiguous, rather than interwoven in the same conceptual space. This is a coarse representation that separates the attended from the disattended too starkly. Second, frame suggests a somewhat unbalanced representation of attention and disattention. While Goffman pioneered the sociology of disattention, conceptually speaking, the metaphor of a frame—which focuses on the distinction between some "relevant" content (a painting, for instance) and that which it is not (the surrounding wall, everything outside of the picture frame)—primarily brings analytical focus to what is "in frame"; everything else is lumped together as "out of frame." As a result, the frame metaphor directs attention to those details that are marked as relevant, but does not invite the same kind of specific analysis of what is "irrelevant" and disattended because the space outside the frame is infinite and undefined. In reality, however, backgrounded information has its own shapes, patterns, and configurations.[81] Analytically, then, it is essential to systematically identify both the figure and the background.

A disproportionate analytic focus on attention over disattention also applies to the concept of a *schema*, which is typically used to describe a rapid and unconscious mental "filling in" of expected attributes based on the perception of a small number of highly marked cues. As such, conceptually speaking, schemata emphasize what is seen and what is mentally "added" based on what is seen, but not what is overlooked and ignored. Further, as I mentioned above, the concept of a *schema* does not provide a clear metaphorical structure to direct an analysis of attention and disattention. The same critique applies to the concept of *habitus*. While Bourdieu states that habitus should be understood as a "principle of selection," he relies on the notion of a schema to describe *how* habitus shapes perception.[82] In any case, while generally evocative of selective attention, neither concept provides a concrete spatial image that can guide a proportionate analysis of both attention and disattention.

I emphasize this point about bringing analytic focus to what is normally *not* seen because identifying the disattended is uniquely valuable for constructionist analysis. What remains unnoticed, after all, is the evidence and detail supporting alternate perceptions and categorizations. Attending to such alternatives helps unravel obviousness and self-evidence. If sociology's task is in part to examine self-evident ideas,[83] a conceptual system explicitly conceived to highlight the disattended is an exceptionally useful tool. Such inversions of the normative structure of attention preclude self-evidence, as "a reality can hardly seem self-evident if a person is simultaneously aware of a counterreality."[84]

Beyond frame, schema, and habitus, several other concepts that come to mind as natural choices for an analysis of visual perception are *lens*, *screen*, and *perspective*. The concept of *perspective* certainly conveys the idea that one never sees everything; however, in this case the things unseen are actually outside the physiological limits of one's vision. What *perspective* does not capture, therefore, is that even within one's visual field, much of the available information is disattended. This is one of the virtues of the metaphor of a *lens*, which works within one's field of vision. Indeed the notion of a *cultural lens* has been used to capture the idea that social norms can act as distorting prisms for our perceptions, as in the idea of the "lenses of gender."[85] Whether conceived as the lenses of the eyes or as a camera's lens, the metaphor refers to focusing—bringing some things into relief and blurring others—which does capture selective attention to some extent. However, given the earlier discussion of denial, it is insufficient to think of the disattended features of reality as merely fuzzy or out of focus. They are effectively invisible.

The mesh of a screen in a window or door is used to "screen out" some things, such as bugs, while allowing others—a nice cool breeze—to pass through. In light of this, *screen* seems like a particularly fitting metaphor for selective attention. However, this meaning for screen is in competition for a number of other meanings, such as a movie screen, a computer screen, a "touch" screen, and so forth. These other types of screens do not specifically convey the dynamics of blockage and passage that a mesh screen does, making the term *screen* somewhat ambiguous in its metaphorical structure.

One alternative that captures this "screening" effect equally well, but without invoking as many competing meanings, is the metaphor of a *filter*. When using the term *filter*, I specifically have in mind a mental "strainer," or "sieve," through which visual stimuli pass before they are consciously perceived, letting in culturally meaningful details while sifting out the culturally irrelevant. *Merriam-Webster Dictionary* defines the function of a filter as "holding back elements or modifying the appearance of something" and *The American Heritage Dictionary* offers that a filter is "any porous substance through which a liquid or gas is passed in order to remove constituents."[86] Filters in general function by allowing selected elements to pass through a set of holes while blocking others. Although the size, shape, and number of openings vary, all filters perform this function of "straining," or "sifting." Thinking in terms of filters thus specifically directs our analysis to questions about which features or details pass through and are attended and, perhaps more importantly, which are blocked by the filter and thus remain unnoticed.[87] Unlike metaphors that disproportionately emphasize what is "in frame" and attended, a filter highlights what is seen *and* what is ignored because its metaphorical blockages and holes explicitly represent the dialectical relationship between attention and disattention (see fig. 2).

One further benefit of the filter metaphor is that it may provide a common language with cognitive scientists, who draw on the same idea to talk about the brain of the perceiver. Cognitive scientists and visual neurobiologists periodically use the term *filter* to describe how information flowing in from the senses is cognitively reduced by extracting certain features while ignoring others.[88] While not specifically applying the metaphor of a filter, other brain researchers have looked at the neural correlates of selective attention using electroencephalogram (EEG) recordings[89] and studied visual attention and disattention by tracking eye movements, demonstrating that sometimes even when the eye rests on something it remains unperceived.[90] Still others have studied the extent to which selective visual perception of different

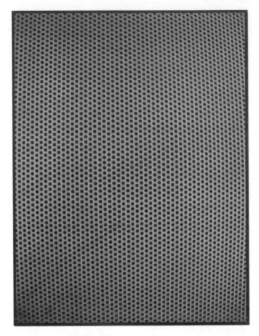

FIGURE 2 Filter analysis: A new metaphor for perceptual construction. Holes represent attention, and blockages represent disattention. The figure brings analytic focus to norms of attention and disattention. (Image by Jennifer Lawrence for the author.)

properties of shapes can be traced to cultural differences in exposure.[91] If it is the case that a process of filtration takes place at the level of the brain and in the social organization of perceptual processes (as well as, arguably, in memory and cognition more broadly), this common form may provide a useful basis for exploring the similarities and differences among these filters and an opportunity to explore the mirroring of biological and cultural processes.[92]

In fact, the notion of an attention filter originates with the cognitive scientist Donald Broadbent, who used it to explain that, as a result of the limited capacity of our nervous systems, we are only able to consciously perceive a small number of the many different types of sensory stimuli that normally surround us.[93] Broadbent describes various properties of stimuli that make them more likely to be selected by the attention filter for further processing, including intensity, novelty, and spatial location. Broadbent thus primarily emphasizes the features of the *stimulus* that make it "relevant" or "irrelevant." When he does address the state of the *perceiver*, relevance is framed in the language of "drives," understood as biological states (e.g., hunger).[94] My approach is to borrow the concept of filtration, but to extend our understanding of selective attention to include *social* rules of relevance that create in the *perceiver* a mental state predisposing him or her to select particular sensory details over others. The Russian linguist Nikolai Trubetzkoy used the concepts of a *phonological sieve* and *phonological relevance* to capture this process by which the perceiver filters out "irrelevant" sounds in language perception, emphasizing that, because relevance is defined differently in different languages, meaning inheres not in the sounds themselves but in the perceiver's system of filters or sieves.[95]

Several sociologists have also alluded to the metaphor of filtration, though no one has presented a sustained theoretical examination of the concept. The most fully articulated use of the term comes from Murray Davis, who explicitly uses *filter* as opposed to *frame* in his typology of different sexual worldviews. His explanation for why he prefers the term *filter* is the following: "The term 'frame' directs the reader's attention to the different organizations of experience within and without a boundary. I prefer the term 'filter,' which directs attention to the modifications experience undergoes as it passes through a contextual scheme."[96] Davis also hints at the important dimension of "disattention" or "blocking" in the filter metaphor when he writes that "filters obscure all but a few aspects of sexual experience and activity."[97] While it is clear that Davis was aware of many of the nuances of the filter metaphor, and used it quite deliberately, readers must infer a lot from his descriptions to fill out a portrait of the analytic tool from what amounts to an extremely suggestive sketch. Zerubavel is one of those readers of Davis who sensed the richness of the concept of filtration, quite deliberately borrowing the language.[98] However, while his broader argument in *Social Mindscapes* played a central role in my thinking about filters, he himself did not explicitly undertake the project of theoretically exploring the concept. In their recent book on the sociology of the senses, Phillip Vannini, Dennis Waskul, and Simon Gottschalk also repeatedly use the filter metaphor when discussing the social work of perception—for instance, stating that the *process* of somatic work is to "filter" all the material that reaches our conscious perception and thought.[99] They further argue that such "ritual sensations" are "not to be confused with mechanical sensory responses to material stimuli, but are rather body techniques that guide the material of perception, *much like a filtering mechanism*."[100] Despite repeatedly using the filter metaphor, as well as mentioning the concept of *attention* several times, they do not focus on *how* this filtering process that "guides" perception actually functions, or why this is the best metaphor for the mechanisms of somatic work.[101] Other sociologists who have used the term *filter* in an informal way, without explicit theoretical reflection, include Alfred Schutz and Thomas Luckmann, Jeffrey Alexander, and Ron Eyerman.[102]

In the chapters that follow I further illustrate the analytic benefits of filter analysis by using the metaphor to explore the perceptual construction of the body, specifically, visual perceptions of male and female bodies. I chose to study sex because historically sex and the matter of the body more broadly proved to be a stumbling block for constructionist theories. In taking on one of the "hard cases" of social construction, the unique insights facilitated by filter analysis are all the more apparent. The distinctive focus of this approach is to demonstrate that empirical reality is always richer and more complex than what we perceive and thus experience. Things in the world exceed any and all filtered perceptions of them, which always represent just one possible version or selection of elements. The form of constructionism promoted by filter analysis therefore focuses on the question of *how*—by what kinds of cognitive and sensory *practices*—the social construction of material reality is accomplished.

TWO

Selective Perception and the Social Construction of Sex

Visual perception is always partial and selective, despite the common presumption that when we see, we see everything. The truth is that we never fully attend all of the information technically available to our eyes, let alone what is available through the other four senses.[1] One question raised by this selectivity is, what determines what is seen and what is unseen (not to mention what is not heard, smelled, tasted, etc.)? Empirical salience may account for some of this; that is, we are more likely to note sensory stimuli that are relatively large, bright, loud, or those with a strong smell or taste, and to overlook what is more difficult to see, hear, taste, and smell. At the same time, however, we are visually encultured into various optical *norms* that play an important role in organizing our perceptions, adding *social* forms of salience to the empirical world. In fact, social salience can at times override empirical salience, leading us to attend to perceptually subtle but socially important information.

Sex is no exception. When we visually perceive someone as male or female, their materiality passes through one or more mental filters that sift and sort the body, marking certain details as "relevant" and important to note, and others as "irrelevant" and "uninformative." The result is a visual perception in which certain bodily details get foregrounded, while others are backgrounded and unseen, or technically seen but not consciously noticed. These dynamics of corporeal visibility—and, arguably more importantly, erasure—need to be charted and interpreted for both intellectual and political reasons.[2]

In fact, it bears mentioning that even our ability to talk about "parts" of the body at all is an effect of our social filters. A truly un-filtered perception of the body would presumably be much more ho-listic, blurring the shapes and boundaries we normally perceive. One of the most productive contributions of filter analysis is that it high-lights the ways we perceptually carve up the body, essentially by speci-fying what is marked as "relevant" in any given perception. This does two things: It gives us an opportunity to ask *why* particular details are marked as important, highlighting the normative character of our at-tention. It also leads to questions about other possibilities. That is to say, analyzing selective attention encourages thinking about what is *not* attended.

Sexpectations and Sociomental Control

Beginning at birth, the social world sends an unambiguous and relent-lessly repeated message about sex differences: that they are both self-evident and uniquely important. As Jake (age 48), one of the intersex people I interviewed, put it, "From the moment we are born and la-beled with a sex we are thrown into two completely different worlds." Even parents who consciously try to avoid exposing their children to gender stereotypes are unable to shield them from subtle and not-so-subtle differences in clothing, toys, and how *other* people (grandpar-ents, teachers, doctors, strangers) relate to little boys and little girls. And of course, the reality is that many families are not skeptical of gen-der norms and continue to teach them to their children uncritically.

While both groups I interviewed commented insightfully on the transmission of social norms about sex differences in the context of family life, the transgender and intersex respondents tended to have particularly strong memories of sex differences being rigidly enforced and reinforced in childhood, likely because these messages were fre-quently in direct conflict with their intense desire to explore ambigu-ity and fluidity.

I used to make clothes for my teddy bear, but also I played with trucks and such. My daddy went crazy whenever I did anything that girls would do. (Alex, an intersex person who appears socially as male, no age provided)

I started cross-dressing at around probably like two or three [. . .][3] and for me it was just like totally normal back then, like I never thought of it—ooh I'm cross-dressing—you know? It was just like I used to just wear my sister's clothing and play around. And over time, I would get into trouble, and kept getting into trouble. (Sarah, MTF transsexual, age 28)

In the basement I found in a box some of my mother's old clothes from when she was a child. There was this yellow sundress and I just had to put it on, and I did. And my father beat me badly because of doing it [. . .] and then hundreds of times after that throughout my life. (Liz, MTF transsexual, age 56)

While the tension and conflict surrounding sex difference in these respondents' childhoods may have intensified the message, both in terms of frequency and emotional investment, all children are confronted with what Harold Garfinkel calls the "natural attitude," the taken-for-granted view that everyone who has ever lived and will ever live is either male or female, and that this dichotomy is natural, normal, and functional.[4]

In addition to parents, influential figures in the rest of children's social worlds, such as teachers, doctors, relatives, and peers, often help communicate these cultural messages about the unique importance and naturalness of sex differences. For instance, Annette, a transwoman in her mid-40s, recalls her kindergarten teacher's negative response to her desire to challenge norms about play: "I can actually remember back in kindergarten when I was wanting to stay inside and play in the kitchen with all that stuff and playing house, and the teacher forcing me to play outside with the guys in the sandbox with the trucks. I just didn't want to do that but that's what they forced me to do, and I had temper tantrums on the floor crying and everything else." Karin Martin's ethnographic research in preschools similarly shows that teachers begin communicating messages about the differences between males and females at a very young age—even encouraging boys and girls to move and experience their bodies differently.[5]

At the same time, beliefs about the importance of sex differences are reinforced outside of the classroom. For instance, Kathy, a 67-year-old MTF transsexual, shared the following anecdote about the mother of her childhood friend, who made a strong impression with her angry and hurtful reaction to a male child's desire to wear her daughter's clothes: "When I was quite young, me and the girl next door were playing, and I had the strongest urge to want to try on her clothes, which she thought would be funny, so she let me. We were in a tree house that my brother built. Later she told her mom about it and she flipped out, wouldn't let me near her daughter for quite a while. She called me a 'dirty little boy' and that hurt deeply, something that stayed with me all my life." Even if the mother's response was not a reaction to this respondent exploring "girls'" clothing but to a little boy seeing her daughter naked, this is also a form of marking the significance of sex differences, since she presumably would not have had the same intensity of response if the child was the same sex as her daughter.

These ideas about the unique importance of sex differences circulate in our social worlds from birth, ultimately becoming the expectations through which we understand and perceive men, women, and their bodies—our sexpectations, so to speak. I use the term *sexpectations* to extend the generic idea that social expectations create an intersubjective state of "perceptual readiness" to quickly recognize socially expected cues to our perceptions of bodies and specifically to the perception of sex differences.[6] Conceptually, *sexpectations* highlights the role played by gender norms in shaping perceptions of sexed bodies. More specifically, it draws attention to the considerable social pressure to focus on sex differences and ignore, avoid, and deny sex similarities. In this way, *sexpectations* emphasizes the relationship between sex and gender, as opposed to the distinction. This relationship is particularly apparent when gender is understood as a "cognitive schema" or mental filter we use to perceive and make sense of human bodies.[7]

Perhaps even more influential in establishing children's sexpectations than the parental figures and other adults in the above anecdotes, however, is the English language, which emphasizes sex differences over other forms of bodily difference. Consider the fact that, in English as well as many other languages, one must speak of people as "he" or "she." As a result, it is virtually impossible to even refer to another person without first attributing sex. In some languages (e.g., Hebrew and Russian), sex determines not only the pronouns used but also the form of verbs. In such cases, speakers must take into account someone's sex to speak to or about him or her at all. This is not true of other differences; there is no comparable grammatical category for eye color, hair color, skin color, height, weight, or any other visual variable. If there were, we would likely perceive people differently.

This point was recently reinforced for me as I settled into a new job and became acquainted with a new group of colleagues. Long before I had learned everyone's names and roles, I knew with certainty whether they were male or female, whereas it took me over a week to register that one of the people I was working most closely with has one brown eye and one blue eye. Of course, if language were organized around eye color rather than sex, I would have been unable to ignore it. These conventions of language help create the expectation that all human bodies are either male or female, and that this is a significant difference, more important than other, equally perceptible differences.

Expectations regarding the salience of sex differences may be initially established in childhood, but they are also reinforced throughout life. For one thing, a disproportionate emphasis on sex differences suffuses many social institutions, including scientific and other academic institutions. If we tend to be blind to the sameness between men and women, then it is in part because of a lack of available evidence to the contrary, as some of the major sources of "evidence" or "truth" in our culture do not publish findings of sameness as often as they publish findings of difference. Yet this is not because such data do not exist or could not be collected.

A number of gender scholars have noted this academic bias in favor of data that demonstrate sex differences. Anne Fausto-Sterling, for example, reviewed biological research on purported sex differences and identified numerous studies that technically also demonstrate sex similarity.[8] Carol Tavris summarizes this asymmetrical attention to sex differences as follows: "Typically, when scientists haven't found the differences they were seeking, they haven't abandoned the goal or their belief that such differences exist; they just moved to another part of the anatomy or a different corner of the brain."[9] They do not, however, generally publish a finding of "no sex differences." As Anelis Kaiser and her colleagues reported in a study of brain research on sex differences in language processing, the general preference for publishing "positive" findings in scientific journals is exacerbated in sex/gender research by assumptions in the design and analysis of studies that "inevitably lead to the detection of differences rather than the detection of similarities."[10] Similarly, in social scientific research on gender it is an institutional norm that finding no gender difference is tantamount to having no finding, and as a result there is a high level of nonreporting of "negative" data. In most social scientific research comparing men to women, the majority of the data does not reveal significant gender differences. In fact, most variables suggest that there are more similarities than differences between men and women. Yet these results do not often appear, or at least are not the data that are highlighted, in journal articles and books. What is of interest from the standpoint of having "findings" to report and publish is the much smaller number of variables showing statistically significant gender differences.[11]

These discourses that elevate sex differences over sex similarities also circulate outside of the academy—for example, in the health-care system, where physicians and other health-care providers transmit ideas about the naturalness and fixity of sex differences in the context of patient care. One admittedly extreme example is the medical "standard of care" for transsexuals, which explicitly incorporates such messages in both the psychological and surgical phases of transition. A number of my transgender interviewees mentioned that at a certain point their psychotherapists pushed them to avoid ambiguity and fully inhabit either one sex category or the other. In fact, something called a "real-life test" or "real-life experience," where one is encouraged to move out of ambiguity and live full-time as one's sex of transition for a period of time prior to sexual reassignment surgery, is strongly recommended by the World Professional Association for Transgender Health (WPATH), formerly known as the Harry Benjamin International Gender Dysphoria Association (HBIGDA), widely viewed as the authority on the standards of medical care of gender variant individuals.

In addition, some surgeons who perform sex reassignments feel that they have an obligation to preserve the sex binary even while assisting people to change sexes. For instance, one surgeon explained that "although a number of his ftm patients seeking breast reduction/chest reconstruction tell him that they do not wish to have their nipples or aureole reduced, almost all patients *need* such reductions" (emphasis added). Another reportedly stated that he will not allow his FTM phalloplasty patients to retain their vaginas, because to do so would be to make "a chick with a dick—and no one would want that!" In such cases, doctors act as gatekeepers, refusing to blur the sex categories and carefully preserving the social reality of bodily dimorphism.[12]

Although to this point I have focused my discussion on examples from science, medical practice, and academic research, ideas about the importance and naturalness of sex differences are also institutionalized and communicated through religion and law. For example, Judaism at least implicitly promotes the belief that sex is fixed because it is created by God, and Christian ideology similarly includes ideas about "the divine purpose of sexual difference and scripturally derived gender roles."[13] Consider also the whole realm of law and legal documents, the vast majority of which require one to claim membership in a sex category. An *M* or *F* is listed on birth certificates, passports, and driver's licenses, providing people with a binding legal sex and implicitly supporting the view that sex is distinct from other aspects of the body— more important, more self-evident, more fixed, and more natural.

Further, our most common sexual identity categories and hegemonic ideas about sexuality are conceptually rooted in—and in turn transmit—beliefs about fixed, natural sex differences. More specifically, we can only think of people as "homosexual" or "heterosexual" because we can think of them as "male" and "female." These terms are meaningless unless we can see bodies in two categories.[14] Of course, the prefixes *homo-* and *hetero-* technically just mean "the same" and "different," and could be construed much more broadly than sex. For instance, interfaith marriage is a form of heterosexuality, and a sexual relationship between two people of the same race or nationality could be considered homosexual. It is only because we are hyperattentive to the sex distinction that we define heterosexuality and homosexuality so narrowly.

In addition to our sexual identity categories, heteronormativity—dominant assumptions about the naturalness of heterosexuality—contributes to the experience of a sex-differentiated reality. As an illustration, consider the photograph taken from behind of two people with their arms draped over one another's shoulder and waist in figure 3. This particular image is an interesting test case because it eliminates some of the most common sex-attribution cues—for instance, hair length (both figures have long hair), body hair (none is visible on either person), and facial hair/makeup (neither is visible from the back). It is still "obvious," however, that the figure on the left is female and the one on the right is male. For one thing, the person on the left is wearing very feminine clothing (a short sundress and a ribbon in her hair). She is also slightly shorter and smaller than the person on the right. But it is certainly possible that the person on the right is also a female; he or she has no visible body hair, is not particularly large-framed or muscular, has long hair, and is dressed very neutrally in jeans and a white T-shirt. Yet assuming the context was not marked explicitly as gender-bending or nonheterosexual, we respond not with the sense that this person *may* be a male. The perception is that anything else is inconceivable. Heteronormativity plays a powerful role in that judgment, especially when we see two people together and touching. Under heteronormative logic, because the figure on the left is very clearly female, the figure on the right is automatically male.

In light of how many different social forces all simultaneously demand categorization in terms of sex differences, our sexpectations are best understood as "overdetermined"—they are created by multiple forces simultaneously, any one of which alone may be enough to account for the observed effect.[15] The overdetermination of sex difference

FIGURE 3 Heteronormativity in sex attribution. (*Glamour*, May 2003.)

raises questions about how best to conceptualize the power dynamics sustaining its salience. Namely, how should we understand who or what maintains the hegemonic view of sex differences? For example, are the biologists and other academics researching sex and gender intentionally distorting their findings or trying to hide something when they disproportionately emphasize sex differences? Or is it more accurate to say they are socialized into the cognitive and optical norms of the prevailing culture, and thus subconsciously define as "irrelevant"— and therefore ignore—data that do not demonstrate sex difference? As Roger Lancaster put it, following Thomas Kuhn and Ludwik Fleck (among others): "The eye of the scientist, like that of everyone else, is a *trained* eye that has *learned* to see."[16]

In this view, dominant ideas about the significance of sex differences are not strategically promoted and imposed by elites who benefit in some way from hyperattention to difference. It is not that the "bad guys" impose the binary, while the "good guys" expose it. On the contrary, the power dynamics securing the prevailing norms regarding sex differences are better described as a form of "discursive power," meaning dominant discourses coordinate and shape our perceptions (and our bodies) through ideas about normality. As such, no one person or group is imposing these ideas, and neither is anyone outside of their reach.[17]

Judith Butler has drawn on Michel Foucault's notion of discursive power to illustrate how power functions through gender norms. In this view, power is not held or exercised by one social group (men, elites, whites, etc.) that defines gender in a manner that serves its interests and then restricts other people to that definition.[18] Instead of repression, discursive power relies on the viewpoint of the objective and the normal as the mechanism of power's enforcement. In other words, the "force" of discursive power is to constitute the realm of the thinkable. Rather than policing our behavior through restriction (you can't act that way, you can't look that way), gender constrains our behavior through the circulation of ideas about what is "normal" and "possible." Cultural discourses about sex differences also function as a form of "socio-mental control" dictating how we see male and female bodies.[19]

I intentionally chose to interview two groups whose circumstances logically should (and do, to some degree) make them uniquely aware of the nonnecessity of the sex categories. Blind and transgender people arguably have access to more nondichotomous information and may even have the opportunity to see the world without sex difference to an extent. Yet one of my unanticipated findings is that this does not really disrupt their investment in sex as a natural binary, highlighting the way that dominant beliefs can perform sociomental control even on people whose social position predisposes them to "deviant" perceptions.

I also expected to find a lot of variation between the blind and transgender respondents—particularly in light of some of the differences between vision and other senses, such as touch and hearing, identified in previous research. For one thing, since touch requires contact with the object perceived, it may be less prone to distortion.[20] In addition, hearing and smell may not allow for as precise distinctions as sight.[21] As Yi-Fu Tuan describes, "When we open our eyes, a diffuse ambience of sounds and smells yields to a sharply delineated world of objects in space."[22] Making a similar point, Andy (age 61), who has been blind since birth, told me that if he were suspended in a hot air balloon to touch the carvings on Mount Rushmore, even if he could tell that they were human faces, he would not be able to tell that one of them was George Washington.

Given these potential differences, I expected that touch and hearing might lead to perceptions of bodies less influenced by the prevailing discourses regarding sex differences. While in certain ways this is true (and I will not ignore these interesting differences), it is also evident the blind respondents "know" sex is obvious and have the expectation of perceiving it unproblematically, and that this knowledge colors the way they perceive bodies through hearing, smell, and touch just as it shapes the visual perception of sex by the sighted. For example, Andrea (age 30), who began losing sight at age 12, described something akin to sociomental control when she explained that blind people and sighted people categorize bodies in the same way because what we perceive is an effect of social conditioning (which we all share):

But in terms of the way we categorize people and size them up, because I think that's so much social conditioning, most of what you're actually seeing. I really think we pretty much do it the same. People say, you can't be racist because you're blind and you can't see color, but it's really not about the physical characteristics. It's all of the learning that we've attached to those characteristics. Blind people, we're conditioned just like everyone else. We might have to find sort of alternative ways of finding out that information, but we still categorize people and size them up just like everyone else.

Everyone—blind or sighted—is socialized into the prevailing discourses regarding the unique salience of sex differences. Accordingly, a sense of deep certainty of the reality and "obviousness" of sex differences was present in the narratives of many of the blind respondents:

I can always tell. [. . .] There is a certain something. It's hard to put into words, but you can generally just tell. It's almost instant as well, if that gives you an idea. It's not like I even have to really try all that hard to know, almost instinct. (Tim, age 33, blind since age 3)

It is very easy to decipher between the sexes 99 percent of the time. (Simone, college age, lost vision at age 15)

Most of the time, it's really incredibly easy to distinguish a male from a female. (Jackson, age 24, mostly blind since birth)

Further, most of the blind people I talked to care profoundly about sex differences and take the task of sex attribution very seriously—so much so that they frequently stated or implied they feel uncomfortable and anxious when sex attribution is difficult. In the example below, Owen begins by describing the cues he typically uses to determine sex. Then in the middle of the passage he shifts to describing an instance when someone's sex was not self-evident.

Sometimes I can see if she's got long hair, and most guys don't. Earrings, if large enough, and bright enough, are a possibility. And sometimes, you can tell by the way a woman moves. I can't get that every time, but once in a while. [. . .] Now, I should admit something, I went to the school for the blind here in Iowa from ninth grade on. There was this kid there, probably twelve or thirteen at the time. It took me three or four months to realize this person was a female. (Owen, age 28, blind since birth)

The experience of sexual ambiguity is described as something he has to "admit to," suggesting that there is something wrong or shameful about not finding sex obvious. In the next example, Andrea portrays perceiving sex ambiguity in similarly negative terms as something that "weighs on you" and is "disconcerting." "There was one [. . . person] who a lot of us knew, and we would get really disconcerted because with his voice we couldn't tell if he was a male or a female, and his name was 'Jackie' so we couldn't get a cue from the name either, so it was really interesting. [. . .] It's interesting because it is sort of so important. It kind of weighs on you not knowing. [. . .] You just keep wanting to know" (Andrea, age 30, began losing sight at age 12). The implicit logic of these accounts is that perceiving sex as self-evident is correct, whereas perceiving ambiguity is somehow wrong. This anxiety about ambiguously sexed bodies is of course not unique to blind people. When a sex attribution is problematic, or in very rare cases impossible, most sighted people also feel at least somewhat uneasy. This is largely because to acknowledge that sex is anything but totally self-evident is a violation of the natural attitude, which dictates that sex must be attributed in every interaction. Such violations make us feel embarrassed and uncomfortable, as if something has gone "wrong" with the interaction.[23]

The blind respondents' descriptions of sex as "obvious" also raise two further questions: (1) *How* is the sense of obviousness and necessity created, cognitively and perceptually? And (2) *why* sex differences? Why is this particular way of understanding bodies so strongly emphasized? Answering the *how* question is one of the central aims of this book, and I will return to it throughout. In essence, though, my argument is that sex is only perceptually self-evident if we selectively attend sex differences and selectively disattend sex similarities. However, the question of *why* this happens, why we are culturally obsessed with determining sex and marking it as the most important and obvious difference among human bodies, deserves some discussion as well.

There are many ways to answer the question of why the male/female distinction is such a heavily emphasized social and cognitive organizing principle. For example, biologically oriented theories typically explain the importance of gender differentiation as a requirement of reproduction; that is, we need to attend to (and become attracted to) the differences between males and females in order to become aroused and engage in heterosexual intercourse. While some feminists have taken this to mean that it is only through the elimination of women's reproductive function that they will achieve equality with men,[24] others criticize the idea that human reproduction requires such "excessive sex-distinction" at the level of cultural discourse, arguing that the real reason for compulsively socially differentiating men from women is to create and maintain women's subordination.[25] In this view, the reason we are socialized to be hyperattentive to sexual difference is to create and maintain a system of social inequality between males and females. A Marxist explanation, by contrast, would maintain that gender inequality is an epiphenomenon of a more fundamental process of emphasizing the differences between the sexes in service of the capitalist mode of production.

There is also a sociocognitive answer to the question of why sex differences are so rigidly emphasized, which is mental anxiety about ambiguity.[26] From a cognitive sociological perspective, this anxiety about sex ambiguity is just one instance of a more general mental discomfort with uncertainty and the desire to maintain the mental "purity" of a rigidly classified universe. One way we manage this cognitively is to disattend ambiguity in order to create dichotomies.[27] In addition to quelling our mental anxieties regarding indeterminacy, the creation of clear-cut dichotomies is also about avoiding cognitive and perceptual "overload," since "a world with no lines is a chaotic world."[28] While these simplified perceptions protect us from being bombarded by undifferentiated stimuli, as one may expect, this is achieved only at a cost. The trade-off is that, for the sake of comfort and simplicity, a lot of the world's variety, diversity, and ambiguity are essentially eliminated from our perceptions.

In eliminating so much complexity from our perceptions, norms of disattention make certain ways of perceiving bodies "obvious" and others "impossible to imagine." In other words, not only do we collectively perceive sex as "obvious," we also cannot see human bodies as other than male and female, as coming in more or fewer than two categories. That is to say, it is almost impossible for us to be blind to sex.[29] A number of gender scholars have commented on this failure of imagination when it comes to (un)sexed bodies, arguing that sex difference functions as a "necessary background to the possibility of thinking, of language, of being a body in the world,"[30] such that "alternatives are virtually unthinkable."[31] While it is admittedly often a struggle to conceptualize nondualistic ways of thinking in general, sex seems to totally close down our faculties for creative thinking. To capture this resistance, sex has been called an "incorrigible proposition,"[32] and "a limit beyond which thought cannot go."[33]

Peter Berger and Thomas Luckmann used the terms *externalization, objectivation, internalization,* and *reification* to capture the process by which human activity attains the characteristic of objectivity.[34] Prior to them, Fleck specifically stated that to "objectivize" something is to draw the *work of interpretation* into the background.[35] In the case of seeing sex, not only are sexed bodies obvious to us and unsexed bodies unimaginable, but we also do not experience sex difference as socially imposed on us from without, or as created through human action or thought. Rather, we tend to feel that our perceptions of sex are rooted in and verified through our experiences, which we take as objective representations of "Reality." Stated differently, our optical socialization in the cultural context of the overdetermination of sex creates particular perceptions of sex that in turn serve to validate the reality of sex difference in a kind of closed circuit. Maurice Merleau-Ponty described this circular process of perceptual construction as follows: "Our perception ends in objects, and the object once constituted, appears as the reason for all the experiences of it which we have had or could have."[36] Of course, what gets overlooked in this formulation is the intervention of social norms and expectations in the act of perception, which shapes our sensory experiences in socially shared and socially acceptable ways.

The culmination of all of the various social forces simplifying and synchronizing our perceptions of bodies, restricting our awareness to sex differences, is that sex becomes self-evident and taken for granted. Sex difference is experienced as irrefutable common sense—everybody knows, it's obvious—and the myriad of social forces relentlessly highlighting and disproportionately emphasizing sex differences drop below the level of social visibility. Despite this invisibility, or more precisely because of it, from a sociological perspective, that which is self-evident is what most needs to be called into question. In fact, it is arguably one of the discipline's defining tasks to expose and study the taken-for-granted, even if doing so is always a challenge, as ethnomethodologists and symbolic interactionists have made clear. In the spirit of Garfinkel's famous "breaching experiments," which were conceived as "aids to a sluggish imagination," learning to see bodies differently requires that we imaginatively distance ourselves from the perceptual norms of the sex-difference paradigm—to the extent that this is possible—and treat as problematic that which is normally taken for granted.[37] My suggestion is that filter analysis can facilitate this. When we conceptualize sex difference as a mental filter, the salient question becomes, what is attended and what is ignored when we see bodies as "male" or "female"? Answering the latter part of this question—what is ignored when we see sex?—directly confronts us with "the reality of other possibilities, as well as the possibility of other realities."[38]

Sex Difference as a Social Filter

A number of scholars have previously provided descriptions of sex/gender that are evocative of a sociomental filter in their pointed emphasis of attention and disattention. Butler, for instance, describes a "grid of legibility" that "defines the parameters of what will and will not appear within the domain of the social."[39] Linda Nicholson similarly highlights sociomental dynamics of attention and disattention when she describes perceptions of sex differences as "missing much": "Like a lens that only illuminates certain aspects of what we see by shadowing others, these visions kept from sight the many contexts that we as women and men deviate from the generalizations these analyses generated."[40] Selective attention is also the key mental process underlying Kessler and McKenna's concept of a *gender schema*. For instance, consider the following characterization of the gender-attribution process: "The attributor contributes to the accentuation of gender cues by selective perception. For example, members of our culture may look for facial hair, while in other cultures this might not be considered something to inspect. In learning to look for facial hair, the attributor perceives in greater detail signs of facial hair than would be the case if facial hair were not a cue."[41] Based on this description, gender attribution is essentially a form of selective attention. As they put it: "Certain differences take on importance, while others are seen as irrelevant . . . [and] may be ignored."[42] The metaphor of a filter offers significant analytical precision and richness when it comes to identifying these crucial processes of selective perception.

Several of the transgender people I interviewed likewise described sex attribution as a process of selective attention. In the following comments, for instance, note the way the perceiver disattends—"filters out"—sex ambiguities:

I read once that for every male attribute you need to have two other feminine attributes to compensate—to tip the balance in the other direction. (Jamie, MTF transsexual, age 18)

Like there are plenty of biologically born women who have big shoulders or are like six foot five, but they have other things where it kind of cancels out. (Ali, MTF transsexual, late 20s)

It's like a point system for taking someone's license away. I couldn't tell you how it breaks down. It's jewelry, makeup, what does your face look like, deportment. I think that deportment gets overlooked. [. . .] It's kind of a pass/fail test, which is why everybody says passing. (Susan, MTF transsexual, age 30)

The idea that certain physical attributes "cancel out" others, or that a determination of sex can be cognitively "tipped," highlights the centrality of cognitive processes in sex attribution. More specifically, these ideas suggest that we disattend many of the ambiguities and complexities of bodies when categorizing them as "male" and "female." This is precisely the logic of a "pass/fail" test or a "point system," both of which allow for some amount of ambiguity to be present but "irrelevant."

It is not especially surprising that transgender people have a keen awareness of these processes of cognitive exclusion, since one defining feature of transgender identities is the inability to fit into the available categories—or to fit only by denying ambiguous or contradictory (according to the available categories) aspects of themselves. In Jacob Hale's words, "Those of us who live in borderzones constituted by the overlapping margins of categories . . . do so because our embodiments and our subjectivities are abjected from social ontology: we cannot fit ourselves into extant categories without denying, eliding, erasing, or otherwise abjecting personally significant aspects of ourselves."[43] Without this denial, elision, and erasure, he explains, "lost in language and in social life, we become virtually unintelligible, even to ourselves."[44] To some extent, however, this is true of everyone. We all fall somewhere in the "overlapping margins of categories" Hale describes. Bodies are always "classified into simplistic *social* categories (for example, male/female, black/white, upper/middle/working class) which ignore overlaps in, and stress the differences between, human bodies."[45]

Whenever we see bodies, we note certain details while ignoring others; we never take in all of the technically available information. Depending on his or her optical socialization, education, and training, one person will notice details to which another person is blind. Dermatologists, for instance, can differentiate between healthy and dangerous moles that look identical to an untrained observer. (Experienced mushroom hunters can likewise distinguish edible from inedible mushrooms that to the uninitiated are impossible to tell apart.[46]) One can continue in this vein virtually indefinitely: podiatrists notice feet, chiropractors notice posture and spinal alignment, orthodontists notice jaw alignment, dancers notice leg alignment, aestheticians notice pore size, and so on. And at the same time that members of each of these different groups attend to the particular details of bodies they are socialized to find salient, they are of course also not seeing other details. The body is only ever seen selectively, through one or more filters.

While each of the filters alluded to above relates to subcultural conventions of attention and focusing, specifically the optical norms of different occupations and hobbies, norms of visual attention operate much more broadly as well. I know I am not alone, for instance, in the way that I frequently do not register someone's eye color, but I virtually always notice whether he or she is male or female. Likewise, it is not unusual for me to say "I remember him as taller"—or heavier, or fairer—whereas it is highly unlikely that I would say "I remember him as female." Just like the optical filters of an occupation or hobby, when we focus on those details of bodies that provide information about sex differences, we are attending only to certain features of the body. Strictly speaking, selectively noticing sex differences (which also requires selective inattention of sex similarities) is no less conventional than these other, distinctly subcultural ways of seeing bodies. This normative attention to sex differences is clearly not the *only* way we see bodies, as the above-referenced examples of subcultural norms of perception make clear. While not monolithic, selectively seeing sex differences is nonetheless a hegemonic perceptual norm, reflecting the demands of our sexpectations.

In light of this, one can think of sex difference as a "foundational" influence on attention, directing our analytic focus to the ways that culture, in a macrolevel paradigmatic sense, impacts the attribution of meaning in social life by blocking some information from our awareness while allowing other information to "pass through."[47] *Foundational filters* structure our attention and the attribution of meaning, organizing what we see and what we know (as well as what we do not see and what we do not know), as adherents of broad worldviews. At a less foundational level, exemplified by the occupational norms of attention discussed above, the concept of *contextual filters* highlights the way our perception is structured by different social contexts. Here I understand context broadly to include environments or times that establish a clear field of relevance within which our attention is structured—and meaning is attributed—in a particular way. As opposed to the foundational level of experience, which is unbounded and omnipresent, contextual experiences are bounded temporally and/or spatially.[48]

Whether foundational or contextual, it is important to emphasize again that these patterns of selective attention are all—at least in part — a reflection of *social norms*. It is not simply that certain body parts are more available for us to inspect, and it is therefore those empirically salient details that we attend. Although some details may in fact be more visually salient, that alone cannot account for what we notice. At times, in fact, social norms of attention direct us to seek out and attend physical details that are far from obvious and to ignore those that are technically more salient. For instance, breasts and facial hair are not really any more empirically salient than elbows, noses, and earlobes, yet their social salience leads us to pay them more attention.

Further, through selective attention, our sexpectations influence not only what bodily details we notice, but *how* we perceive different parts of the body, including whether we view those parts as given for life or malleable. For example, when people adjust their crooked teeth using braces and even sometimes oral surgery, we do not continue to believe that they have crooked teeth (and are falsely representing themselves as "straight toothed"). Though malocclusion is a biological "fact," orthodontic interventions can permanently alter biology. However, other body parts are viewed as fixed for life. Consider in this light the sex reassignment surgeries undergone by transsexuals. Technically these interventions are at least as permanent as orthodontic adjustments—even, arguably, more permanent, since without consistent, long-term use of a retainer, one's teeth can shift back to their original state after braces are removed. However, due to the prevailing belief that sex is a fixed and essential aspect of personhood, even after surgery transsexuals find that there exists an assumption that they remain their birth sex on some fundamental level. This is to say that sex is viewed as part of one's essence in the classical Aristotelian sense of that which is unchanging and constitutive of a person or thing. Jake, a 48-year-old intersex person, also touches on the notion of sex as essence when describing the root of his mother's lack of acceptance: "Seeing as I am not completely male or female she views me as invalid as a human being." Other parts of the body, such as one's teeth, weight, or hair color, are by contrast merely "accidental," and one can alter them without challenging prevailing beliefs about the irreducible core of the self.[49]

To put it another way, orthodontic interventions "count," whereas sex reassignment surgeries "don't count" as a legitimate biological transformation, given that sex difference is singled out among all the various parts of the body as the irreducible essence of a person.[50] This view implicitly underlies the following comments from both Jamie and Sam about their friends' and family members' difficulty making the cognitive and perceptual switch required by their transition:

So many of my friends have known me for so long as [male. . . .] I don't feel like they're ever really going to see me as female [. . .] even if everyone else in the world just kind of is like "hello miss." [. . .] The assignment's been there for a really long time; it's not going to shift that much. [. . .] They'll look at my face and still see [. . . a male] face. There's still going to be all these masculine attributes that they had seen previously, which wouldn't necessarily be masculine, but they would attribute them just because they knew that those were there before. (Jamie, MTF transsexual, age 18)

There are a few who are very diligent about using male pronouns with or about me, but that's because they care about my feelings. [. . .] Most are having a very difficult time using appropriate pronouns. I think a small part is simply habit, but a large part is changing the perception. And don't get me wrong, these people are supportive and do try. It's just difficult for them to flip that switch. (Sam, FTM transsexual, age 37)

In large part, "flipping the switch" when it comes to sex is so difficult for people because, when compared with the rest of the body, our emotional and moral investment in the reality and fixity of sex is much stronger. Consider a comparison with another medical intervention, bariatric surgery. If one's child or friend became thin after this or a similar medical procedure, it would be surprising if one continued to perceive them as fat (disregarding their new medically created bodily appearance as "false"). Perhaps more to the point, when a woman has breast reduction surgery, we do not insist that she still has large breasts. Neither is someone forever seen with a crooked nose after rhinoplasty. Yet this idea somehow seems perfectly logical in the case of sex differences. Of course, making these distinctions among different body parts requires ignoring the commonalities between sex and other bodily differences and focusing only on what makes sex unique.

We are not only socialized to see sex as more fixed and essential than other aspects of the body. We also learn to see the pelvic area as more private and sexual. It would be possible—that is, given different social norms and expectations—to experience the genitals as the sexual equivalent of the ears or the elbows. Joan Emerson makes this point explicitly when discussing the medical view of genitals in the context of a gynecological examination: "In the medical world the pelvic area is like any other part of the body; its private and sexual connotations are left behind when you enter the hospital. . . . Their [the medical staff's] nonchalant pose attempts to put a gynecological examination in the same light as an internal examination of the ear."[51]

The broader point to take away is this: when we see male and female bodies, what we see is never a direct mirroring of empirical reality. Social norms and expectations intervene between the perceiver and the perceived. Consequently, we should not think of sex as purely biological: sex is always perceived through the interplay of social norms, cognition and matter. Considering that cognition and perception are such important mechanisms of the social construction of sex and the body more broadly, they have received surprisingly scant attention in the current upsurge of interest in the body in both sociology and gender studies.

Perception and the Social Construction of the Body

While notable earlier works certainly exist, both sociology and gender studies have recently seen a remarkable increase in attention to the body. Bryan Turner's *Body and Society* was truly path blazing when it was first published in 1984, and only since then has the body emerged as a central and distinct area of both theoretical and empirical research in sociology. The first sociological journal explicitly devoted to the investigation of the body, *Body and Society,* was founded in 1995 to capture this new interest in the social and cultural aspects of the body, but it was not until 2009 that the American Sociological Association added a section on the body and embodiment.[52]

Within sociology and in the broader interdisciplinary field, gender scholarship now constitutes one of the most sustained and systematic attempts to take embodiment seriously. When writing about the ways the body is shaped and transformed by the social structure of gender, however, the role of cognition and sensory perception in the social construction process receives relatively little focus. Further, while gender scholars have written effectively and extensively about social practices that "gender" the body, until recently "sex itself" was often explicitly excluded from their accounts.[53] An unexamined conceptual boundary seemed to separate sex from the rest of the body—sex was portrayed as an exception to the social construction of gendered bodies and the omnirelevance of gender, reinforcing the idea of sex as more essential than other aspects of embodiment.[54] Ironically, at the same time, many gender scholars have criticized essentialism and have acknowledged that understanding sex as a fixed biological dichotomy hinders the acceptance of their conclusions about the social construction of gender.[55] As Raewyn Connell put it, ideas about natural sex differences are "the lion in the path of social theories of gender."[56]

More recently a number of key gender scholars have argued that it is important to problematize hegemonic understandings of sex as well as gender. This growing body of research on the social construction of "sex itself" is the closest in focus to this study. There are many different answers to the question of how sex is socially constructed. My approach is to highlight the role of cognition and perception, but previous work has pointed out the exceptions to binary sex (such as intersexuality), identified historical differences in conceptualizations of sex, and analyzed the ways gender norms frequently influence scientific findings about sex differences.[57]

Kessler and McKenna's *Gender: An Ethnomethodological Approach* prefigures my approach to the social construction of sex in several important ways. Their most noteworthy contribution, a shift to conceptualizing gender as a mental schema, has been described as follows: "What is important about Kessler and McKenna's conception of gender is not merely their insightful account of the mechanics of gender attribution, but their subtle shift of gender's terrain. Gender moves from a stylization of the body to a category of the mind. It is, in an important sense, an immaterial substance—an intangible idea with palpable consequences, an a priori category that structures the phenomenal world."[58] Kessler and McKenna's book thus initiated the important work of studying the cognitive and perceptual dimension of gender. When they write that "the constitutive *belief* that there are two genders . . .

creates a sense that there is a physical dichotomy,"[59] for instance, Kessler and McKenna provocatively highlight the sociocognitive dimension of our experience of male and female bodies. In fact, as they put it, "most of the work is done for the displayer by the perceiver."[60] My analysis adopts precisely this notion of gender as "an a priori category that structures the phenomenal world," in addition to extending their focus on the perceiver rather than the displayer.

In the course of their analysis, Kessler and McKenna make several crucial points about the social *rules* of sex attribution. For instance, they point out that visual sex attribution is never based on genitals, even if we believe they are the basis for our categorization.[61] In reality, we do not normally see each other's genitalia, so the attribution process depends on "cultural genitals"—more visible "gender clues" (e.g., hair or clothing) that stand in as proxies for anatomical genitals.[62] This idea raises several of the key questions I aim to address, including: What are these proxy genitals specifically, and what are the other cognitive mechanics of the "gender attribution process"?[63]

Kessler and McKenna's overlay experiment, in which they created images of people with different combinations of "male" and "female" body parts and asked research subjects to decide whether the resulting figures were male or female, was designed to capture the relevance of different body parts in sex attribution. However, the insight this experiment can provide is limited by certain elements of the study's design, which presupposes some of what it sets out to investigate because it includes a number of unexamined assumptions about what is and is not relevant for sex attribution. The only body parts Kessler and McKenna varied in the experiment were genitals, breasts, body hair, head hair, and hips. They did not change the faces, arms, legs, hands, feet, necks, overall stature, or any other feature of the bodies in the images shown to their participants. Their experimental design thus presupposes that genitals, breasts, and hair are "relevant," whereas faces, stature, arms, legs, hands, necks and feet are "irrelevant." They also assume that there are in fact "male" and "female" hips, hair, breasts, and so forth; how else could they mix "male" and "female" body parts to create "ambiguous" figures? As one of my goals is to challenge the prevailing cultural logic about which body parts are "relevant" in sex attribution (and even which body parts can accurately be considered male or female), it is important for me to consider the entire body, especially those parts that seem intuitively *irrelevant*.[64]

Further, despite the fact that Kessler and McKenna highlighted the important role of the perceiver in sex attribution over thirty years ago, these questions about how—by what cognitive and sensory processes—perception contributes to the social construction of male and female bodies have yet to motivate significant in-depth study. Kessler and McKenna's observation that you "see someone as female only when you cannot see them as male" remains one of the few available explanations.[65] Much of current gender theory instead hangs on the notion of performativity, the enactment of sex and gender norms through reiterative acting out and display.[66]

Most famously, Butler argued there is no "naturally" sexed subject who preexists the performance of gender. The sexed body that is assumed to be behind any display of gender is "performatively constituted by the very 'expressions' that are said to be its results."[67] While Butler's efforts to theorize the social construction of sex are commendable for their complexity and attention to gender norms and the psychological mechanisms by which these norms operate to form our experience of ourselves as having a fixed sex, her account of the social construction of sex is limited in two important ways. First, as she herself confesses, her analysis rarely actually takes the physical body as its explicit focus.[68] Both Butler's suspicion of the category *sex* and her tendency to slip past the physical into other realms reflect the intellectual strengths and limitations of queer (and other radical social constructionist) theory more generally.[69] Moving forward, it will be important to create research projects that maintain some of the insights of this important body of work while engaging more directly with the materiality of the body.

Second, conceptually speaking, gender performativity captures only one aspect of sex attribution and the social construction of sex—the construction and performance of a sexed subjectivity. In practice, however, cultural norms work to construct sex difference from several directions simultaneously—organizing not only our sense of ourselves as having a fixed sex, which we then display through norms of grooming, adornment, and bodily demeanor, but also our sensory perceptions of other people's bodies. Yet while our understanding of the display side of the interaction has become quite complex and interesting, the experience of the perceiver is much less understood.[70]

This is particularly problematic since the body's material properties, while important, are largely meaningless unless individuals attend to them—unless they are both sensed and made sense of.[71] Indeed, "from a very young age, human beings are trained to visually process and meticulously read bodies—our own and others—for social cues about love, beauty, status, and identity."[72] In fact, sensory perception is arguably the context for our entire experience of bodies, both other people's and our own, whether as the displayer, the perceiver, or both. As such, perception represents an interesting case to explore in relation to criticisms that research on the social construction of the body (and sex specifically) is usually overly textual and, ironically, rather disembodied. Perception is actually *doubly* embodied. Not only is it our primary mode of experiencing bodies, but it is an embodied experience in and of itself, automatically overcoming the mind/body bifurcation.[73]

Part of what makes it difficult to study the perceptual dimension of the social construction of sex, however, is that, as we have seen, the visual experience of bodies as always either male or female is profoundly taken for granted. The sighted trust vision uniquely among the senses; we typically believe that what we see is a complete, objective representation of empirical reality. When we see people as sexed, then, it is usually without any consideration of the sociocognitive or perceptual *processes* that may create that experience. To really think critically about sex difference, we need an ontological and epistemological jolt—an alternate perspective that, if acknowledged, so strongly challenges our expectations that it forces us to problematize the seeming perceptual "obviousness" of sex. I have tried to construct this break both methodologically (through the study's design) and analytically (through filter analysis).

Blind people provide access to an "outsider perspective" on visual sex attribution that brings to light aspects of the process that we may otherwise take for granted as sighted people. Stated another way, I studied blind people as a case that can illuminate more universal dynamics. My goal is to capture the cognitive and sensory process by which they attribute sex and to compare that process to visual sex attribution to learn how much of the dominant understanding of sex is specific to sight. This is not to say a blind phenomenology of male and female bodies is necessarily any more (or less) accurate than the sighted experience, but it does provide access to an alternate perceptual reality that challenges taken-for-granted assumptions about the "self-evidence" of visual differences.

Transgender people, on the other hand, provide access to a perceptual experience of sexed bodies that is similar in its sensory content to the dominant experience (in that it is primarily visual), but with a significantly elevated awareness of the intricacies of all that is involved in seeing sex. Accounts by and research on transgender people suggest that they tend to be hyperaware of how sex and gender are constructed.[74] In order to live in a sex different from the one they were assigned at birth, they have to be. The stakes for them are much higher, in that their very lives may depend on their knowledge of how people "read" bodies as male or female.

Analytically, I argue that reconceiving sex as a mental filter provides unique insight into what is going on cognitively and perceptually when we see sex. The filter metaphor is organized around a dialectic of attention and disattention in which certain details of empirical reality pass through our filters and are attended, while others are socially blocked from our awareness. Attention and disattention are well-known dynamics of categorization that have not been fully mined for their conceptual insights regarding sex attribution and seeing bodies more broadly. By highlighting the centrality of disattention, filter analysis pushes us to recognize and define how social relations enter into and transform the body in ways that have not been fully theorized.

One of my central claims is that focusing on selective perception using filter analysis represents a new way to conceptualize the interaction of biology and culture, one that acknowledges obdurate material reality without simply taking it at face value. While perception is not her main focus, Alice Dreger highlights my exact point of entry into these debates about social construction and materiality: "Certainly we can observe some basic and important patterns in the bodies we call 'male' and the bodies we call 'female.' And the *patterns* we *notice* depend in part on the cognitive *and* material tools available at a given moment."[75] In other words, it is not necessary to espouse a "pure constructionist" or "blank slate" position to develop a useful and interesting constructivist account of bodily sex difference. Filter analysis acknowledges material structures—physical similarities and differences that provide the raw sensory data and play some role in perceptually distinguishing socially meaningful entities. Given this, I locate the social construction process in how we cognitively and perceptually "deal with" those features through socially organized practices like selective attention. This approach allows me to tread a path between radical social constructionism and the formulations that are variously called "weak" constructionism, "foundationalism," and "cautious naturalism," which, while not necessarily determinist, typically do take sex as one of a limited number of "givens of biology."[76]

Further, social norms of cognition and sensory perception actually underlie many—if not all—other areas of sociological research on sex (and other aspects of the body). For instance, when investigating the social construction of sex through scientific research, the actual mechanisms of social construction are arguably cognition and perception. To take just two examples, in her study of scientific research on sex hormones, Nelly Oudshoorn argues that "the prescientific idea of sexual duality" was a "major guideline structuring the development of endocrinological research," and Melanie Blackless and her collaborators similarly argue that "if one relinquishes an a priori belief in complete genital dimorphism, one can examine sexual development with an eye toward variability rather than bimodality."[77] Both of these claims highlight the sociocognitive dimension of scientific research, specifically the way that social norms regarding the unique salience of sex differences have limited scientists' thinking—and their literal sensory perceptions. The same is true of studies of different historical constructions of sex. For instance, when the historian Thomas Laqueur argues that until the end of the eighteenth century male and female bodies were seen as more similar than different, what underlies this observation is social norms of cognition and perception. As he puts it, "To be sure, difference and sameness . . . are everywhere; but which ones count and for what ends is determined outside the bounds of empirical investigation."[78]

In the chapters that follow, with the filter metaphor as a guide, I use the perspectives of blind and transgender people to provide a grounded illustration of the role of cognition and perception in the social construction of the body. Identifying the parts of the body that are attended—as well as those that are disattended—when we see bodies as male or female allows me to provide detailed descriptions of the social construction process that directly address the matter of the body. I begin by focusing on norms of attention, highlighting the ways that socio-optical filtration and polarizing display practices both create perceptual bias in the same direction—attention to sex differences—and thus function together to obscure other possible perceptions of bodies. Then I explore the complementary norms of disattention by asking the defining question of filter analysis: What is being filtered *out*?

THREE

Selective Attention—
What We Actually See
When We See Sex

The fundamental question to be addressed by a sociological analysis of attention in the context of sex attribution is, what information do we actually perceive when we see sex, and why? Although certainly not a definitive list, the transgender and blind people who participated in this study offered many ideas about what bodily cues are "relevant" for sex attribution. For totally different reasons, members of both populations are able to shed light on the parts of the body that are most frequently attended when seeing sex. Many transgender people actively and consciously present themselves as female (if they were determined to be "male" at birth) or male (if originally assigned a "female" sex), making them aware of cues that cisgender people take for granted. This is both because the stakes of successful sex attribution are higher for them, and because they are often still in the process of learning norms that cisgender people also learned, but so long ago that the practices may feel "natural" and unremarkable.[1] Blind people, on the other hand, do not participate in visual sex attribution (at least as perceivers). Their descriptions of the sensory cues relevant for them in identifying a person's sex at times provide an instructive contrast to the visual experience, illustrating the key benefit of a multisensory approach to knowledge: when we generate enough different ways of perceiving the same thing, it becomes very difficult to view one as more self-evident or valid than the alternatives.

Transdar and Transition: Transgender "Expert" Knowledge of Sex Cues

One topic of discussion that consistently revealed the transgender respondents' elevated awareness of which body parts are the most important sex cues was what several of them referred to as "transdar" (a variant of "gaydar" in which one can pick out who is a transgender person). Joan, a 67-year-old MTF cross-dresser, defined *transdar* as follows: "We know what to look for, the things you can't change. The size of the hands and wrists. That's really the first thing. And of course if someone still has an Adam's apple, that's a clue, or if someone is covering up an Adam's apple. There isn't too much you can do about the width of your shoulders." Other respondents offered similar descriptions of transdar as a keen understanding of the most important sex cues. Jacqueline, a MTF cross-dresser in her mid-60s, put it this way: "I can get on the subway, and there are a fair number of transgendered people on subways now. [. . .] I can tell. I know. [. . .] Adam's apple, skin roughness, oh, another big one is hands. [. . .] A lot of men have the thick spatula hands. That's a giveaway. [. . .] Shoe size, big feet. [. . .] We know what's harder to disguise." Based on these and other similar descriptions, the transgender respondents view themselves as experts on sex cues who are much more aware of them than nontransgender people.

The logic underlying the concept of *transdar* is that firsthand knowledge of transition brings with it a heightened awareness of the major differences between male and female bodies—overcoming those differences, after all, is the most challenging barrier to passing. In light of this, one particularly rich source of information about the key indicators of sex was the transgender respondents' descriptions of what they believe makes other people perceive them as one sex over the other.

Hair is big. General facial features. And your body motions. Sitting like a female is generally very different from sitting like a guy. Walking too. Because I didn't have huge bone structure. I didn't have the chiseled facial features men sometimes have. (Cynthia, MTF transsexual, age 45)

Chest is now flat, body is more muscular and thick, voice is deeper, facial hair is prominent, haircut is more "male." (Joe, FTM transsexual, no age provided)

Well number one is definitely the face, including hair, facial structure. Number two is height. I would say number three is, um, I don't know if it's attitude, but presence? How you walk, or your body motions, things like that. (Ali, MTF transsexual, age 27)

For the full range of their answers to these questions about what makes them "read" as one sex or the other, as well as more general questions about what they feel are the relevant cues for assigning someone to "male" or "female" (not just in their specific cases, but more broadly), see the list of cues in table 1. I constructed this list inductively from the interview transcripts and recorded the number of respondents mentioning each cue. In cases where someone mentioned a particular cue multiple times, I only counted the first instance.

The transgender respondents seemed to agree on a small handful of reliable cues for determining sex, particularly demeanor/deportment,

Table 1 Transgender respondents' list of sex cues (n = 41)

Cue	Number of respondents who mentioned the cue
Body motion / deportment / demeanor	31
Head hair	28
Breasts	22
Voice	22
Body shape / silhouette	22
Facial hair	19
Facial features overall	18
Makeup	18
Body hair	14
Clothing	14
Hand size	13
Stature	13
Eyebrows / brow ridge	11
Shoulder size	10
Hip size	9
Legs	9
Adam's apple	8
Shoe style	7
Nose shape	6
Eyes	6
Lips	6
Butt size	5
Foot size	5
Skin texture	5
Chin size	4
Jewelry	4
Arms	3
Jaw line	3
Waist size	2

which was mentioned by all but ten of the forty-one respondents, as well as head hair, breasts, voice, and silhouette, all of which were mentioned by over half of the respondents. However, they also raised a range of less commonly recognized cues (everything from chin size to nose shape to shoe style). On the one hand, this suggests that many different parts—the greater proportion even—of the body can serve as sex cues, at least some of the time. On the other hand, the great majority (twenty-four out of twenty-nine) of these cues were mentioned by less than half the respondents (and in fact sixteen of the twenty-nine total cues were actually mentioned by less than a quarter of the respondents). Considering this, what did not emerge from these data is a stable set of clearly defined, mutually agreed-upon biological indicators of sex. Further, approximately a third of the cues they mentioned are indisputably social and have little if anything to do with natural bodily differences between males and females, (e.g., makeup, jewelry, and clothing). Among the remaining cues, many, while biological, are arguably quite variable within the sexes, such as waist size, skin texture, and nose shape.

While table 1 simply presents the universe of cues they mentioned, I also asked approximately half of the transgender respondents to complete a survey designed to provide more specific insight into the relative salience of different body parts. I primarily used the survey in the in-person interviews (and a few of the e-mail exchanges). It was not used in the phone interviews, although I always covered essentially the same ground verbally. There were also a few cases where I did not use the survey in a face-to-face meeting in a public place when I sensed that the respondent was concerned about drawing attention to the fact that he or she was being interviewed. Participants ranked the importance of twenty-three body parts, which I provided to them in a list, on a scale from 1 to 10, where higher scores indicate higher relevance for sex attribution. The mean relevance scores for each body part (as well as the full range of responses) are summarized in table 2, and a copy of the survey is available in the appendix.

Most of the cues ranked highest in the survey—chest, hands, hair, eyebrows, and several other facial features—roughly correspond with those that came up most frequently through coding the interview narratives. (They are all among the top ten most commonly mentioned parts of the body.) However, this may suggest somewhat more consistency than the data support. For one thing, many of the body parts receiving the highest scores on the survey were also assigned the lowest scores by other respondents. As an illustration, consider the range of

Table 2 Survey results—relevance scores assigned to twenty-three body parts by transgender respondents (n = 19)

Body part	Relevance for seeing sex (mean score, out of 10)	Range of responses (1–10)
Chest	8	3–10
Hands	8	5–10
Head hair	8	6–10
Buttocks	7	4–10
Eyebrows	7	3–10
Shoulders	7	5–10
Cheeks	6	1–10
Chin	6	3–10
Feet	6	2–10
Forehead	6	1–10
Lips	6	2–10
Neck	6	2–10
Abdomen	5	1–10
Calves	5	1–10
Genitals	5	1–10
Lower arms	5	1–10
Thighs	5	2–10
Upper arms	5	1–10
Ankles	4	1–10
Ears	4	1–10
Knees	4	1–10
Elbows	3	1–5
Shins	3	1–8

responses displayed in table 2. Of the twenty-three body parts listed, ten received the full range of possible responses (1–10), and an additional five body parts received nearly the full range of responses (either 2–10 or 1–8). Further, with the exception of elbows and shins, each body part with a mean score of 5 or below was assigned the highest score by at least one respondent (and shins received scores as high as 8).

This variability brings to mind Suzanne Kessler and Wendy McKenna's argument that the key to understanding sex attribution may not lie in identifying a set of mutually agreed-upon cues. As they put it, the attribution process "cannot be reduced to concrete items that one might list as differentiating women from men." "Members need to know, for example, when to disregard eyebrows and look for hand size."[2] Nonetheless, I believe it is still enlightening—particularly epistemologically—to create a list of possible cues, which provides a rare opportunity to break the body down into parts and specifically consider their sex dimorphism (or lack thereof).

However, if sex attribution is not a mechanical application of a set of rules but a more complex process of "mental weighing," wherein particular cues "count" only in some circumstances, or "don't count" in combination with certain other cues (e.g., long hair generally signifies femaleness, but if combined with other cues that signify maleness, such as facial or body hair, it does not "count"), then creating a list of sex cues alone is not enough; it is also necessary to identify some of the mechanics underlying the more complex sociomental processes by which we interpret the cues.[3]

As a starting point, if we can use a range of different cues to attribute sex, some of them not at all biological, and some of them quite variable within the sexes (and therefore presumably only sometimes informative), this suggests that the *content* of sex attribution—what we actually see when we see sex—is at least somewhat *flexible*. That is, we can perceive sex in a number of different ways, using different combinations of cues. What is much less flexible, reflecting the rigidity of our sexpectations, is the compulsion to see sex (however that may be achieved in practice). We may then think of sex attribution as a cognitive process by which perceivers take in a range of stimuli—perhaps even attending to totally different cues in different cases— and yet seem always to come to the same conclusion: male or female.

One implication of this flexibility in the content of sex is that the dominant *ideology* of sex difference is quite different from the everyday *practice* of sex attribution. Perhaps the best example of this disjuncture between social beliefs about sex and the actual practice of sex attribution has to do with the role of the genitals. Kessler and McKenna made the argument that, while sex attribution is essentially a decision about whether someone has a penis or a vagina, it is almost always made in the absence of information about genitals.[4] My data basically support this view of genitals as a highly marked but functionally irrelevant sex cue. In fact, two respondents actually assessed the importance of the genitals as 0 on a scale of 1 to 10 on my survey, while five additional respondents assigned them either a 1 or a 2. There is widespread awareness in the transgender community that not all transsexuals (particularly FTM transsexuals, for whom the constructed penis is often less functional) choose to undergo sexual reassignment surgery, and yet they still "pass" unproblematically. Others delay the surgery for a long time—sometimes decades—while they live as their sex of transition. Genitals are culturally marked as highly relevant for knowing someone's sex, but they almost never actually serve as a cue in practice.

While cultural discourses present sex as a self-evident and unchanging feature of the body—something that exists in a concrete and stable way that we then "read off" the body—in practice, the sex-attribution process may be much less uniform and fixed, drawing on different cues in different cases. Several FTM transsexuals, for example, mentioned they almost always read as "male" in small towns, whereas in metropolitan areas, where the cultural context provides the category *butch*, they can also be read as "butch-females." In the first case, wearing "men's" clothing and having short hair are sufficient signifiers of maleness, and other characteristics such as stature or hand size are irrelevant and not noticed. In the latter context, these aspects of appearance are considered important cues ("tells"), whereas dress and hairstyle may be viewed as insufficient information for sex attribution (since there is an expectation that both males and females can wear "men's" clothing). The difference lies not with the individual's bodily display but rather the shape, structure, and quantity of the holes in the perceiver's cognitive filters.

That a determination of sex can be achieved using a wide range of sensory cues is even more obvious when considering nonvisual sex attribution. Blind people describe an entirely different universe of sex cues that overlaps very little with those cues I have been discussing up to this point, serving as a powerful reminder that any suggestion that we might all agree on the most salient differences between the sexes fails to acknowledge the validity of the sensory realities inhabited by blind people.

The Sound of Sex

When describing how they determine whether someone is male or female, the blind respondents' near-universal first response was "tone of voice." Jack, age 38, who has had macular degeneration since birth, describes the differences in voices as follows: "Masculine voices are usually a little bit deeper and run at a lower decibel rate. I think [that] is probably a way to describe it. And they are sometimes more gravelly although not always. I tend to think of feminine voices as being a little higher pitched, so the pitch has something to do with it. For me, masculine voices are heavier and feminine voices are lighter." Another common response was that the sound of someone walking—the type of shoe and the sound of the footfall—can often serve to indicate sex. Further, due to blind people's expertise in sorting out aural information, they can also use a wide range of surprising (at least to a sighted person) sound cues to decide whether someone is male or female in the absence of voice—for instance, the sound of a skirt on someone's legs, a sneeze or cough, or even a cell phone ring:

Usually I pick up on subtle things like the sound of their shoes to identify their gender. Also, girls are usually more chatty when they enter the room so it's easy to tell. Or, if they cough or sneeze, or laugh, I can tell. [. . .] As I mentioned, I can usually pick up on one's gender by little cues they make with their voice, or other alerting sounds like sounds of a girl's skirt brushing against her leg as she walks, a man's heavy boots hitting the ground, or even their cell phone ring sometimes. (Simone, college age, blind since age 15)

Sometimes by the sound of their walk, like if a woman is wearing high heels, and sometimes men tend to have a heavier walk. (Juliana, age 23, visually impaired since birth, totally blind since age 16)

I would notice, I suppose, how fast they walked. I might infer from that some approximation of how tall they were. I would be able to tell if they were carrying a plastic bag, or wearing a backpack. The backpack would make noise as it rubbed against their shirt. (Jackson, age 24, blind since birth)

Basically without exception, the blind respondents told me that this highly developed sense of how sex sounds is the primary way they attribute sex.

However, any discussion of a blind phenomenology of the body would be incomplete without acknowledging the role of smell; almost all of the respondents mentioned that scent cues played some role in sex attribution, as well as in their perceptions of people's bodies more generally, and in their daily experiences navigating from place to place. Many mentioned perfume, cologne, scented lotions, and other scented beauty products as cues that alert them to whether someone is male or female.

I could figure it out if the person was wearing perfume or cologne. Not a whole lot of guys wear Tommy Girl. And not too many girls wear English Leather. (Jackson, age 24, blind since birth)

If the subject is wearing cologne or perfume, I could tell between a man and woman. (Owen, age 28, visually impaired since birth)

Speaking more broadly, others noted that smells are often integral to their experience of physical spaces like buildings. Simone, for instance, who has been blind since age 15, relies heavily on scent cues when walking across her college cafeteria:

Without sight, it is very common for me to depend on my smell to identify objects and even locations. [. . .] At the university I attend I have to walk through the main eatery on campus several times a day to get to various places. The area is very large and sometimes confusing. Through my sense of smell I can identify my position based on the smells around me. For instance, as soon as I smell coffee, I know I am near the stairs and the doors that lead outside, because the coffee shop runs parallel to these areas. As the smell of coffee becomes stronger, I know I am approaching this area.

Others mentioned that they are sometimes surprised that sighted people do not experience smells as intensely as they do. "I have a friend and she used to be married to this guy, and [. . .] he just had the foulest BO [body odor]. He just smelled like sweat all the time. And—because we were like best friends—I said to her, 'How can you have sex with him? He's so gross smelling'" (Anna, age 37, blind since birth). These comments collectively suggest that the blind respondents rely on scent to categorize and describe people, as well as to aid in spatial orientation.

While I recognize that they do not typically attribute sex through touch in everyday life—my respondents were all very quick to point out that the stereotype of the blind person feeling someone's face is not a real reflection of how blind people recognize another person—it is still interesting to think about what parts of the body are sex dimorphic through touch and to learn more generally what blind people believe they can know about bodies through touch. Considering that the skin is the largest sensory organ, tactile information about sex differences is rarely discussed and undervalued when compared with visual information. Further, as I already mentioned, some scholars contend that touch is less prone to distortion than vision because it requires contact with the perceptual object.[5] The suggestion is that, as a result of this proximity, "the tactile sense does not encourage intellectual leaps."[6] Not to mention, blind people do of course touch the human body, and probably more frequently than sighted people, since they often hold on to a person's elbow or shoulder when they walk with them as a "sighted guide." For these reasons, I was particularly interested in exploring the blind respondents' tactile perceptions of bodies.

Just as they seemed able to find much more useable information in sound and scent cues, many respondents told me that just by touching a person's arm or hand, they can determine his or her approximate height and weight.

I can actually tell quite a bit about someone just by walking holding their arm, [. . .] things like height, sometimes a guesstimate on weight, how muscular, etc. (Lucy, age 25, blind since birth)

I learn how tall they are. Just yesterday I went to the dentist and the dental assistant walked me in, and I said to her, "My goodness, have you lost some weight?" And she had. Because I had taken her arm before and it was very sort of firm, and now it was thinner but [. . .] kind of soft. (William, age 61, blind since birth)

Specifically regarding sex attribution, the question is, does touch provide blind people with a very different phenomenal experience of male and female bodies?

To capture some of these tactile experiences of bodily sex differences, as part of the interviews I asked the respondents to participate in a thought experiment. I described a hypothetical scenario in which they would be presented with a line of people—a mix of males and females—and asked to decide where to touch the people to most reliably determine their sex. This is clearly an artificial set of circumstances, and therefore the responses cannot be taken to capture naturally occurring interaction. Simply from the perspective of exploring sensory differences, however, it is interesting to consider which body parts they felt would provide the most tactile information about sex differences. A very small number of respondents stated or implied that they would first touch the genitals—although interestingly most did not mention them, possibly assuming that they were not "allowed." Beyond that, some respondents wanted to begin with facial hair, some with head hair, some with height, some with "midsections," and some with legs. Andy (age 61, blind since birth) explained his view as follows: "If you said touch whatever you want to, I would touch their cheek because with a man you would immediately feel—even if he had just shaved. Yeah, there are women who have facial hair, but that would be the most accurate I think." Now contrast his perception of the "best" sex cues with the following responses:

I believe I would have the easiest time if I were able to touch their midsection or their legs. (Simone, college age, blind since age 15)

Height would be a way to start to sort a little, facial features (hair, shape, etc.), throat area (Adam's apple, etc.), and that's just with the face and head. (Arlo, age 33, blind since age 3)

A few people also mentioned skin texture and chests, one mentioned shoulders, and one mentioned hair texture. Clearly there was a lot of variation in their responses, perhaps because they do not routinely rely on their sense of touch for sex attribution.

In table 3 I summarize all of the sex differences the blind respondents raised during the interviews. I culled this list from the transcripts, and included both the cues they reported using most often to attribute sex—for instance, voice, scent, and footfall/type of shoe—as well as their responses to my hypothetical questions about the sex differences they perceive through touch (even though in practice they rarely rely on touch for sex attribution). In cases where a respondent mentioned the same cue more than once, I only included the first instance.

Although it seems "obvious" from an emic perspective, from an etic perspective it is interesting that the blind respondents completely excluded taste from their descriptions.[7] It is also noteworthy that because they rarely use touch for sex attribution in natural interaction, blind people do not typically base their decisions about sex on the matter of the body at all—its shapes, surfaces, or appearance more generally. Erving Goffman's distinction between "manner" and "appearance" provides some useful grounding here. The "front" we perform includes two conceptually distinct dimensions, according to Goffman. One's "appearance" is a fairly stable set of signs (mostly bodily—e.g., posture, facial expressions, and gestures) that communicate one's status; that is, who one is, including one's sex. "Manner" refers to signifiers of how one wants to be perceived within one's role, or status—for example, passive, haughty, dominant, and so forth.[8] Blind people do not usually have access to facial expressions, gestures, and body language—the key elements of "appearance" as Goffman describes it.

I'd like to understand body language better, but I can't because there's so much of it that you have to see to know. (Betty, mid-50s, blind since birth)

I think I'm aware that they [gestures] exist. [. . .] I told somebody one time, I want you to teach me how to give dirty looks. I want you to teach me how to look impatient. [. . .] But I'm not very successful with that. But I know that gestures exist. [. . .] I know gestures exist, but I probably don't know what they are, and unless I'm

Table 3 Sex differences, blind respondents (n = 27)

Sex difference	Number of respondents
Hearing	
Voice	21
Speed/weight of footfall when walking	10
Sound of shoe (e.g., high heels)	10
Name	9
Content of conversation (subject, word choice, intonation)	4
Sound of clothing	2
Laugh	2
Cough/sneeze	1
Cell phone ring	1
Bracelets	1
Scent	
Products (e.g., perfume/cologne, shampoo, lotion)	15
"Natural smell"	3
Touch	
Body/facial hair	12
Head hair	10
Hand size	7
Skin texture	6
Arm/elbow size	6
Jewelry	6
Type of clothing	5
Ear size	5
Nose size	5
Height	4
Weight	3
Leg size	2
Muscle mass	2
Neck size/Adam's apple	2
Shoulder size	2
Breasts	2
Foot size	1
Hip size	1
Buttocks	1
Bra strap	1
Overall body shape	1

touching the person, I probably wouldn't know that they made them. (Andy, age 61, blind since birth)

Body language such as shaking your head yes and no. Stuff like this, such as waving at someone if you're riding in a car—do you show them the front of your hand or the back of your hand? What is that gesture? Those are things that you [blind people] learn because you're taught, not because you see other people doing them. (Jack, age 38, macular degeneration beginning at birth)

Based on Goffman's definition, then, one may say that blind people do not perceive appearance, and rely on manner, particularly as conveyed by voice, to indicate both one's role, or status (who one is), and how one wishes to be perceived in terms of attitude and behavior. At the same time, however, a multisensory approach to social research also suggests a critique of the concept of *appearance*, and even the visual root of the term itself, as failing to acknowledge the extent to which category membership is conveyed nonvisually (e.g., through the sound of a heavy footfall, or a feminine scent or voice). Even those cues normally assumed to be strictly visual almost always have other sensory dimensions—for instance, a person's height, which many respondents reported perceiving through both sound (by noting the point of origin) and touch.

Nonetheless, my respondents occasionally relied on an ocularcentric understanding of "body" and "appearance" themselves. William (age 61, blind since birth), for instance, said: "I don't have any perception of them, their body, or what they're like if they're just walking by. I'm mainly concerned with not bumping into them." Of course, William surely has *some* perception of other people's bodies as they walk by, most notably the sound of their footfall, yet he defines body only as visual appearance. The following comment from Jesse (age 50, age of onset of blindness not provided) similarly indicates an implicit visual definition of body: "Actually physical characteristics really don't mean anything to me, because then you get into the questions of what is beautiful, what is ugly, so I really don't pay that much attention to people's physical characteristics. I don't really care." Again, when he states that "physical characteristics" don't mean anything to him, Jesse understands what counts as "body" in purely visual terms, since characteristics such as scent, voice, and other nonvisual mannerisms do presumably matter in his interactions.

Similarly ocularcentric assumptions were also evident in some respondents' discussions of sex attribution specifically. As Andrea (age 30), who began losing her vision at age 12, put it, "In the blind community it is not uncommon for there to be a lack of awareness of gendered ways of presenting one's self." While this may be true of visual cues, such as hair or makeup, as we have seen, blind people are highly aware of voice, scent, and other nonvisual sex cues. This once again signals an unmarked visual norm that falsely suggests that the information available through the other senses provides only indirect information about what is understood—even by some blind people—as an essentially visual reality. Prior research similarly shows that blind people tend to have a visual understanding of race, which they feel they access only indirectly, using "proxy" cues.[9] However, even if blind people themselves often define the body, including sex and race, in visual terms, it is important to point out that there is no empirical reason that the visual appearance of sex or race is more "real" or meaningful than other sensory information. That is, the experience of sex or race through hearing, touch, smell, and taste are just as real and accurate as visual perceptions but less culturally validated.

In this vein, explicitly complicating the tendency toward ocularcentrism I've just described, a number of respondents questioned what the sighted may miss by relying largely on vision. Rowan (age 24, with ongoing vision loss) framed this criticism of ocularcentrism, or any form of monosensory perception, this way: "I believe that, if you rely on any one sense for all of the information you receive about something, the potential for inaccuracy exists." In other words, because sighted people so heavily privilege visual appearance—as James (age 54, legally blind since birth, totally blind since age 3) put it, "Our culture is very high on looks and appearance and visual attributes" (age 54, legally blind since birth, totally blind since 30s)—we not only miss the wealth of information that is available through the other four senses, but we can be "hindered" and "consumed" with appearances. Anna (age 37), who has been blind since birth, elaborates on this point in the following comments:

Usually my husband is more than happy to just blurt out what someone looks like because he's more consumed with that as a visual person. I think one thing I observe with him is that vision can sometimes be a hindrance in being consumed with what somebody looks like. It's like, "she's fat"—and he's just got a thing about fat people—and I don't necessarily have that. And I can figure it out. If I grab onto somebody's arm, I can tell if they're fat or thin or short or tall. You know, that type of thing. But I'm not consumed with it. It doesn't hinder me. If I like a person, I'm not going to sit there and worry about if they're fat. [. . .] But it is a hindrance to my husband at times. It gives a lot of people prejudice against them. What are they going to be like because they're fat, they're lazy or whatever. I just don't have that kind of thing going on.

I also interviewed the wife of one of my blind respondents, and one of the things she most emphasized in her comments was that her husband has made her aware of how much more sensory information is out there beyond what the sighted typically notice. "Before I only found a scenic location beautiful for what I can see. In February we went to a bed and breakfast and walked around a nearby creek. I loved listening to the sound of the water and animals. We skipped rocks around the pond and enjoyed the sounds that different size rocks made, and [. . .] the smell was wonderful and refreshing as well."

Sidney (age 54, blind since birth) summarized the same set of ideas as follows, bringing the question of what the sighted miss specifically to the body: "If you got to touch someone or look at them, how is the information you're going to get out of it different? I think that they would be, and I don't have any way to compare, but I know that touching someone I can learn a hell of a lot." Sidney went on to argue that the information our sense of touch provides about other people is important and underutilized. He pointed out that, even for the sighted, there is a threshold of intimacy where vision "crosses over" to touch because touch can convey different and valuable information. "And what's interesting is sort of the crossover between [vision and touch. . . .] We use that [visual display] to attract or appeal or entice, but what is fascinating though is that at some point that switches over or results in touching, which becomes more intense or [. . .] a stronger way to express one's self or feelings, and yet in the normal discourse of daily events touch is sort of taboo or it's not used. It is I think underutilized in some way."

In addition to underscoring the importance of adopting a multisensory approach to social research, these comments on the limits of monosensory perception also call to mind the earlier discussion of flexibility in the content of sex attribution. It is undeniable that blind people rely on much different information than the sighted to determine someone's sex, and that their phenomenal experiences of other people's bodies are significantly different even beyond sex attribution. At the same time, despite substantial differences in content, the *cognitive process* of sex attribution, organized by the expectation that sex differences are real and important, is common across all modes of perception. Blind people take the task of sex attribution seriously and share in many broad social beliefs about the importance and self-evidence of sex differences (and, by extension, their cognitive and perceptual effects). In the following comment, for instance, Andrea highlights the way that she shares the same mental "boxes" as sighted people but fills them using different information. "I think blind people, we're raised with the same social conditioning as everyone else. [. . .] The difference is that sometimes we have to sort of find clues to put people in their proper boxes, if that makes sense." In other words, there is a shared set of expectations, but those expectations are met with very different sensory information. This also returns us to the element of socio-mental control in our cognitive processing. Even though the sensory information available to us in any particular instance of sex attribution may be distinct (whether because of the characteristics of the particular body being perceived or the mode of perception employed), all sex attributions are still organized by a mental filter resulting from shared sexpectations.

A Sex Cue Can Be Anything (as Long as It Provides Information about Sex)

Considering the transgender and blind respondents together, I collected a wide array of different answers to the question of what cues are most relevant for sex attribution. As I have been arguing, one way to make sense of the range of responses is to shift the terrain of the question being asked; rather than a fixed set of mutually agreed-upon cues, what if it is actually this significant flexibility in content that can help clarify the sociocognitive dimension of sex attribution? That is to say, in terms of the specific sensory content of our perceptions, there seems to be a lot of room for variation; in this view, anything that *can* indicate sex is relevant *if* it indicates sex in that instance.

In addition to highlighting the commonalities between visual and nonvisual practices of sex attribution, this formulation can also extend beyond the mode of perception one employs. For instance, different information is used when categorizing a naked body than a clothed body. Cues are also rendered salient by cultural context, such as when transmen report being perceived differently in small towns than in major metropolitan areas. Further, different cues must be used depending on the characteristics of the particular body being categorized—for example, some "female" bodies do not fit stereotypes about the sex dimorphism of hair, stature, or breasts, so different cues are used. While there is significant flexibility in content, a common—and quite *in*flexible—sociocognitive filter applies across these different cases, creating a binary perception no matter what kinds of cues are available. This explains how sex attribution is always simultaneously practical, in flux, and situated, and yet remarkably consistent in its outcome.[10] It further underscores the fact that the categorical perception we ultimately experience does not reflect the empirical variability in the bodies being perceived.

To put it another way, one of the implications of the analysis in this chapter is that sometimes a nose may serve as a sex cue and sometimes a nose is just a nose. That is, specific body parts are not necessarily consistently sexed, but may exhibit a spectrum of sex ambiguity. Body parts that are indicators of sex in some circumstances are ambiguous in other cases. This ambiguity is theoretically interesting but does not practically disrupt the sex-attribution process (because uninformative attributes are mentally and perceptually filtered out as "irrelevant"). Even if all body parts come in a spectrum of sex dimorphism, sex attribution still functions efficiently because even normally informative body parts are disregarded when they are uninformative. This is how the system cognitively "deals with" ambiguity without it becoming a threat to the binary social categories.

If this is true, the sex-attribution process is not fundamentally about describing the body but about efficient categorization. This formulation actually represents a renewal of Kessler and McKenna's insight that social practices, rather than body parts, are the foundation of sex attribution.[11] It also supports Judith Butler's well-known statement that sex is always already gender.[12] Indeed, contrary to the organizing principle of the sex/gender distinction, neither sex nor gender directly reflects the body itself, which may actually present us with significantly more ambiguity and variety than the cultural logic of "two and only two."

Thinking of sex cues as a system of signs that can be studied semiotically can shed more light on this dynamic in which the actual bodily cues are flexible while the social meaning remains rigid. A sign really consists of two separate things, the signifier and the signified, where the one recalls the other in our minds. The signified is the concept represented, while the signifier is what represents it.[13] The meaning of a sign does not come from any necessary relationship between the concept signified and the specific signifiers that represent it. Rather, the meaning of a sign is the result of socially shared conventions regarding the relationships between different signifieds. In the words of the linguist Ferdinand de Saussure, "Concepts are purely differential and defined not by their positive content but negatively by their relations with the other terms of the system. Their most precise characteristic is in being what the others are not."[14] The meaning of a sign, then, is based in the opposition between the signified and other related signifieds. By extension, if we analyze our bodily sex cues as a system of signs, the rigidity is in the relationship between the two signifieds—the syntactic separation between the concepts *male* and *female*. The signifiers that represent that difference are flexible. The semantic relationship between the various signifiers of maleness and the concept *man* is arbitrary (i.e., it only holds insofar as the signifiers of the concept *man* maintain their opposition to the signifiers that represent the concept *woman*).

In light of this, consider that even the cues we have been most strongly socialized to believe are very informative of sex are ignored when they are ambiguous. For example, one of the most "reliable" cues, according to both groups of respondents as well as some of the other available evidence, is head hair:

I can have every male sign removed, all my makeup, all my jewelry, and without the hair, the hair is like the final crown. [It will] make or break you. [. . .] No matter what else I did, [without the hair] I wouldn't pass. (Annie, MTF cross-dresser, late 50s)

I had a hair transplant [. . .] sort of in preparation. [. . .] Hair is big. (Caroline, MTF transsexual, 40s)

My best attribute, that would have to be my hair. (Sandra, MTF cross-dresser, age 54)

I'm not sure if you've ever noticed, but to me, women's hair just seems to be somewhat of an entirely different feature than a male's hair. I can't explain it, but they're just not the same. (Owen, age 28, blind since birth)

Sociologist Betsy Lucal likewise emphasizes the importance of hairstyle in her account of her own experiences being perceived (and not) as female: "I again let my hair grow out for several months, although I did not alter other aspects of my appearance. Once my hair was about two and a half inches long (from its original quarter inch), I realized, based on my encounters with strangers, that I had more or less passed back into the category of 'woman.' Then, when I returned to wearing a flat top, people again responded to me as a man."[15] An advertisement for Thermacare (fig. 4), a disposable heating pad that adheres to the body, similarly demonstrates that hair alone can be a strong enough cue to induce us to interpret a body as female. The fact that the human figures in the ad are otherwise identical is not really noticed because the long hair serves as such a strong signifier of femaleness. The *New Yorker* cartoon that follows (fig. 5) similarly plays on the way apparently female hair is immediately recognized as a meaningful sex cue to the exclusion of attention to other equally real but ambiguous, uninformative details (in this case, the fact that the doctor is actually a man in a feminine wig).

Despite the widely held expectation that hair is an important, infor-

FIGURE 4 Hair as a powerful sex cue (Thermacare ad). (*Newsweek*, April 14, 2003, special advertising section, p. 10.)

*"Many women are more at ease with a female doctor.
That's why I'm wearing the wig."*

FIGURE 5 Hair as a powerful sex cue (*New Yorker* cartoon). (With permission of the *New Yorker* [originally appeared February 2, 2004, p. 39].)

mative sex cue, in instances when it is ambiguous, we easily disregard it. Hair is "irrelevant" on a woman when it is very short (or we probe instead for the subtle details that make it a short feminine style while ignoring the ways it is similar to men's short hair). As Caroline, a MTF cross-dresser in her 40s put it, "You could shave your head and you'd still be a woman, because you have the other attributes." Likewise a man with long hair is a man despite his "feminine hair." Even if it is something we have been socialized to understand as a key indicator of sex, in other words, when a cue is uninformative in practice, it is ignored. What this demonstrates is that, once again, the flexibility of the content of our sex attributions rarely disrupts the categorization process in practice.

Breasts are also widely regarded as a particularly reliable and informative sex cue. Recall, for instance, that chest received the highest mean relevance score in table 2, and was the third most frequently mentioned sex cue behind hair and demeanor/deportment in table 1. To take another example, in her autobiographical book chronicling her experimental attempt to pass and live as a man, Norah Vincent describes an interaction during which she had to "prove" to someone that, despite appearances, she is a biological woman. The cues she emphasized to make her case were the absence of an Adam's apple and the presence of breasts.[16] Yet breasts are only relevant when informative of sex. A female with a totally flat chest is still unproblematically seen as female. Rather than disrupting the sex-attribution process, or bringing the sex categories into question, her flat chest is quite easily ignored as uninformative. For instance, one of the transgender people featured in the documentary *Gendernauts*, Stafford, said that she is never taken as female (her birth sex), even if "I'm just wearing a T-shirt and I have breasts showing." At six feet tall, she explains, her height is taken as a secondary sex characteristic that overwhelms the other "female" cues. Similarly facial hair can "outweigh" breasts if both are present, a point Kristen Schilt illustrates in the following description of one of the transmen she interviewed: "Because most people expect that biological sex differences are written on the body, they overlook any visible female cues when facial hair is evident. During our interview, Stephen and I took a break to get some coffee. He had not had chest surgery at that time and was not wearing a binder—a tight, flexible top that flattens breasts. Though he had visible breasts, everyone in the store called him 'sir' because he had a goatee."[17]

What these examples illustrate more generally is that we are primed by our sexpectations to scan bodies in a socially structured way. Rather than allowing the particular details of the body itself to determine what is most salient, our expectations direct us to zero in on the most likely indicators of sex first, such as hair, breasts, and stature. In doing so, we look past any similarities between the sexes, rather than "counting" them as evidence that sex differences are questionable. At the same time, we disregard even these likely indicators if they turn out not to provide clear information about sex. The effective result of this filtration process is that we cognitively create as many sex differences as possible in each instance without taking into account the relative proportion of bodily ambiguity. At the same time, this perceptual bias in favor of sex differences is further exaggerated by the cognitive distortions I examine in the next section.

Cognitive Distortions in Seeing Sex

I have argued that, in perceiving sex, some body parts (those that demonstrate sex difference) are attended, and others that are equally real and empirically available are ignored. However, in addition to the question of *what* we see, it is necessary to consider *how* we see it. Our perceptions of the body are subject to a number of cognitive and perceptual distortions, all of which influence our perceptions in the same direction: toward seeing (or sensing) sex differences as more prevalent than they are empirically. The two perceptual distortions I present here are *topological perception* and *sex seepage*.

As Eviatar Zerubavel describes it, topological perception "leads us to mentally inflate distances across boundaries."[18] Such mental inflation involves highlighting differences across social boundaries and downplaying differences within boundaries. Zerubavel also refers to this process as "lumping" and "splitting." He explains lumping as follows: "As we group items in our mind (that is, categorize the world), we let their similarity outweigh any differences among them."[19] Splitting, by contrast, involves heightened attention to information that separates the members of different social categories. Another way of saying this is that we perceive *in more detail* those differences that are relevant for categorization, regardless of their empirical salience. This is in contrast to metric perception, which refers to standardized units of measurement such as millimeters or ounces, and is unaffected by category membership.

Both groups of respondents described male and female bodies in markedly topological terms. Note the inflation of sex differences in the following description of hands, for instance: "A man's hands are typically more rough than a female's. The bone structure throughout the hand is generally thicker in the male's hand and more petite in the female's hand. [. . .] A man usually has thicker hair on their fingers and their nails are wider" (Simone, college age, blind since age 15). While perhaps an accurate description of sex differences in hands, the details this respondent emphasizes—differences in size, skin texture, and hair—are all examples of small differences in a context of greater similarity. Even if these sex differences all exist, in other words, there are also many similarities that are totally ignored in such topological descriptions, as well as wide variation *within* each of the sexes. Within-sex variation and between-sex similarity are not defined as relevant by our sexpectations, however, and are mentally and visually deflated, while sex differences are inflated. The same analysis applies to many other supposedly categorical sex differences; relatively small distinctions in a context of much greater similarity are viewed as categorical because they are differences across a very heavily emphasized social boundary.

The topological inflation of sex differences can also expand into sex seepage, in which the entire human body is viewed as sex dimorphic. As an illustration, consider this description of facial differences from Ali, a transwoman in her late 20s:

Nose shape is pretty important. [. . .] A lot of girls have smaller noses that kind of point upwards or are very small at the tip. Guys sometimes have a really big ridge. [. . .] There's also lips. If you have a masculine face, if you have really big lips, it's kind of feminizing, typically. Everything, really, if you want to analyze it. Guys have bigger chins. Women tend to have really pointy smaller chins. The jaw line is usually more rounded on a female, especially where the ear is. This is not really noticeable, but guys have an extra bone behind their ear, too, that you can feel.

In fact, several of the transgender respondents replied to my questions about what body parts are the most sex dimorphic with statements like "What *isn't* different?" The following comments from Tim (age 33, blind since age 3) also illustrate sex seepage: "In general women would have different shapes of almost all things than men so you might be able to tell in lots of ways. Some I'd think would be less effective, but I do think you could tell though from just about everything." In each of these comments, sex differences are not limited to the primary and secondary, or even the "tertiary," social behavioral sex characteristics but are perceived over the entire surface of the body.[20]

The effect of both topological perception and sex seepage is to exaggerate social norms of relevance and selective perception. In other words, it is not simply that sex-dimorphic body parts are "relevant" and thus noticed more; we also see sex differences *in body parts that are empirically ambiguous* by picking out subtle differences and distorting their degree of salience in relation to sex similarities. Because we are hypersensitized to sex differences, we see them much more readily than sex similarities—even when the similarities are equally, if not more, empirically prominent.

While these distortions occur on the perceiver's end, they are also buttressed by *polarizing practices* which disproportionately *display* sex differences. That is to say, the exaggeration of sex differences on the part of the perceiver is supported (and maybe even surpassed) by the exaggeration of sex differences by the displayer. Up to this point, I have artificially separated two social processes that are in practice experienced simultaneously and feed off of one another. It is difficult to talk about "relevance" in perception without also discussing the social norms of self-presentation that highlight certain parts of the body as meaningful signs ready to be perceived. The salience of sex differences is thus produced and reproduced through a dialectic of perception and display.

Polarization

While my primary objective in this chapter is to capture the parts of the body that are cognitively and perceptually marked as relevant in sex attribution, quite deliberately highlighting only the role of the perceiver, which has previously received disproportionately little attention, complementary though distinct rituals and norms of self-presentation operate simultaneously with our sociocognitive filters. Social norms regarding grooming, dress, adornment, comportment, and body shape and size all help facilitate seeing difference. We manipulate the appearance of body parts that are naturally similar for males and females—body parts that exist in a natural continuum rather than a dichotomy—to display difference rather than resemblance.[21] Through these polarizing practices, body parts are ritually prepared to be seen, and to pass unproblematically through the binary sex difference filter.

Gender scholars have periodically highlighted the social display of difference on and through the body as a pivotal aspect of the social construction of gender. For example, Kessler and McKenna referred to a "dichotomization process," Candance West and Don H. Zimmerman argued that "doing gender" is essentially the creation of difference, and Raewyn Connell introduced the concepts of "negation" and "transcendence" to describe the cultural creation of physical gender differences where none exist "naturally." The work of these and other gender scholars reminds us that the body is a gendered cultural product; the social construction of gender extends to the body, to the creation of dichotomous differences in behavior and appearance.[22]

Dress, for instance, can function to make sex difference more visible in several different ways. Certain types of clothing, such as plunging necklines, highlight by revealing. Clothing can also highlight sex differences by what it covers: "women's" bathing suits cover the breasts while "men's" do not, drawing attention to—and in the process helping to construct—the "difference" between male and female breasts. Clearly, clothing is culturally variable, and it is difficult to generalize about whether dress always functions to emphasize sex. In cultures where it is customary for women (and men) to be topless, for instance, highlighting the distinctness of female breasts by covering (or revealing) would not apply. Further, highlighting sex differences by revealing does not appear to apply in certain Muslim cultures in which women traditionally wear a full body veil (*burqa* or *abaya* and *niqab*). However, a variant of emphasizing sex differences by covering could still apply, since veils function as categorical signifiers of sex.[23] As one woman who wears a veil put it, "We don't cover our womanhood. On the contrary, we underline it."[24] Ironically, it is particularly effective to mark sex difference by fully covering the body, because it eliminates all visual ambiguity. To a lesser extent this is also true of modified forms of veiling, which, for instance, cover only the hair. Wearing a headscarf is an unambiguous cue indicating femaleness. No matter what the hair that is covered actually looks like (it could even be a crew cut), covering it with a headscarf makes it "female."

Sex-differentiating display practices also extend beyond clothing to the matter of the body: Male and female eyebrows are not very different naturally, but females frequently pluck and style theirs, creating difference. Similarly, male and female head hair is not naturally different, but social convention dictates that we cut and style it to display difference rather than similarity. Women who have facial hair almost always remove it. Men who have breasts disguise them. Women also tend to moisturize and otherwise take care of their skin in different ways than men, a point raised repeatedly by the transgender women I spoke with:

A lot of being feminine is just personal hygiene. It really is. [. . .] I take care of my skin. [. . .] I use alpha-hydroxy everything. (Liz, age 56)

[Part of my transition was] really concentrating on skin care. When I can afford it, getting facials. I still use some of the products, like every morning I use a special serum, like vitamin C kind of stuff, special moisturizers. (Caroline, 40s)

The suggestion is that it would be possible, given different social conventions of grooming and dress, for men and women to look much more similar than they do. This point is powerfully illustrated in Lucal's account of being consistently perceived as a male because she is "a woman who does not do femininity."[25] Similarly illustrative is Carol Barkalow's caption to a photograph of a group of first-year West Point students in regulation dress with short haircuts, which challenges the reader to locate the only woman in the room.[26]

These gendered grooming practices and conventions of dress have no apparent function aside from eliminating the underlying sameness between male and female bodies; their exclusive purpose is polarization (see fig. 6). Polarizing grooming practices create sex differences where there are none "naturally" or significantly exaggerate subtle differences, thus reducing the proportion of human commonalities male and female bodies would otherwise share (represented by the space of overlap between the curves in fig. 6). Polarization effectively disambiguates male and female bodies by reducing their similarities while simultaneously increasing their differences.

Our understanding of polarizing practices can be further enhanced by viewing them as "rituals of separation" that play up the crossing of

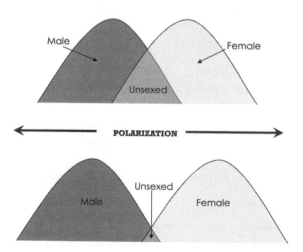

FIGURE 6 Gender display as polarization.

sociomental divides in order to make them seem more "real."[27] Such rituals "substantiate" or "enhance the experience of discontinuity."[28] Norms of grooming materialize the social distinction between males and females by creating more sex differences. While a small number of body parts differentiate the sexes prior to polarization, conventionally groomed female and male bodies are actually much more different than similar. Through these norms of self-presentation, the balance shifts and more body parts display difference than similarity. (Compare tables 4 and 5).

While one can certainly disagree with my categorization of individual body parts as sex dimorphic or non–sex dimorphic, or identify

Table 4 The ungroomed body

Sex dimorphic	Non sex dimorphic
Facial hair	Head hair
Adam's apple	Forehead
Breasts	Eyebrows
Body hair	Eyelashes
Overall stature	Eyes
Hips	Nose
Genitals	Lips
	Ears
	Nape
	Collarbone
	Shoulders
	Armpits
	Elbows
	Insides of elbows
	Wrists
	Hands
	Abdomen
	Back
	Buttocks
	Thighs
	Knees
	Backs of knees
	Shins
	Calves
	Ankles
	Feet

Notes: The use of the terms *sex dimorphic* and *non–sex dimorphic* here is for emphasis only and is undoubtedly an overstatement. The body parts in the left column, even when artificially polarized by grooming, are not fully sex dimorphic. And in some circumstances, the apparently nondimorphic body parts in the right column are actually relied upon to attribute sex. Thanks are due to Judith Gerson for pointing this out to me.

Table 5 The groomed body

Sex dimorphic	Sex dimorphic only when groomed	Non–sex dimorphic
Facial hair	Head hair (cut, style)	Forehead
Adam's apple	Eyebrows (plucking, waxing)	Nose
Breasts	Eyelashes (makeup)	Elbows
Body hair	Eyes (makeup)	Insides of elbows
Overall stature	Lips (waxing, plucking, makeup)	Abdomen
Hips	Ears (jewelry)	Back
Genitals	Collarbone (jewelry, neckline of clothing)	
	Nape (jewelry, collar / neckline of clothing)	
	Shoulders (exercise, cut of clothing)	
	Armpits (shaving, waxing)	
	Wrists (jewelry)	
	Hands (nails, jewelry)	
	Buttocks (cut of clothing, type of underwear, shoes [e.g., high heels])	
	Thighs (shaving, waxing, cut of clothing)	
	Knees (shaving, waxing)	
	Backs of knees (shaving, waxing)	
	Shins (shaving, waxing)	
	Calves (shaving, waxing)	
	Ankles (jewelry, shoes)	
	Feet (nails, shoes)	

parts of the body I have overlooked, the overall proportional shift is undeniable. What is more, even some of the body parts that are still not sex dimorphic after grooming can be socially enlisted in other ways to mark the difference between males and females. Many social conventions of comportment and style are singularly devoted to reinforcing gender distinctions. For instance, in the aggregate, males and females learn to hold or gesture with their fingers and wrists in different ways, even further polarizing the presentation of human bodies.[29] My transgender respondents spoke extensively about these additional polarizing behavioral norms for males and females:

I think you generally can make a woman because she's more graceful. Because her facial expressions are more emotional and interesting: the smile, the look. Men tend to be more deadpan looking. [. . .] And also body language. Men tend to be flat. (Jacqueline, MTF cross-dresser, 60s)

A man would never hold a pen like that. (Dee, MTF cross-dresser, age 55)

Sitting like a female is generally very different from sitting like a guy. Walking too. (Cynthia, MTF transsexual, age 45)

In short, through conventions of grooming and other norms of bodily adornment and presentation, the greater part of what is naturally the same about "male" and "female" bodies is eliminated. Lindsey, a 19-year-old transwoman, described the effect of these polarizing norms of self-presentation as follows: "There is definitely a continuum. [. . .] There are very few people in the very center." Tay, who is intersex, made the same point from a different perspective, explaining that no social norms of self-presentation exist for those people who are between male and female: "There are no norms for me to adhere to, unlike if you were one or the other. I have found society polarizes women and men."

These polarizing norms support, and are supported by, the perceptual filtration process. In other words, just as gender is an interactional accomplishment,[30] seeing sex involves both the "reader," the person whose visual perception is structured by the sex-difference filter, as well as the person perceived, whose presentation of self is expressly designed to allow them to be seen unproblematically through this filter. "Concrete displays are not informative unless interpreted in light of the rules which the attributor has for deciding what it means to be a female or a male. As members of a socio-cultural group, the displayer and the attributor share a knowledge of the socially constructed signs of gender."[31] The binary sex-difference filter thus works to enact sex difference from two directions simultaneously—it organizes perception as well as our norms of grooming, adornment, and bodily demeanor. When we shape and style our bodies, we are presenting ourselves to viewers who are well-schooled in the same perceptual and semiotic language—they share the same sexpectations and mental filters.

Stated differently, polarization is filtration preparation. Grooming and other forms of bodily socialization are fundamentally about preparing the body to be seen as sexed. There is a mutually reinforcing dialectical relationship between filtration and polarization that *makes selective attention to sex differences not feel selective*. Polarization increases the empirical salience and obviousness of sex differences (and eliminates ambiguity), and thus assists in easy and unproblematic perceptual filtration and categorization.

While we may experience maleness and femaleness as "obvious" and self-explanatory, then, this "obviousness" is the product of a number of different social processes, all of which emphasize and draw attention to the singular distinction of sex difference. Although here I have focused my analysis at the level of interaction, I have already discussed the ways that sex differences are also relentlessly emphasized and institutional-ized at much more macroscopic levels, including medicine, academic research, childrearing, and education. Without these multiple forms of social reinforcement, sex would not appear to us as the indisputable reality of bodies.

Furthermore, seeing bodies as male or female, or, more broadly, see-ing anything *as* something, requires *not* seeing the other possibilities. Our perceived reality is always filtered through various interpretive frameworks. We never simply *see*. Whether consciously or subcon-sciously, we are always *looking*. The distinction between looking and seeing has been alluded to by a number of other scholars, all of whom emphasize that looking is an "essentially social act" distinct from "sim-ple observation."[32] As such, "the act of looking, and what is sought, af-fects what nature discloses."[33] In other words, the body does not tell us which details to look for; rather, we construct the body in the shape of our expectations by the act of looking for socially relevant features. In the case of sex, we do not simply *see* human bodies; we *look for* "male" and "female" bodily cues. Because we expect sex differences, that is the information we seek out, and thus what "nature discloses." Of course, what unavoidably remains *unnoticed* are the evidence and details that would support other perceptions and categorizations—and by exten-sion other social worlds, organized around different rules of relevance. In the next chapter I use my interview material to try to peer around the mental filter that encourages us to see sex difference—and bracket the polarizing practices that make sex differences more empirically sa-lient—in order to access some of these normally disattended alternate perceptions of bodies.

Blind to Sameness

It is a useful exercise to imagine how a human body might look if we were blind to all the details that indicate sex differences, and what we noticed instead—what "stood out" to us perceptually—were sex similarities. We would register people's foreheads, eyes, elbows, and ears, for instance, but ignore their hair, breasts, and makeup. When I try to imagine how a person would appear to me through such a filter, what comes to mind is a series of line drawings in which noses, elbows, ears, eyes, and foreheads are rendered in great detail, whereas head hair is uniform and schematic, and breasts are de-emphasized, if they are included at all. These are the fundamental questions motivating this chapter: Suppose we did not perceive bodies with the expectation of sex difference but through a different mental filter? How differently would the body appear to us? What would we see, or hear, or feel, or smell, or taste that we usually do not?

One example of such an alternate filter is the "one-sex model" described by historian Thomas Laqueur. Laqueur contends that in the past, specifically prior to the nineteenth century, male and female bodies were seen very differently than they are today. As opposed to the two distinct sexes that seem so self-evident to a contemporary observer, through the mental filter of a one-sex model, "male" and "female" bodies were more similar than different. The vagina was seen as an interior penis, for instance, and the ovaries as testicles. Here I further explore the idea of sex sameness, essentially asking what bodily evidence adherents of a one-sex view might have drawn on to substantiate their beliefs. In other words, with a one-sex model as a mental filter, what bodily details were considered relevant? What sensory information did people selectively seek out and attend, and what did they ignore as "irrelevant"? Laqueur himself provides a starting point when he explains that, under the one-sex model, the differences between male and female bodies were often overlooked as irrelevant: "No one was much interested in looking for evidence of two distinct sexes, . . . anatomical and concrete physiological differences between men and women, until such differences became politically important."[1]

Primed to perceive sex differences, today we are much more likely to ignore sex similarities. As an illustration, consider Michael Messner's observations about a group of parents watching two soccer teams, one all boys and one all girls: "In the entire subsequent season of weekly games and practices, I never once saw adults point to a moment in which boy and girl soccer players were doing the *same* thing and exclaim to each other, 'Look at them! They are so *similar!*' . . . In fact, it was not so easy for adults actually to 'see' the empirical reality of sex similarity in everyday observations of soccer throughout the season."[2] Reversing this normative structure of attention, this chapter brings sex similarities into the foreground. Drawing on blind people's rarely acknowledged nonvisual perceptions of bodies, and transgender people's expert knowledge about those parts of the body that are *not* relevant for appearing as one sex or the other, I map out some of the key commonalities between male and female bodies.

This is not to say that the blind and transgender people I interviewed do not share at all in the hegemonic belief in sex difference and the cognitive practice of backgrounding sex similarities. As I described in chapter 3, they easily identified many sex differences. More broadly, they seem to believe sex is obvious and to have the expectation of perceiving it unproblematically. Most directly pertinent to the subject of this chapter—disattention—they also tend to view as "irrelevant" any similarities between male and female bodies that do enter their awareness. This came out in the interviews in several different ways: For one thing, both groups of respondents initially seemed quite dumbfounded by my questions about what elements of the human body are the same between males and females. For example, when I asked Annette, a 71-year-old MTF transsexual, if there are any parts of male and female bodies that are the same, she said: "Now that's a tough one. I don't know. I've never thought about that. I can't answer that." When I probed further, asking about specific body parts, such as the back, she said she "never gave it much thought." Iris (MTF transsexual, age 48) seemed equally at a loss when discussing knees, ankles, and shins: "Knees. Hmm. I never thought about that one. [. . .] I mean, it's not something I notice. I notice like hands and things like that, the big stuff. [. . .] Ankles. Is it important? Not really. [. . .] Shins. Never thought about that one. [. . .] I haven't even heard anybody talk about that." One way to interpret this bewilderment is that it indicates that these respondents have unconsciously assigned sex similarities the status of "irrelevant," and they are confounded when these similarities are unexpectedly brought to the fore of their attention. In fact, both groups of respondents occasionally expressed surprise (and sometimes even laughed) when I brought up some of the more androgynous parts of the body, such as knees, noses, ears, shins, and elbows, in the context of a discussion of sex. For example, when I mentioned noses and ears it elicited the following reactions from two blind respondents:

That's a funny question! Ears. Ears I couldn't tell. If I were able to get the nose without touching anything else or without factoring the height into it I couldn't tell. [. . .] I never thought about that! But I'm certainly gonna be thinking about it the next time! [. . .] That would be funny! (Betty, mid-50s, blind since birth)

Hmm . . . nose and ears?? I guess I never considered either of these places. (Simone, college age, blind since age 15)

Notably, the tone of uncertainty and surprise in these responses is totally different from their assertions of the obviousness of sex differences, which were typically expressed with great confidence.

The concept of a cognitive "blind spot" can be helpful here. Like scotoma, the physiological blind spots—such as the one created where the optic nerve attaches to the retina—that prevent us from perceiving some portion of the visual field, cognitive blind spots *mentally* block certain technically available sensory information from entering our awareness. Reframed in the conceptual language of filter analysis, blind spots are essentially the blockages of a perceptual filter—those places where the sensory data cannot get through. Daniel Goleman argues that these blind spots, which he refers to as "lacunas," typically emerge to help us cognitively avoid anxiety-evoking information.[3] Normally when one imagines the parts of the body that are most likely to create anxiety, what comes to mind are the sexualized body parts, such as the breasts and genitals, which we even explicitly tell children are "private" or "bad touch" areas. In the context of sex attribution, however, it may be that the parts of the body that produce sufficient cognitive unease to manifest as blind spots are not the genitals but sexually ambiguous body parts such as the elbows, ears, and knees. Obviously, elbows and knees are not inherently threatening (nor are the breasts and genitals, for that matter). Rather, we are socialized to have these specific blind spots about bodies, to banish certain body parts to the background of our attention—often because they threaten social norms. In this case, the threat is to the self-evidence of sex differences.

Both groups of respondents demonstrated this normative blindness to sex similarities. However, at the same time, the underlying presumption that similarities between male and female bodies do not exist, or are not particularly salient in comparison with sex differences, often seemed to be maintained in great tension with other features of their knowledge and experiences. By mining for these moments of dissonance, I was actually able to find out quite a bit about the similarities between male and female bodies.

Transgender Narratives and the Filter of Transition

Transgender people have a unique perspective on sex differences because they view the human body in light of the possibility of transitioning between sexes. That is to say, their knowledge of the transition process changes their disposition to notice and believe certain things about human bodies. Integrating this observation into the conceptual language of filter analysis, one may say that the defining experience of and investment in transition forms an additional subcultural sociomental filter that gets layered on top of the hegemonic filter of sex difference. As a result, certain physical features take on new prominence and centrality ("relevance"), moving from the background into the foreground of their perceptions. While in some ways it focuses them even more intensely on sex differences (consider my earlier discussion of transdar), transitioning can also elevate their awareness of sex similarities.

For example, the following reflection illustrates an idea that came up repeatedly in the interviews, which is that it is *easy to pass*. Note the way that Annette (MTF transsexual, mid-40s) specifically explains the ease of her transition by referencing her preexisting androgynous—even feminine—physical characteristics. "I have nice cheekbones, so that makes it easier to pass. [. . .] Because I have naturally those features, those things aren't major things for me: facial features, body shape, and chest size." Below Tara, a transwoman in her early 40s, similarly reflects on the lack of difficulty she faced in her own transition. Implicit in her comment is the belief that gendered "mannerisms" very effectively differentiate otherwise similar body parts. "I guess this is obvious to you, but the relative ease to cross over, at least in cursory appearance, if you work on your voice and your mannerisms, who's gonna know? It's a lot about how you display it. I could go like this [gestures with her arm], or I could go like this, and it looks fairly different." For many of the transgender respondents, then, the knowledge that it is not only possible but at times quite easy to shift in appearance from one sex to the other was associated with a heightened awareness of physical similarities.

In fact, some respondents told me that the experience of transition so powerfully influenced their beliefs about human bodies that they are no longer able to unproblematically perceive sex differences. For example, Tilly, a 29-year-old transwoman, told me that for people who have transitioned: "You can make people out to be either sex. You might see a woman and say, okay, if you cut your hair short, and with men, a little different, a little different. You just have a sense of how fluid it is, and it's hard to go back to the sense that most people have where those are very strictly defined things." This description beautifully captures the way transition can enact a cognitive and visual shift that heightens attention to the ambiguities of sex.

Another related theme that emerged from the interviews is how "male" and "female" features are copresent in all bodies but exist in a "balance," "proportion," or "percentage." As Ali (MTF transsexual, age 27) put it: "Things don't have to be completely perfect, but you need to have a certain percentage of things looking like a female side in order to be passable." Sex differences always exist amid sex similarities, in other words, but "on balance" bodies tend to lean one way or the other. In the same vein, another MTF transsexual in her early 30s, Lena, mentioned that one impediment to passing she has observed in some transgender people is having surgery to make all of their features uniformly sexed; the result is that, in failing to acknowledge the natural androgyny of human bodies, they become not passable in a new way. As she put it, "Sometimes it's better to leave a few things that are neither/nor." Based on her experience, then, not only is ambiguity always present, it is actually part of what makes a body look typically sexed. In other words, sex sameness is the necessary background of any unproblematic perception of sex difference.

The idea that, as these comments suggest, sex differences and similarities coexist in all human bodies serves as an important reminder that transitioning is not about changing bodies per se. Transitioning is about changing body *parts*, which means that a lot of the body remains the same pre- and posttransition and does not interfere with sex attribution. For example, when Sam, a 37-year-old transman, reflected on the parts of his body that remain the same, he concluded that the transition was actually limited to just a handful of features: "I had a bilateral mastectomy, so there's that. I've been on hormone therapy three and a half months; my voice has dropped quite a bit. There really aren't any other significant changes other than a bit more hair on my chin." Kathy, a 67-year-old transwoman, described the unchanged parts of her body as follows: "I'd say that one's skeletal structure is unaffected by all this as to mass and shape. I can't think of what else to say [. . .] ears, eyes, nose, toes." One of Jason Cromwell's interview respondents similarly highlighted just how small sex differences are in relation to the rest of the body when he described himself as "a man in every way [except] the lower part of his body."[4] Cromwell further emphasizes the very small proportion of the body that is relevant when considering sexual reassignment surgery: "Many [transsexuals] are dissatisfied with having breasts and menstruating, neither of which accounts for the entire body. The majority of FTMs and transmen do not have gender dysphoria. What many experience, however, is body-part dysphoria, which focuses on elements such as breasts and menstruation that are quintessentially female."[5] Again, the point is that transgender people do not exchange a "male" body for a "female" one. More often than not, what they change is some combination of breasts/chest, genitals, and hormones. Many MTF transsexuals also remove their facial and body hair using electrolysis, and a subset have plastic surgery to make their facial features more "feminine." Less frequently, they may also have liposuction, or have a rib removed, or undergo other similar procedures to reshape their silhouette. Nevertheless, even in the most extreme cases, they still retain the vast majority of their bones, muscles, organs, and much more. One implication of this insight is that the "wrong body" discourse, so prominent in the medical "standards of care" for transsexuals, among its other problems,[6] also helps reinforce sex seepage, the distorted view that the whole body is sexed.

Implicitly challenging this idea that changing one's sex does not entail changing one's entire body, several respondents expressed the belief that hormone therapy changed virtually every part of their bodies. For example, one MTF respondent mentioned that her endocrinologist told her that, after taking estrogen for seven years, every cell in her body would have changed. Another MTF transsexual, Bettina (age 50), listed the many changes she observed from her estrogen treatments: "Hormones make a big difference. The difference in my face from even a year ago is unbelievable. Hormones have made such changes. I've also lost weight. [. . .] Absolutely changed the shape of my face. [. . .] Obviously you grow breasts. My waist has narrowed. I have a shape. My hips have gotten wider, my butt's gotten rounder. Hair growth is unbelievable. I'm Italian. I was a bear. [. . .] The hormones definitely soften it up and cut the growth." In this context, other respondents also mentioned changes in nails and skin texture, as well as changes in sexuality, such as erectile dysfunction ("with the hormones on my side, the hydraulics don't work no more") and increased skin sensitivity. Yet at the same time, these claims about the widespread effects of hormones were tempered and complicated in the narratives by other reflections (sometimes from the very same respondents) on the *limitations* of hormone treatments. For example, Bettina, who is quoted above as saying "hormones make a big difference" also offered, "[I] could probably put a suit on right now, cut my hair, and look pretty close to how I used to look." Another transwoman, Samantha (age 36), similarly described the effects of hormone treatments as too subtle to significantly enhance her passability as a female. "I'm not taking the estrogen to feminize. I don't think it would be effective. If it softens things up a little bit, that's fine. If there's a little bit of weight redistribution, that's fine. I don't think it's going to do that much." At least in some cases, then, hormonal changes are actually quite subtle, and in any case, to say that taking estrogen or testosterone "changes everything" ignores the fact that many of the fundamental structures of one's body remain the same in spite of changes in hormone levels.

A small subset of the transgender respondents, those who identify as intersex, spoke particularly eloquently on sex similarities and bodily ambiguity. In this case, their heightened awareness of sex sameness is not due to experiencing sex transition but to living outside of the binary sex categories. One intersex respondent, Alex, who is perceived as male but regards that as a distorted view, spoke at length about the fallacy of the hegemonic view of sex differences, framing his beliefs explicitly in terms of his experiences living as neither male nor female.

I think that being intersex and intergender has made me more resistant to this brainwashing. [. . .] I don't buy all this "men are from Mars, women are from Venus" nonsense. I am from planet Earth. People forget that sex itself is a social construct. There are not just two sexes. Most people are a mixture, not just one or the other. But we all try to fit into this norm for male or female, and it mutilates many people, not just intersex people. I have thought about this a lot, and frankly, I have come to the conclusion that most people are making a big deal out of very minimal differences in many cases. [. . .] We learn a lot of it. I am convinced of this. It is mostly culturally imposed on us. Not totally, but I would bet that cave people would not make such a big deal out of all this supposed difference because it simply is not there.

Another respondent, Tay, similarly emphasized that his experiences living as an intersex person provided the perspective that drew his attention to sex sameness. "Intersexuality has made me more aware of perceptions of male and female. My gift as a two spirit helps me to see through this veil of control. I would say the bodies are more similar. Some men's bodies actually look better than women's if you look at them form-wise. Some women have a man's buttocks and vice versa, for one example." Tay further illustrated his belief in the prevalence of physical sex similarities by reflecting on the androgyny of his own body. "I am perceived as a male because of the way I dress in public I suppose. My legs and arms look female. Sometimes it messes men up, because they get excited by my legs when I wear shorts. I don't have any body hair, and the little patches that are there, I get rid of to make myself look neat and clean."

In short, whether through the experience of transitioning between the sex categories or the experience of having an intersex body, the transgender respondents share a heightened awareness of the physical similarities among human bodies. Given their unique points of view, I analyzed their narratives to identify the specific body parts these respondents collectively perceive as androgynous. As I already mentioned, many examples of neutral or unsexed body parts emerged in discussions of physically passing (or *going stealth*, a term a number of my respondents used that avoids some of the implications of acting, fraud, and evasion associated with the term *passing*[7]). The following reflections on what makes it easier and more difficult to read successfully as one's sex of transition provide a sense of the range of sex similarities they identified in this context:

I didn't begin with a female "figure." My body shape and general appearance was pretty androgynous before hormones, so it didn't take much to "jump" the boundary between female and male. [. . .] I never had a narrow waist and wider hips as do most females. My face Is kind of round, even a little squared. I closely resemble my dad and the other men in his family. I also never picked up mannerisms that are stereotypically female (walk, hand movements, etc.). I've always been a bit more broad in the shoulders and had hands just a little larger than "normal" for women. Men's pants always fit me better than women's, due to the cut and my shape. (Sam, FTM transsexual, age 37)

A lot of males are very thin framed and feminine to begin with, and if they are inclined to become a woman, it's easier for them to pass. (Angela, MTF cross-dresser, 50s)

My face is, thank god, pretty feminine as it is. I mean I haven't had any facial surgery. (Bettina, MTF transsexual, age 50)

There are a lot of women who have lower voices. Right now, I'm in the middle. (Nicky, MTF cross-dresser, age 45)

Taken together, these four respondents mentioned the following body parts as potential locations of sex similarities: face, voice, frame size, body shape, shoulders, waist, hips, and hands. In figure 7, I represent all of the body parts designated by the transgender respondents as potentially androgynous on a map of the body. I gathered this information inductively from the transcripts, looking both for body parts they explicitly stated were similar and those they implied are often the same. My goal was to create a visual image that foregrounds sex similarities and backgrounds sex differences.

Many respondents pointed to examples of sameness on the head and face (with over twice as many mentions as any other area of the body), but beyond that, the similarities are approximately evenly distributed over the surface of the body. There were fewer references to the back, although this is in part an artifact of how I placed the dots, as the shoulders, for example, could just as easily be represented on the rear view. The same thing applies to the arms and legs, as well as the hair, which are all just as much a part of the rear view as the front view. In this context I should also note that I divided the dots between the left and right limbs, rather than concentrating them on just one side, which may give the impression that the shoulders, arms, hands, legs, and feet were mentioned less frequently than they actually were.

Additional information about the parts of the body the transgender respondents find the most androgynous is available in the survey data.

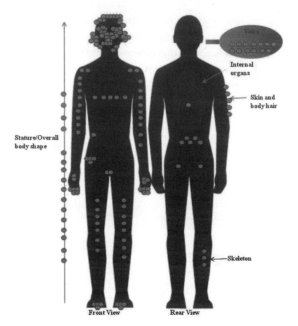

FIGURE 7 Map of sex similarities mentioned in interviews, transgender respondents. Each oval represents one respondent. (Image by Jennifer Lawrence for the author.)

Of the twenty-three body parts participants ranked from most to least likely to indicate someone's sex on a scale of 1 to 10, those body parts receiving the *lowest* mean score—indicating that they are not normally informative of sex—were elbows and shins, followed by ankles, ears, and knees (see table 6).

These results differ somewhat from those generated through coding the interview narratives. Whereas there the sex similarities were most dense around the head, here the legs are the most common site of ambiguity, with shins, ankles, and knees emerging as particularly indistinct. By contrast, the ears are the only body part on the head that received a low relevance score. One factor that may help explain this discrepancy is that being presented with a list is a very different experience than spontaneously mentioning parts of the body, and it provided an opportunity for participants to reflect on the salience of body parts they might not have otherwise thought to mention. On the one hand, then, providing a list might have helped disrupt taken-for-granted assumptions about what body parts are relevant and worth raising for discussion. On the other hand, providing a list also limits my ability to capture the respondents' operative beliefs about what body parts are so irrelevant they would never mention them. The fact that the two sets of results differ also further underscores a theme that emerged repeatedly from the data, which is variability in the content of sex. In fact, not only did the responses regarding the most common sex similarities vary depending on the form of data used, but participants characterized many of the same body parts as both sex cues and sites of sex similarity (see table 7, which compares the sex cues and sex similarities identified in the interview narratives).

The same point is illustrated using the survey data in table 8, which is a comparison of the body parts assigned two of the lowest relevance scores (reflecting the respondents' assessment that they are not important for passing) and those receiving the two highest scores. In the table, the body parts that are in bold appeared in both lists; that is, these body parts—all eighteen of them—were given one of the two highest scores by one or more respondents and one of the two lowest scores by at least one other respondent. In short, all but two of the body parts receiving the two lowest scores also appear on the list of body parts

Table 6 Survey results—lowest relevance scores assigned to twenty-three body parts by transgender respondents (n = 19)

Body part	Relevance for seeing sex (mean score, out of 10)
Elbows	3
Shins	3
Ankles	4
Ears	4
Knees	4
Abdomen	5
Calves	5
Genitals	5
Lower arms	5
Thighs	5
Upper arms	5
Cheeks	6
Chin	6
Feet	6
Forehead	6
Lips	6
Neck	6
Buttocks	7
Eyebrows	7
Shoulders	7
Chest	8
Hands	8
Head hair	8

Table 7 Interview data—comparison of androgynous body parts and sex cues, transgender respondents (n = 41)

Body part	Number of respondents stating it is androgynous	Number of respondents stating it is a sex difference
Arm / elbow / shoulder	22	13
Leg/shin	15	9
Voice	13	22
Nose	13	6
Hair	11	28
Body shape / silhouette	10	22
Facial features overall	7	18
Stature	6	13
Feet	6	5
Chest/breasts	5	22
Body hair / skin	5	14
Hands	5	13
Eyebrows	4	11
Hips	4	9
Eyes	3	6
Butt	2	5
Jaw/chin	2	4
Waist	1	2

Table 8 Survey results—comparison of body parts assigned the lowest and highest scores (n = 19)

Body part	Number of respondents who gave it one of their two *lowest* rankings	Number of respondents who gave it one of their two *highest* rankings
Ears	**10**	1
Elbows	10	0
Shins	9	0
Ankles	7	1
Genitals	7	5
Knees	7	2
Abdomen	5	2
Forehead	4	4
Lower arms	4	3
Upper arms	4	3
Feet	3	4
Lips	3	7
Calves	2	5
Cheeks	2	6
Chin	1	5
Eyebrows	1	11
Hands	1	10
Neck	1	5
Shoulders	1	3
Thighs	1	1

Note: The body parts in boldface appear in both lists.

receiving the two highest scores, indicating disagreement about what body parts are the most important sex cues.

The fact that the respondents identified many of the same body parts as sex cues and sex similarities returns us to the point that body parts are not *either* sexed *or* unsexed in all instances but come in a spectrum of dimorphism. A forehead or an arm could be totally ambiguous in terms of sex, or it could err in one direction or the other. For instance, head hair and voice were two of the most frequently mentioned sites of ambiguity; as I discussed earlier, however, they are also among the most highly cited sex cues, indicating that they must be very informative of sex, at least some of the time. I argued in chapter 3 that the content of our perceptions of sex—the actual body parts we use as cues—is flexible, and it depends on the mode of perception being used and the particular body being perceived, among other things. The data in this chapter underscore this flexibility, in part by highlighting one reason the content of sex attribution is so variable, which is that even the most informative sex cues are ambiguous some of the time. By implication, the notion of "self-evident" sex differences is more a feature of our minds than a feature of our bodies. It is not something we "read off" of naturally dichotomous bodies, but something that precedes and structures our experience of the material world. In the next section, I further illustrate this point by mining my blind respondents' narratives for examples of the nondichotomous body.

A Blind Phenomenology of Sexed Bodies

When a person, blind or sighted, encounters someone for the first time and wants to classify him or her, there is a lot of sensory information potentially available—the sound of the voice, the texture of the hair or skin, the smell of the breath, and so forth. Theoretically, one could differentiate people through any of these sensory experiences. However, part of the socialization of sighted people involves learning to privilege visual information, especially in relation to classifying human bodies in face-to-face interaction.[8] By privileging vision, however, one might say the sighted miss a lot.

For one thing, the temporality of nonvisual sex attribution is slower and more deliberate, which may allow for the perception of more complexity and ambiguity. According to the philosopher Hans Jonas, such temporal differences are one of the defining distinctions between sight and the other senses. He argues that, because we can visually survey a wide field in a moment, sight is intrinsically less temporal than the other senses and thus tends to promote fixity and stasis over dynamism and ephemerality.[9] Elizabeth Grosz similarly contrasts the successiveness of the impressions gained through touch and hearing with the synchronic nature of vision.[10]

Several of my blind respondents also emphasized these temporal distinctions, describing their impressions of bodies as being built diachronically, as they encounter different features and characteristics individually over time.

The one thing I can tell you is when you as a sighted person, when you met me for the first time, all of the idea of what I look like would hit you at once—my height, my approximate weight, my hair, [. . .] you'd have all those impressions at once, whether you wanted them or not. Whereas for a blind person, if I met you, I would gain impressions of you one thing at a time. If I held your arm that would be one thing, but I would have no idea what your hair was like, or if you were wearing earrings. Whereas if you saw me, all those things would be impressed upon you at once. For a blind person, they come piece by piece. So I might, for example, know how tall a woman is but have no idea what her hair was like. And that wouldn't happen to you. Unless you just plain forgot what his hair was like or her hair was like. So it's a piece-by-piece physical impression that you gain as opposed to the entire impact when you see someone for the first second and it all hits you at once. (William, age 61, blind since birth)

James, who has been legally blind since birth, and totally blind since age 3, used the parable of the blind men and the elephant to illustrate this idea of a "piece-by-piece physical impression": "I assume you know the story of the [. . .] blind men who try describing an elephant. One man is feeling the trunk, another man is feeling a leg, another man is feeling the tail. The difference between folks like me and most folks is that I describe the tail without asserting that it is an elephant. After I've groped everything in the area [. . .] *eventually* I figure out what is elephant and what is circus floor" (emphasis added). As opposed to a holistic gestalt that impresses itself upon them rapidly and all at once, these respondents describe blind people as building their impressions of bodies much more slowly and deliberately. As Lou put it: "You can glance and see. I can't glance and see; I have to listen." What all of these accounts suggest is that the sensory "maps" of bodies created diachronically through touch and hearing incorporate more complexity and ambiguity, and do not lend themselves as easily to fast, sharp, static identification.

It is also important to point out in this context that many social norms governing the display of sex and gender are visual, and these norms are automatically bracketed for blind people. One way to illustrate this point is to return to the dialectic between perception and display in sex attribution discussed in chapter 3. In a blind phenomenology of bodies, the initial process of polarization through display is mostly limited to voice, and as a result, the blind perceiver is faced with more ambiguity when categorizing bodies (see fig. 8).

Further underscoring the point that they contend with a significant amount of bodily ambiguity, a number of the blind respondents described sex attribution as a "draining" process, a puzzle that is occasionally a struggle to piece together, indicating that for them bodies can be sufficiently indistinct in terms of sex to be difficult to interpret and categorize. "It [sex] is not always obvious. Sometimes it works, sometimes it doesn't, but I gather information through whatever I hear—their movements, the way they walk, and, of course, the way they speak; and from what I smell. Yeah, it's pretty draining a lot of time" (Tim, age 33, blind since age 3). Betty (mid-50s, blind since birth) explained that it can take some time—and sometimes even someone else's help—for her to sort out whether a person is male or female: "It took a little while to

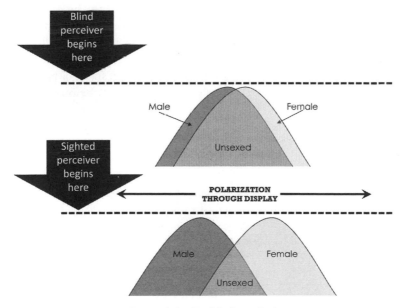

FIGURE 8 Sex attribution without polarization (blind perceiver).

sort it out, or I just shut up and listened and waited for someone else to clue me in. [. . .] You can be confused." Others framed the same point in terms of intention, explaining that they often have to *intentionally try* to figure out someone's sex, particularly if they are not interacting with the person directly. For example, one respondent offered this description of how she determines the sex of those around her in her college classes: "I try to introduce myself to those around me. I pay close attention to names when the professor is taking role. I like to have an idea of who is in the class. I tend to listen to what is going on when we are doing group work. What I mean by listening is, pay attention to how the people around me interact or who is sitting near me by their voices" (Juliana, 23, visually impaired since birth, totally blind since age 16). The implication is that, without this conscious, concerted effort, Juliana would not know the sex of many of her classmates.

The fact that making nonvisual sex attributions is frequently difficult and draining helps to reveal the *work* of sex/gender attribution, even for sighted people. Here the blind help us to reconsider the notion of "doing gender" in a new light, reminding us that, not only is attributing gender an interactional accomplishment, it can actually be difficult work.[11] Stated another way, it is rarely recognized that the typical visual self-evidence of sex is likely achieved only by resolving some amount of empirical ambiguity. The blind navigate sensory paths where ambiguity remains prominent. Acknowledging the validity of these nonvisual sensory realities—weighting them more evenly with the visual experience of sex—makes clear that sex is not *naturally* easily attributable.

In fact, the ambiguities of sex reported by these respondents directly challenge dominant cultural assumptions about the "obviousness" and "self-evidence" of sex. In this vein, many participants stated or implied that they are not aware of the sex of *most* of the people they encounter in the course of their daily lives—unless they explicitly interact with them, or they intentionally try to figure it out.

I usually don't try to tell their gender unless I am trying to decide out of self-interest, e.g., feeling social, wanting to make a friend, or feeling flirty. [. . .] It really depends on the situation. [. . .] Out of the hundreds of people I pass throughout the day, I probably know the gender of ten of them. (Simone, college age, blind since age 15)

If I'm not interacting with someone, I don't really think about his or her gender; it simply doesn't cross my mind. I don't think, "Hmm, I wonder if that's a man or a woman," or anything like that. I might pick up on something, high-heeled shoes and perfume, for example, and realize that a woman is walking by, but that's about it. (Louisa, age 19, blind since birth)

As a result, the everyday experiences of blind people, particularly their "unfocused" interactions—those in which individuals within one another's visual and aural range are going about their activities without a shared point of attention—are notably less punctuated by sex difference.[12] "If they don't talk at all, to me or anyone else," Lucy (age 25, blind since birth) explained, "then really there's no way for me to know [someone's sex]." While sighted people almost always immediately identify every human being we encounter as either male or female (regardless of whether we interact with the person, even just passing on the street), blind people are usually aware of the sex of strangers only when they are directly interacting with the person, or when they intentionally try to figure it out. "Well, I don't try to figure it out. Every once in a while you'll notice by the scent of somebody's cologne. Or, like I said, footfall, type of shoes. So sometimes I can tell a woman is walking by me because she's wearing high heels, but it has to stick out. It's got to obviously stick out or intrude into my consciousness [. . .]" (Betty, mid-50s, blind since birth). This comment also returns us to the differences in temporality between visual and nonvisual sex attribution, as the implication is that "figuring it out" frequently takes some amount of time.

Based on the above descriptions, one characteristic of a blind phenomenology of bodies is that strangers often remain androgynous in situations of simple copresence without direct interaction. By implication, if sighted people did not so strongly privilege vision, sex differences would become a less prominent feature of our phenomenal experience as well, largely restricted to focused interaction. It is worth addressing further what this observation means generically. Most centrally, it suggests that, when sight is not privileged over the other senses, sex differences are not necessarily among the most salient features of the perceptual landscape. This supports what many in the queer theory and transgender literatures would like to accomplish—highlighting the instability and discursive production of the sex and gender categories[13]—not through the stories of people who display ambiguous or androgynous genders, but through the experiences of people who perceive ambiguity in the "normally gendered" due to their reliance on nondominant modes of sensory perception. When the sighted encounter someone who may be transgender or who is intentionally queering sex/gender, we do the hard work of trying to attribute sex. The additional dimension being added here is that, without sight, the sex of nontransgender people is also ambiguous—at least until the point of direct interaction. In other words, studying nonvisual sex attribution brings new insights to transgender studies and queer theory by providing an additional approach to reveal the ambiguity in everyday assumed-to-be unambiguous displays of sex/gender.

Before discussing the specific parts of the body that emerged in the interviews as sexually ambiguous for my blind respondents, however, I must once again reiterate that, at least initially, many stated that a person's sex is usually "obvious" to them. Their commitment to the obviousness of sex differences, a belief that does not seem to reflect their everyday phenomenal experiences of sex, is a powerful illustration of the way dominant cultural messages about sex can perform "socio-mental control."[14] In such cases, cultural beliefs and expectations about the self-evidence of sex override what is actually there in terms of perceptual cues (which, as we have seen, are actually indicative of a great deal of ambiguity).

This sociomental control is not absolute or seamless, however, and in the moments of dissonance between the blind respondents' cultural beliefs and their sensory experiences, a more complex portrait of human bodies was sometimes available. For instance, I observed an interesting tension in the narratives between this initially stated obviousness and the ambiguity the blind respondents revealed when I probed for the details of their sensory experiences of particular body parts. Consider the following exchange with Simone (college age, blind since age 15) in this light (emphasis added).

AUTHOR. If I lined up a bunch of men and women and you were told that you could touch them to identify their sex, do you think that you could do that easily?
SIMONE. There is no question in my mind that I would get 999 right out of a thousand. [. . .] I believe that typically every part of the body would alert me to a person's gender.
AUTHOR. Okay. I'm going to ask you to specifically consider several parts of the body and tell me how you think they would tell me whether someone is male or female. The first one is hands.
SIMONE. A man's hands are *typically* more rough than a female's. The bone structure throughout the hand is *generally* thicker in the male's hand and more petite in the female's hand. When examining a hand to determine gender I would

most likely pay close attention to the fingers. A man *usually* has thicker hair on their fingers and their nails are wider.

AUTHOR. Okay, thanks. What about elbows?

SIMONE. As a blind person I hold onto a person's elbow very often, as this is how they guide me. A man's elbow, again, is typically broader and hairier. *I have found this particular area to be more difficult when determining gender especially when the person is heavier.*

While Simone begins from a very strong position of certainty and obviousness—"no question," "999 out of a thousand," "every part"—she shifts into more qualified language as soon as she considers specific body parts. This progression from an initial default assumption of obviousness to a later description that includes significant qualification and uncertainty was present in a great many of the interviews. The following excerpt from my interview with Tim (age 33, blind since age 3) provides one more example of this slide from obviousness to ambiguity (emphasis added):

TIM. In general women would have different shapes of almost all things than men so you might be able to tell in lots of ways but some I'd think would be less effective. I do think you could tell though from just about everything. Even something as simple as skin texture might be a hint.

AUTHOR. What about noses?

TIM. Noses, hmmm. I don't have a large cross section of noses to work with but noses *might* give clues by women's noses being finer and smaller than male noses but yeah *I think it would be hard to tell.* Same with ears. Again smaller *might* be an indicator but *not with 100 percent accuracy on its own.*

Given that most of the blind respondents strongly believe sex differences are obvious, I sometimes had to read their narratives "against the grain" to access the evidence of sex similarities that is present. In many cases, including those I just discussed, this evidence was located in the hedges and qualifications in their descriptions. Two additional examples are provided below. Both comments are intended to communicate that it is easy to attribute sex, but they can also be read for the references to ambiguity they contain.

I am *usually* aware if someone is a male or a female. It is *sometimes* unclear at first, e.g., *some women I know have low voices*, but once I find out the person's name and hear him or her talk for a bit, things are *no longer* unclear. I have never been in a situation where I gave up on figuring out whether someone was male or female. (Louisa, age 19, blind since birth, emphasis added)

[. . . Y]ou *might* be able to tell *something* about somebody's shoulders, *although there are a number of women who are athletic who've got really strong, broad shoulders.* So I'm thinking that's a *possibility,* but I wouldn't rely on that as much, but I would say face, yes, *if* you can tell if someone shaves or not, then, you know, the *majority* of men have facial hair and the vast *majority* of women don't. (Sidney, age 54, blind since birth, emphasis added)

I treated these kinds of qualifying comments as evidence of sex similarity along with the blind respondents' direct statements that particular parts of the body are androgynous.

Hedges and qualifications aside, there were approximately fifteen parts of the body, including hair, feet, noses, backs, and shoulders, that the blind respondents explicitly identified as sites of androgyny. The following examples roughly capture the range of tones and body parts in these direct statements of similarity.

A person's back or legs or feet, particularly if they're covered by clothing, but even without it, I think those would be the most difficult parts of the body to make assumptions about. (Tina, age 24, blind since birth)

The shin, I wouldn't have a clue. (Jack, age 38, macular degeneration beginning at birth)

I am not sure I could correctly decipher between males and females based on the feel of their ears. In fact, I don't believe I could with a high success rate. I may have an easier time with the nose, although I still believe it may be difficult. (Simone, college age, blind since age 15)

Most women shave their legs. Most guys don't. But it could be fairly difficult to tell one set of hairy legs from another. I mean, if you got the average woman and a skinny guy side by side, neither of whom had shaved their legs, it would be difficult to distinguish which was a female. (Jackson, age 24, mostly blind since birth)

In table 9, I summarize all the body parts that emerged (via both direct and indirect characterization) as potentially similar or ambiguous in the narratives of the blind respondents.

The first thing to note is that there is a significant amount of overlap between the two columns. Of the ten most frequently mentioned body

Table 9 Ambiguous body parts, blind respondents (n = 27)

Direct characterization	Hedging/qualification
Ear (9)	Ear (3)
Nose (9)	Nose (2)
Voice (8)	Voice (18)
Arm (6)	Arm (8)
Leg (6)	Leg (2)
Elbow (5)	Elbow (4)
Hands (2)	Hands (4)
Body hair (1)	Body hair (10)
Face (1)	Face (3)
Feet (1)	Feet (1)
Hair (1)	Hair (3)
Height (1)	Height (4)
Neck (1)	Neck (1)
Shoulder (1)	Shoulder (1)
Other	Other
Back (3)	Skin (2)
	Facial Hair (1)

Note: The number of people mentioning each body part is indicated in parentheses.

parts, eight appear on both lists. That means, overall, when the respondents indirectly implied that particular body parts were potentially androgynous, these were the same body parts they identified directly. This correspondence suggests some basic agreement about which body parts are unclear in terms of sex, even when the ambiguity is only acknowledged implicitly. This point is also illustrated in figure 9, which is a visual depiction of the sex similarities reported in table 9.

Although the numbers cannot be compared directly, since I interviewed forty-one transgender people versus twenty-seven blind people, here again the largest concentration of responses is around the head (thirty-four mentions), which is the same pattern as the map I constructed based on the transgender respondents' narratives (see fig. 7). However, there is a significant difference in the number of blind respondents that mentioned the arms, hands, and shoulders (thirty-one, as opposed to thirteen mentions by the transgender respondents). One reason blind people may have this area of the body in the forefront of their minds is that they often hold a sighted person's arm, elbow, or shoulder when walking with that person as a sighted guide. For this reason, they are probably more attuned to the spectrum of different arms and elbows than the average sighted person. Further, it is striking that so many of the blind respondents mentioned the voice as a site of androgyny, considering that it is their primary sex cue. Fewer trans-

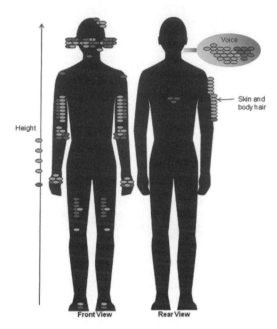

FIGURE 9 Map of sex similarities mentioned in interviews, blind respondents. Each oval represents one respondent. The darker ovals indicate those body parts they directly identified as sex similarities, while the lighter ovals indicate the similarities they alluded to indirectly. For the most part, the two tend to track together. (Image by Jennifer Lawrence for the author.)

gender respondents found the voice to be naturally similar, and a fair number expressed great concern over their voice as an impediment to passing, although several people did mention that it is possible to pass with a voice that is "somewhere in the middle." I suspect they would be comforted by the blind respondents' comments, which suggest that the voice may actually be more ambiguous than they think, even in nontransgender people.

It also bears mentioning that I have included the entire universe of the blind participants' responses here, which is why some body parts were mentioned by just one person. While the low number of responses can be taken to indicate that the body parts in question are not widely understood by the blind participants as sites of sex similarity, it may also be helpful to contextualize these cases in the full set of responses, including both columns of table 9 (i.e., both direct and indirect characterizations) and the interviews with the transgender respondents. For example, while only one blind person directly stated that height is an example of sex similarity, four people indirectly alluded to height as ambiguous, and sixteen of the transgender respondents mentioned stature and overall body shape as a sex similarity. Another example is body hair. Only one blind respondent brought up body hair is an example of sex sameness, but ten blind respondents indirectly alluded to similarities in body hair between males and females, and five transgender respondents mentioned that skin and body hair can be ambiguous. In light of this, it is important not to dismiss body hair as a potential site of similarity. In any case, with the exception of the torso, which was mentioned only a handful of times, what is most striking about this presentation of the data is that—as with the transgender respondents—it illustrates that a great deal, even the greater proportion, of the surface area of male and female bodies can be perceptually ambiguous for blind people.

Sex Differences in Proportion

Collectively the blind and transgender respondents identified a substantial proportion of the surface area of the human body that is ambiguous relative to sex at least some of the time. In fact, there was very little of the body that they did not mention at all when discussing sex similarities. Considering all of the interview data together, then, *minimally* invites the following conclusion: male and female bodies are not nearly as empirically distinct as their typical visual self-evidence suggests; it is more accurately only some fraction of the human body that is universally different between males and females. For this reason, it may make sense to think of sex differences and similarities as a *proportion*—a ratio that contextualizes sex differences in the whole of the human body. In this view, the numerator would represent the number of sexed body parts and the denominator would represent all body parts (see fig. 10). As with all fractions, proportions always have a value between zero (no sex differences) and one (indicating that the body is 100 percent sex differentiated). In other words, bodies always fall somewhere between total androgyny and total sex difference. While my qualitative data do not allow me to precisely characterize the proportion of the body that

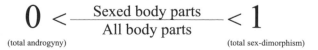

$$0 < \frac{\text{Sexed body parts}}{\text{All body parts}} < 1$$

(total androgyny) (total sex-dimorphism)

FIGURE 10 Sex difference as a proportion.

can reasonably be called sex differentiated, based on my respondents' collective descriptions, much of the body is potentially ambiguous in terms of sex. Despite this significant commonality, we are socialized to be blind to sex sameness, focusing instead on the proportionately smaller sex differences.

Thinking of sex differences and similarities as a mathematical proportion, as I am suggesting, is a "metric" measurement. As I mentioned in chapter 3, metric descriptions of sex can be thought of as a true average using a standardized unit of measurement that takes into account all similarities and differences, whereas the more common topological view is a weighted average, in which certain characteristics, those socially defined as "relevant," are mentally "weighted" and exert a disproportionately large influence.

The concept of "mental weighing" was suggested by Jamie Mullaney to capture the role played by the audience in identity attribution and to specifically highlight the fact that not all acts count equally in our attributions of others' identities. One of the many examples of this process Mullaney provides is directly relevant to the attribution of sex: when perceiving a person with long hair and a beard, we see a man despite the empirical ambiguity of the cues because we know that facial hair "weighs" more than hair length in assigning sex.[15] Karen Danna-Lynch builds on Mullaney's work, in part by emphasizing that mental weighing is also a cultural practice; in her words, "Weight is a cultural anchor." Stimuli are "culturally informed," and the available cultural discourses encourage us to weight certain information more heavily.[16] In this way, she argues, mental weighing is an important illustration of how culture functions (and why culture matters) in everyday life. For one thing, culture helps to create the experience of self-evidence for the perceiver through these practices of adding weight to certain information. When stimuli are heavily culturally weighted, our "readings" of them may seem inevitable, but if we could experience the same factors without cultural weight, it would be possible to arrive at a different interpretation. Applied to the perception of sex differences, what this collection of ideas suggests is that certain features of the body (those that serve to differentiate the sexes) are culturally "weighted," and therefore exert more influence over our interpretations than others that are equally real and empirically available but bear less cultural weight (in this case, sex similarities).

The analytic approach I have been advocating based on the metaphor of a filter is particularly useful when analyzing cultural weight, because it reminds us that it is as important to identify the unweighted, background details as it is to understand what is culturally emphasized, foregrounded, and perceived. In other words, filter analysis specifically directs us to seek out the features and details that are disattended *as well as* those that enter our awareness, thereby gaining a deeper understanding of how culture works on a cognitive and perceptual level. This emphasis on analyzing the disattended is unique to the filter metaphor and constitutes its power as a conceptual tool.

Far from denying the existence of sex differences, then, my suggestion is that we *also* pay careful attention to sex similarities and weigh them more proportionately in our perceptions of human bodies. Such proportionate perception requires the acknowledgment of both similarity and difference. Just as we can learn to see both the vase and the faces in Rubin's famous optical illusion, we can learn to see *both* similarities and differences in human bodies. Cultivating such a "flexible minded" view of the body entails recognizing that there are multiple ways of carving up the body, all of which are, in the end, figments of our minds.[17] The data I collected on blind and transgender people's impressions of the similarities between male and female bodies promotes this mental flexibility because it illustrates the possibility of alternate perceptions, thus calling into question both the assumed veracity of vision and the dominant belief that sex differences are obvious and undeniable.

More broadly, this standpoint is consistent with Roger Lancaster's definition of "a properly thought out constructionism": "A properly thought-out constructionism does not deny the materiality of physical things, but it does suggest that the objectivity of objects is itself the product of a certain highly subjective work. It argues that what marks the object as such is countless unmarked decisions about what to foreground and what to background, what to hold constant and what to see as variable."[18] One can conceptualize the social construction of the body as a process of selectively emphasizing and mentally weighing different bodily similarities and differences. This version of social constructionism does not dispute the existence of biological differences but highlights the cultural work amplifying them. In the case of sex, dominant conceptions of sex are constructed largely in the visual realm through selective attention to sex differences and backgrounding of similarities. Here I have focused on identifying some of these sex similarities that are normally relegated to the background, including those deriving from other sensory modalities.

In the opening paragraphs of this chapter, I raised the question of whether different social expectations would lead us to note different features of bodies. That is, if we "knew" male and female bodies were very much the same, what would we see that we currently do not? I began the process of answering this question by mining my interview data for evidence of normally backgrounded sex similarities. In the next chapter I extend the same question beyond my respondents' narratives: drawing on a number of different forms of data, including body measurements, anatomy textbooks, and drawing manuals, I demonstrate that evidence of physical similarities between males and females is "out there" in the background of cultural discourses and cultural artifacts, ready to be seen—if only we were looking for it.

FIVE

Seeking Sameness

Unlike the transgender people I interviewed, most of us will never perceive bodies through the mental filters created by the experiences of transition or intersexuality, which challenge presumptions about how much of the body is truly sex dimorphic. In the same vein, sighted people can never fully escape the rapid, automatic visual sorting process that reduces the complexity of bodies and experience the relatively slow, diachronic process of nonvisual sex attribution. Given the current cultural context, in fact, it is quite rare to visually perceive a human body except through a filter that essentially blinds us to sex similarities. Nonetheless, it may be possible to analytically adopt a sex-sameness filter, inverting the normative structure of attention by deliberately focusing on similarities. To do so requires ignoring socially created sex differences and actively seeking out the underlying commonality between male and female bodies. Guided by this perspective, I present in this chapter a diverse collection of evidence—from body measurements to figure drawing textbooks—to illustrate sex sameness.

It is, of course, never possible to fully bracket cultural norms and see the "naked" body, and sex sameness is not the singular empirically correct view. It is more accurate to say that, in analytically adopting the filter of sex sameness, I am describing the human form as perceived through a different paradigm of thought, one defined by an expectation of a biological continuum between male and female rather than two separate categories. Perceiving the body through this filter—while it cannot provide a portrait of the "real" body, only *a different* body—demonstrates that sex difference is not the only possibility for seeing bodies and, more generally, reminds us that there are alternatives to the currently hegemonic perceptual paradigm.

Sex without Polarization

When we bracket social norms of perception and self-presentation—intentionally ignoring the cultural practices that normally help disambiguate male and female bodies—what we begin to see is "visually undifferentiated flux," "a boundless, unbroken world with no lines."[1] My goal in this chapter is to present such a "fuzzy-minded" portrait of the body, highlighting only the androgyny of the human form and bracketing those distinctions between male and female bodies that normally seem so "obvious."

As a preliminary foray into a fuzzy-minded view of bodies, consider examples where polarizing practices are absent, or mostly absent—for instance, certain animals, human infants, and the interior of bodies. In such cases, the necessary bracketing is done for us, making it much easier to see sex similarities. Although in some species of animals sex is an obvious and highly marked physical characteristic (e.g., male pheasants possess bright plumage, whereas females are usually a drab brown), in many animals sex is *not* obvious to us at first glance. Zoologists have in fact documented a rather large spectrum of sex dimorphism in animals. On one end is the pheasant, along with the elephant seal, which exhibits extreme sexual size dimorphism, with the male weighing three to five times as much as the female. On the other end of the spectrum is the spotted hyena, a species in which the male and female are visually indistinguishable right down to their genitals.[2] A similar sense of overwhelming sex similarity is also present in the following description of determining a python's sex, which is a minute, hidden difference in an otherwise identical physical appearance. "Karen walked her way hand-over-hand down several feet of python until she came to a little flap on the snake's underside, about three-quarters down its length. 'See this?' she said. 'Boy snakes have two little hooks on either side called 'spurs.' This snake doesn't have them, so she's a girl.'"[3] Further, even *within* the class of birds, there is significant variation in sex dimorphism. In 25 percent of bird species the male is larger, and in 50 percent the female is larger. In the remaining 25 percent, there is no significant sex difference in size.[4]

For the most part, the existence of extensive physical similarities be-tween males and females is both perceptually obvious and cognitively unproblematic when seeing animals that are low in sex dimorphism. A commonplace example is dogs. One intersex respondent, Alex, re-minded me how normal it is for us to ask about a dog's sex—something that is almost never asked about another human. In his words, "When we look at other species this [sex ambiguity] is even more obvious. Peo-ple will ask what sex your dog is, for example, but we make a big to do over it."

It is interesting to consider where human beings fall in this spec-trum of sex dimorphism. Without polarization, in other words, would the sex of human bodies be equally visually ambiguous as the sex of dogs? Human males and females are certainly much more similar than male and female elephant seals or pheasants. Indeed, by some accounts, human beings are very low in sex dimorphism, since their primary sex markers are the genitals.[5] And on the very rare occasion that we do see human bodies absent polarization—one example is infancy—sex dif-ferences are certainly not very visually prominent.

This point was recently reinforced for me while observing a group of children looking at a large-scale sculpture of a naked newborn baby by Ron Mueck (see fig. 11), a sculptor whose work is known for being

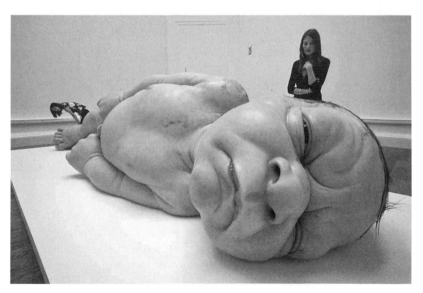

FIGURE 11 The unpolarized infant body. (*A Girl* by Ron Mueck. Reprinted with the permission of the photographer, Murdo McLeod.)

incredibly lifelike, except in its exaggerated scale (this particular sculpture is just over sixteen feet long). The first question the children asked about the sculpture, which is anticipated by Mueck's title (*A Girl*), was whether it is a boy or a girl. The newborn is naked, its genitals clearly visible, but there are no "artificial" indicators of sex, such as clothing, hats, or bows. The children continued discussing this question among themselves for several minutes but were never able to decide on the sex. One possible explanation is that they were simply not yet fully socialized in *how* to see sex. These perceptual skills are still developing in young children, who do not always see sex with the "proper" mental weight applied (e.g., perceiving males with long hair as females). However, without contextual cues, it can be quite difficult for anyone to determine the sex of babies and very young children. In fact, while the children at the museum were discussing the infant's sex, I was standing facing the back of the sculpture, and I had to walk around to the other side to inspect the genitals before I could come up with an answer myself. So much of the infant's body was androgynous—the back, butt, head, neck, torso, arms, legs, feet, and so on—that I could not determine its sex *except* by looking at the genitals.

The degree of sex dimorphism of an infant, then, is arguably much more similar to a dog or a snake than to socialized, groomed, polarized adult humans. Not to mention, it is only in very unique circumstances—consider again the photograph of male and female West Point students in regulation dress with short haircuts described by Carol Barkalow[6]—that adult males and females present themselves totally unpolarized. Nonetheless, one way to bracket a lot of what gets socially added to heighten the differences between males and females is to compare bodies metrically. As I have previously explained, I use the term *metric* in contrast to *topological* to indicate a precise dimension that can be measured in a standardized unit. In advocating a more metric assessment, my point is that similarity and difference can be measured and compared, which would allow us to avoid lapsing into a "topological" (socially distorted) view of sex difference. A recent study called Size-USA, which includes more than 240 anthropometric measurements of 10,000 men and women, provides a rare opportunity to compare bodies metrically. I focus here on the chest, waist, and hip measurements reported in the *New York Times*.[7] What these data reveal—if one is looking for it—is that the mean measurements for men and women of comparable age and race categories are virtually identical (see table 10).

For instance, in the black 18 to 25 category, on average men measured 41 inches in the chest, 34 inches in the waist, and 41 inches

Table 10 SizeUSA body measurements (mean, in inches)

	Chest (men)	Bust (women)	Hips (men)	Hips (women)	Waist (men)	Waist (women)
Black						
18 to 25	41	40	41	43	34	33
36 to 45	43	43	42	46	37	37
56 to 65	43	44	42	46	39	39
White						
18 to 25	41	38	41	41	35	32
36 to 45	44	41	42	43	38	34
56 to 65	44	42	42	44	40	36
Hispanic						
18 to 25	41	39	40	41	35	33
36 to 45	44	43	42	44	38	36
56 to 65	44	44	44	44	38	38
Other						
18 to 25	41	38	40	40	34	31
36 to 45	42	41	41	43	37	35
56 to 65	43	42	41	43	38	36

Sources: SizeUSA (http://www.tc2.com/sizeusa.html); Kate Zernike, "Sizing Up America. Signs of Expansion from Head to Toe," *New York Times*, March 1, 2004.

in the hips, whereas women measured 40 inches in the chest (called "bust," for no reason save to emphasize sex difference), 33 inches in the waist, and 43 inches in the hips. In the 36 to 45 age category, the average chest and waist measurements for black men and women were exactly the same (43-inch chest and 37-inch waist). Over all race and age categories, the largest difference was 4 inches, which occurred in four out of thirty-six reported measurements. A 3-inch difference, the next largest, also occurred just four times. On the other hand, there were eight measurements overall that were *exactly* the same for men and women. Eight additional measures differed by only 1 inch. So out of thirty-six total mean measurements reported in the *New York Times*, sixteen were within 1 inch for men and women. It is also worth pointing out that in the context of a 31-inch measurement (which was the smallest measurement reported), even the largest difference, 4 inches, represented just a 13 percent sex difference (meaning that the measurements were 87 percent the same). Using the most frequent difference, 2 inches, which occurred in eleven measurements, the percentage of commonality was increased to 94 percent.

In addition to the numerical comparisons provided by the body measurements, the SizeUSA data can provide some interesting comparisons of overall body shape. Challenging the assumption that men have little difference between waist and hip measurements, whereas women are "curvy," SizeUSA found that many women share the "straight" shape with men.[8] The buttocks are also commonly understood as a marker of sex difference. However, SizeUSA found evidence of considerable similarity there as well. Not only do some men have a "prominent seat," but there is significant variation among different racial categories, demonstrating that the category *male* is far from uniform (and highlighting the interaction of sex and race cues).[9] In short, based on this study, male and female bodies are quite similar in overall size and shape, and the differences that do appear are much more suggestive of a continuum than two discrete physical categories.

The interior of the human body is another place where social display practices that normally increase the salience of sex differences are automatically bracketed. While my primary argument is that there is a continuum between maleness and femaleness on the surface of the body, the similarities inside of human bodies are even more pronounced. With the exception of gonads, in fact, several different forms of evidence suggest that the tissues, bones, fluids, and other bodily substances inside "male" and "female" bodies are mostly indistinguishable. Angiograms, for example, do not reveal sex differences,[10] and organ transplants regularly occur across sexes.[11] Further, what makes transplants "take"—not be rejected—is that the donor organ cells spread throughout the body of the recipient, cells which often originate in a body of the "other" sex.[12] The implication is that "male" and "female" hearts, lungs, kidneys, livers, bone marrow, and blood do not exist; these organs and other bodily substances are essentially interchangeable between males and females, and a "match" for transplants and transfusions has nothing to do with sex, but with other more biologically important factors. In other words, sex is simply not the most important variable at the level of the cell or the organ. For a visual illustration of this point, see figure 12, a photograph of human fat cells. The caption for this image does not include any indication of sex, suggesting that fat cells are neither male nor female. Note also that the individual fat cells can differ in shape, size, and texture within the same body. These differences, which occur within rather than across the sex categories, are examples of variations that "do not make a difference," illustrating the way that we mentally inflate the importance of some forms of biological difference while ignoring others.

When interpreting any anatomical image presented without identifying information about sex, however, it is important to acknowledge the history of androcentrism in science and medicine.[13] In brief, historically the notion that sex could ever be "irrelevant" has been severely compromised by an unmarked male norm. For instance, as I described in chapter 4, something similar to the singular view of human bodies I have been highlighting in this chapter was actually the dominant understanding of sex from the Greeks until the eighteenth century. This "one-sex" model posited that there is only one type of body; males and females have all the same reproductive organs, but in the female they are located inside the body, rather than outside. In practice, however, this "one-sex" model was solidly androcentric. The "one" body was explicitly a male body, and females were viewed as "unfinished"—not fully developed—males. Androcentric assumptions admittedly could explain why there is no indication of whether the fat cells pictured in figure 12 are from a male or a female body. When a

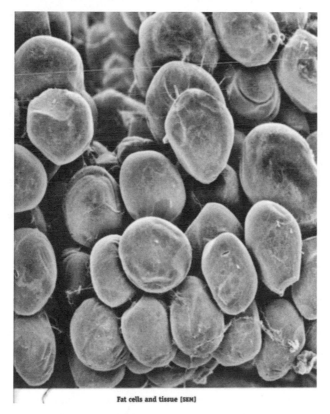

Fat cells and tissue [SEM]

FIGURE 12 Human fat cells. (Victoria Alers-Hankey and Joanna Chisholm, eds., *Photographic Atlas of the Body* [Buffalo, NY: Firefly Books, 2004], p. 17.)

male body serves as the unmarked norm, one need not mention that the image is a male; that is a taken-for-granted presupposition. Indeed, the very act of naming or labeling something usually indicates that it is a "specialized" case distinct from the generic or default form.[14]

Nonetheless, it is worth attempting to disentangle sex sameness from androcentrism, and to consider whether it is possible that fat cells really are most accurately viewed as human—meaning that no indication of sex is logical or necessary. There is certainly enough other evidence that similarities are dominant inside the body that it is plausible to accept that an image of a "human" fat cell with no indication of sex is simply accurate, rather than androcentric. Stated broadly, my suggestion is that by taking a more neutral view, and reconceiving the one-sex model in terms of the human—of which male and female are two minor variations—it may be possible to generate a productive new understanding of the relative salience of sex similarities and sex differences.

One may also object to my current line of argument on the basis that the inside of the body is not available to us in everyday sensory perception, and therefore offers an "unfair" or "misleading" portrait of the information we have to work with in our perceptions of physical sameness and difference. Put another way, this objection suggests that, by necessity, the inside of the body is "irrelevant" in sex attribution; even if the inside of the body were entirely sexless, because it is hidden from us, it plays no role in how we see male and female bodies. However, if seriously considered, the realization that bodies are essentially the same inside can change how we see the relationship of similarity to difference when perceiving the surface of bodies, in keeping with the idea that visual perception is always shaped by our beliefs and expectations. For instance, if we realized that the interior of the abdominal cavity looked like the photograph in figure 13, would it influence our sense of the biological self-evidence of sex differences? Figures 14 and 15 further support the idea that, beneath the skin, human bodies are mostly identical. Neither the gamma camera scan of the knees in figure 14 nor the x-ray of the hands in figure 15 includes any mention of sex, presumably because this anatomy is more or less the same in all humans. Actually, though, I could have substituted an image of almost any cell, tissue, or organ in the body (with the possible exception of the genitals and the gonads) with essentially the same effect.

In this section I have deliberately chosen examples of "unpolarized" bodies—cases where sex differences have not been augmented by gender normative practices of self-presentation. These examples demonstrate that when we restrict our focus to what is essentially untouched

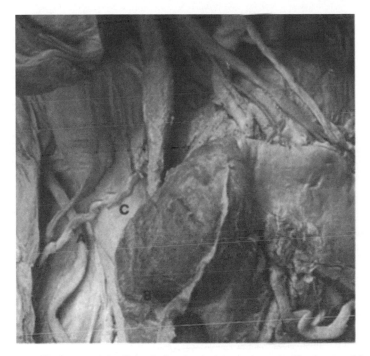

FIGURE 13 The interior of the abdominal cavity: *A*, right ureter, crossed by the gonadal vessels; *B*, descending part of the duodenum; *C*, inferior vena cava. (Robert Matthew Hay McMinn, Ralph T. Hutchings, and Bari M. Logan, *Picture Tests in Human Anatomy* [Chicago: Year Book Medical Publisher, 1986], image 142).

by gender norms, the similarities between male and female bodies are far more "obvious," perhaps even more so than their differences. But it is also possible to find substantial sex similarities when the social norms of display that exaggerate sex differences are in full effect.

Drawing Textbooks: Sameness Despite Polarization

Drawing textbooks, which offer instruction in how to visually represent human bodies, almost always incorporate normative assumptions about sex differences (e.g., that females always have long hair, that males are more muscular than females, or that females have longer eyelashes than males). Yet when read explicitly for sex similarities, they contain evidence of significant underlying anatomical commonality.

I think it is fair to say that the goal of most "realistic" figure draw-

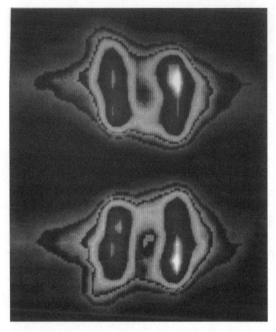

FIGURE 14 Human knees (gamma camera scan). (Alers-Hankey and Chisholm, *Photographic Atlas of the Body,* p. 94.)

ings is to be recognized as "accurate" depictions of either the male or female body; that is, the artist's objective in most cases is for the drawing to "read" clearly as male or female. The point here is that the images of male and female bodies contained in these books, even as they appear realistic (and that realism is typically supported by the use of skeletons, etc., to lend an air of scientificity), are *stylized*: prefiltered for us through our cultural norms and expectations. Precisely because these books are "prepolarized," they provide a conservative picture of the similarities between male and female bodies, yet they reveal a surprising number of body parts that are not sex-specific.

Further, figure drawing artists are experts on the human form. Like the transgender respondents, they have an unusually high level of awareness of the details of human bodies—including both sex similarities and sex differences. Considering the expertise of the artists who produce figure drawing guides, I want to highlight three kinds of evidence for sex similarities: the section and chapter headings, the authors' narrative descriptions of how to draw particular body parts, and the sample illustrations.

The sections and subsections of figure drawing texts are usually introduced by headings stating what they address (e.g., "Drawing the Ear"). Sometimes it is clear from the heading that the author believes the body part in question is sex-specific (e.g., "Drawing the Female Pelvis"). Other times, as in the example of "Drawing the Ear," no sex specificity is indicated. The following list includes just some of the sex-neutral headings I collected from three books: *How to Draw Manga Bodies and Anatomy* (The Society for the Study of Manga Techniques), *Drawing the Head & Figure* (Jack Hamm), and *Draw Real People!* (Lee Hammond).[15]

The Human Skeleton
Various Mouth Shapes
Various Ear Shapes
Various Eye Shapes

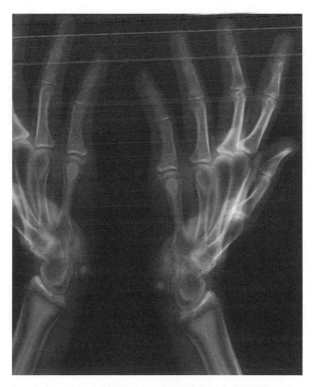

FIGURE 15 Bones of the human hand (x-ray). (Alers-Hankey and Chisholm, *Photographic Atlas of the Body*, p. 95.)

Of course, the lessons following any of these seemingly sex-neutral headings could contain information about sex differences. And in some cases the authors did make reference to differences between male and female bodies: "Sometimes men's lips are very light in color."[16] "Most artists prefer a male figure 8 heads high. Sometimes a petite female drawing as small as 6 heads high is desired."[17] Or, "There is more likely to be a curve between the mouth and nose of the female than the male."[18]

At the same time, however, the authors provide many written descriptions that reveal a fundamental structural resemblance between male and female bodies. For example, Hamm writes, "After one has studied and practiced the opening sequence on the female head, he can employ the same essential approaches in drawing the male head."[19] He also speaks in terms of "average" heads, rather than average male or female heads: "The average head is approximately 5 eyes wide."[20] In a similar vein, Hammond emphasizes the universal shape of the human nose: "The nose is really like three balls hooked together, with one attached to each side."[21] In addition, both Hamm and Hammond discuss ears in sex-neutral terms:

The top of the ear is directly across from the bottom of the eyebrow. The bottom of the ear is directly across from the bottom of the nose. When seen from the side, the ear is about in the middle, between the back of the head and the front of the eyes.[22]

The ears are as long as the distance from the top of the eyes to the bottom of the nose.[23]

Hammond even denies the sex specificity of facial features overall when she writes that "people are pretty similar as far as facial features go. Even though we are all different and have different looks about us, the basic details of our eyes, nose and mouth are very much alike."[24] While all the quotations I have presented to this point deal with the head, comparable statements were made about almost every other area of the body.

On first glance, one possible exception is the legs. Hamm includes a discussion of "the female leg," in which he describes several differences in shape between male and female legs.[25] However, it is important to acknowledge in this context that he only presents the female leg in high heels! In his series of illustrations entitled "Types of Female Legs," every single "type" of female leg he depicts is wearing high heels (see fig. 16). Hamm himself can even be interpreted as implying that some of the sex differences he observes in legs are attributable to high heels in the following comment: "In drawing women's 'flats' . . . the basic rules are quite similar to those used in blocking in men's footwear."[26]

These images of "female" legs notwithstanding, a great many of the sample illustrations accompanying the descriptions of how to draw particular body parts illustrate that male and female bodies are much more similar than different. For example, Hamm includes the following image of varieties of ears (see fig. 17). The text accompanying this image does not mention whether they are "male" or "female" ears. Rather, it refers to "numerous possibilities" and urges the reader to "observe the essentials of the ear's form."[27] When describing how to draw eyebrows and eyelashes, Hammond similarly makes no reference to sex (see fig. 18).

In some cases, even when the author explicitly claims to present illustrations exemplifying sex differences, the sex specificity does not come across clearly in the decontextualized images of particular body parts. For example, Hamm presents a series of images under the heading "Female Noses" and another series under the heading "Male Noses" (see fig. 19), but the differences are not actually very obvious. Further underscoring this point, he himself goes on to present a third series of images that, in his words, "might be either male or female," confirming that the sex differences in noses are far from categorical (see the rightmost column of images in fig. 19).

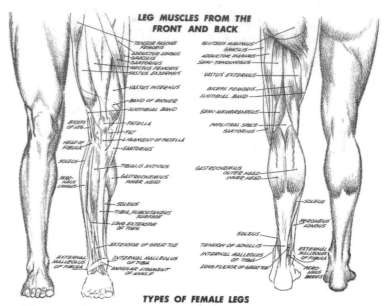

LEG MUSCLES FROM THE FRONT AND BACK

TENSOR FASCIAE FEMORIS
ADDUCTOR LONGUS
GRACILIS
SARTORIUS
RECTUS FEMORIS
VASTUS EXTERNUS

VASTUS INTERNUS

BAND OF RICHER

ILIOTIBIAL BAND

BICEPS OF LEG
HEAD OF FIBULA
SOLEUS
PERO-NEUS LONGUS

PATELLA
FAT
LIGAMENT OF PATELLA
SARTORIUS

TIBIALIS ANTICUS
GASTROCNEMIUS INNER HEAD

SOLEUS
TIBIA, SUBCUTANEUS SURFACE
LONG EXTENSOR OF TOES

EXTENSOR OF GREAT TOE

EXTERNAL MALLEOLUS OF FIBULA
INTERNAL MALLEOLUS OF TIBIA
ANNULAR LIGAMENT OF ANKLE

GLUTEUS MAXIMUS
GRACILIS
ADDUCTOR MAGNUS
SEMI-TENDINOSUS

VASTUS EXTERNUS

BICEPS FEMORIS
ILIOTIBIAL BAND

SEMI-MEMBRANOSUS

POPLITEAL SPACE
SARTORIUS

GASTROCNEMIUS
OUTER HEAD
INNER HEAD

SOLEUS

TENDON OF ACHILLES
INTERNAL MALLEOLUS OF TIBIA
LONG FLEXOR OF GREAT TOE

SOLEUS

PERONEUS LONGUS

EXTERNAL MALLEOLUS OF FIBULA
PERO-NEUS BREVIS

TYPES OF FEMALE LEGS

Below are several different types of female legs. Check out the interior structure on No. 1 and No. 2 by reference to the muscles listed above. No. 3 is an example of subcutaneous fat concealing all but general bone and muscle shape beneath; nevertheless, it is still there. Compare the heavier type No. 4 with the slender No. 5 legs and note how the basic under-pattern is the same.

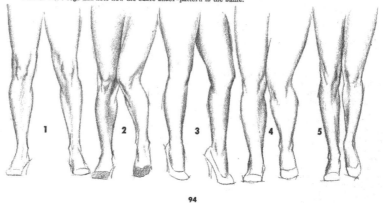

1   2   3   4   5

94

FIGURE 16 "Types of Female Legs." (Hamm, *Drawing the Head and Figure*, p. 94.)

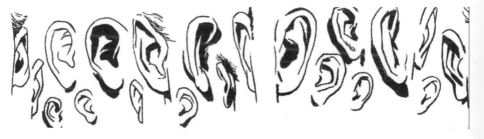

FIGURE 17 "Examples of Ears Done with Pen or Brush Using Ink." (Hamm, *Drawing the Head and Figure*, p. 16.)

EYEBROWS AND LASHES

The line on the left looks hard and straight. The line on the right is softer and curved. It was drawn with a *quick* stroke. Flick your wrist and the line will become thinner on the end.

Eyebrows can be large or small, thick or thin. Just draw the overall shape first.

Start to apply little hairs. Look at the direction they are growing in the picture and apply your pencil lines in that direction.

Continue to draw hairs until they start to fill in, and then take your tortillion and blend the whole thing out.

Add hair strokes again, until it gets as dark as you want it.

To soften it a bit, take your kneaded eraser, put it into a point, and with the same quick strokes, lift some light hairs out. It is this finishing touch that really helps make it look real.

Never just fill in the eyebrow with heavy dark pencil lines.

This is better, but the lines still look harsh and too straight.

These lines work. They are curved and tapered at the ends, more like hair really is.

Eyelashes should not be drawn with hard lines either. These lines are much too hard and straight.

This is the way eyelash lines should be drawn, but eyelashes don't grow in single lines like this.

Eyelashes grow in clumps like this. Watch which direction they curve

Don't ever draw a line all around the eye with lower lashes like this.

This is what lower lashes should look like. They come off the bottom of the lower lid thickness and are shorter than the upper lashes. See how some of them are shorter than others? They, too, grow in bunches.

FIGURE 18 "Eyebrows and Lashes." (Hammond, *Draw Real People!*, p. 37.)

In summary, drawing books suggest human bodies are in fact very much alike—certainly more similar than different. Perhaps, however, this evidence is not totally convincing; these are not, after all, *real* bodies. As I mentioned earlier, my view is that, if anything, drawing texts present a conservative portrait of the similarities between male and

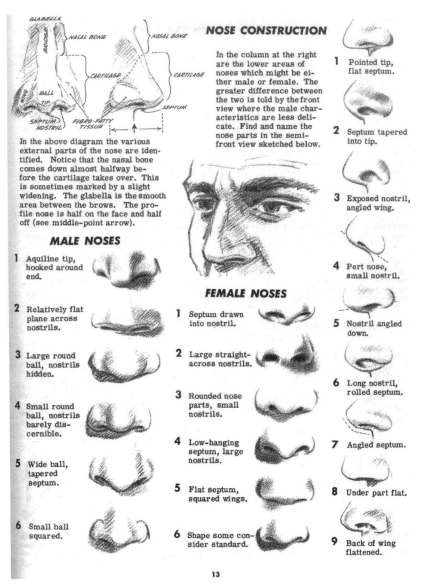

FIGURE 19 "Male Noses" versus "Female Noses." (Hamm, *Drawing the Head and Figure*, p. 13.)

female bodies because of their uncritical portrayal of gender norms regarding appearance. (In fact, one of the texts I included, *How to Draw Manga Bodies and Anatomy*, is known for exaggerated portrayals of feminine appearance, including huge eyes with extra-long lashes and large breasts.) For this reason, the evidence for sex sameness contained in these texts should be all the more convincing. Further, particularly when combined with the body measurements and photographs of the body's interior I presented earlier, both of which *do* deal with real bodies, these books can help establish the existence of significant underlying commonalities between male and female bodies even when polarizing norms are in place (as they clearly are here). As such, they are particularly effective in problematizing the presumption that the self-evidence of sex differences is something we read off of bodies—as opposed to a mental construct we use to interpret bodies—because they demonstrate that even polarized bodies are largely the same.

Genitals, Gonads, and Genes

In a final effort to capture the normally disattended similarities between male and female bodies, I want to specifically consider what for many people constitutes the "hard case" of sex difference: the genitals, chromosomes, and reproductive organs. Even scholars who explicitly challenge assumptions about the pervasiveness of biological sex differences often single these out as the only true, and truly dichotomous, sex differences. One example of such an account is the following, which identifies chromosomes and genitals as the only "real" difference between male and female bodies: "So far as I am aware, the only sex differences that don't overlap substantially (to the point that differences among members of one sex are much greater than the difference between the averages of each sex) are whether one has XX or XY chromosome configurations, vulvas or penises. Plot these out, and I'm sure you will get a beautiful dumbbell distribution, with a big cluster of females at one end and a big cluster of males at the other end, and a scattering of a few anomalous cases in between."[28] My argument does not require committing to the idea that males and females do not differ at all—even genitally, gonadally, or chromosomally. In fact, I am advocating proportional attention to similarities *and* differences. However, I do think that the notion that human genitals—or our genes—are a clear dichotomy can (and ought to) be challenged.

One logical starting point for a critical assessment of the claim that genitals and gonads are fundamentally different is embryonic bisexuality.[29] As Jake (age 48), who is intersexed, described it to me, "Every fetus starts out as female. [. . .] A penis is only an enlarged clitoris. If labia continue to grow and then fuse they become scrotum." Viewed in light of embryonic bisexuality, the claim above that "the only sex differences that don't overlap substantially . . . are whether one has XX or XY chromosome configurations, vulvas or penises" suffers from a polarized way of thinking about penises and clitorises, and scrotums and vaginal lips, which have as many similarities as differences and start out biologically undifferentiated (and the same could be said of ovaries and testes). When thinking about genital differences, then, it is worth remembering that genitals *could* be measured on a single scale and seen as variations on a single category. And this view may even be more strictly biologically correct, given embryonic bisexuality. This idea is part of what is captured by Anne Fausto-Sterling's "phall-o-meter" (see fig. 20), which measures penises and clitorises on the same ruler.

Further, regarding chromosomes, simply put, XX and XY are at least 50 percent the same, and the egg and the sperm actually contain the same sex chromosomes every time both contribute an X to make a female.[30] Sarah Richardson offers a much more scientifically precise version of the same fundamental argument in her critique of recent studies reporting significant genetic variation between males and females.[31]

Sex differences in the genome are very, very small: of 20,000–30,000 genes, marked sex differences are evident in perhaps half a dozen genes on the X and Y chromosome, and, it is hypothesized, a smattering of differently expressed genes

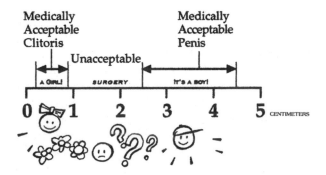

Phall-O-Metrics

FIGURE 20 Anne Fausto-Sterling's phall-o-meter. (Fausto-Sterling, *Sexing the Body*, p. 59.)

across the autosomes. Researchers have doggedly searched for sex-based gene expression differences in dozens of tissues in the human body, including the brain, yielding limited, inconsistent results, and no strong candidate genes for sex differences (Delongchamp et al. 2005; Nguyen and Disteche 2006; Rinn & Snyder 2005; Talebizadeh et al. 2006). In DNA sequence and structure, sex differences are localized to the X and Y chromosomes. Males and females share 99.9% sequence identity on the 22 autosome pairs and the X, and the handful of genes on the Y are highly specific to male testes development. Thinking of males and females as having different genomes exaggerates the amount of difference between them, giving the impression that there are systematic and even law-like differences distributed across the genomes of males and females, and playing into a traditional gender-ideological view of sex differences.[32]

The essential point is this: Males and females are much more genetically similar than different. Whatever the exact proportion of genetic difference to similarity, it is less than 2 percent, although Richardson argues that 2 percent is a significant overestimate.[33] In any case, the fact that males and females are 98 percent genetically identical and yet seen as "opposites" is another illustration of the mismatch between cultural ideas about sex differences and the biological logic of human bodies.

In this chapter I have presented just some of the possible evidence for sex sameness that we normally do not notice, or that we perceive but do not "count," when seeing "male" and "female" bodies. In truth, I only scratched the surface of the "perceptual residue" of dominant conceptions of sex—all the similarities that must be disattended in order to unproblematically see bodies as sex dimorphic. Although not comprehensive, what I have tried to demonstrate by inverting the usual perceptual norms, leaving aside evidence of biological sex differences and actively seeking out information about the body's human commonality, is simply how differently we might see bodies if we filtered them another way. In the final section, I explore the potential benefits of revisiting some version of a one-sex model (but without the androcentric bias) as an analytic strategy.

Sex Sameness as a Rhetorical Strategy

Feminists have debated the intellectual and political utility of the concept of androgyny since at least the 1970s. In these debates, *androgyny* was typically used to connote a lack of social and psychological (though not bodily) differentiation between the sexes.[34] As Alison Jaggar put it, "Androgynous people would remain biologically male or female but, socially and psychologically, they would no longer be masculine and feminine."[35] For the most part, the concept of androgyny has fallen out of favor. Some feminists came to view advocating a mixture of "masculinity" and "femininity" for everyone (and thus implicitly avowing masculinity as legitimate) as an insufficiently politicized goal.[36] Others argued that androgyny failed to leave gender behind,[37] or that, given the cultural context of male dominance, androgyny was likely always to lapse into androcentrism.[38]

Despite these critiques, I find it useful to revisit—and expand, and strengthen—the concept of sex sameness. When I use the terms *androgyny* and *sex sameness*, however, my intended meaning goes beyond the scope of most of these earlier uses to include *physiological* androgyny. Both Monique Wittig and Andrea Dworkin have similarly advocated the traditional feminist ideal of androgyny and extended it to the elimination of the sex distinction itself. In Wittig's words: "Sex is taken as an 'immediate given,' 'a sensible given,' 'physical features,' belonging to a natural order. But what we believe to be a physical and direct perception is only a sophisticated and mythic construction, an 'imaginary formation,' which reinterprets physical features (in themselves as neutral as any others but marked by the social system) through the network of relationships in which they are perceived."[39] The reinterpretation of physical features Wittig describes is precisely what I have tried to capture with the filter metaphor. Part of my motivation for revisiting the idea of *anatomical* commonality between males and females is that the existing accounts of sex sameness have not succeeded in shifting perceptions of bodies, and presumptions of self-evident sex differences retain a grip on our thinking. Ideas about sex differences, as we have seen, are culturally pervasive and recur consistently in science and popular culture, the latest examples being the research on genetic sex differences mentioned above, as well as the recent explosion of studies on sex differences in the brain.[40]

Even if these claims about sex differences are strictly correct, however, they can and should be challenged based on the disproportionate emphasis they place on small sex differences to the exclusion of attention to the much larger similarities between males and females. When studies emphasize statistical differences in the size of a particular region of the brain, for example, it is important to consider what is "filtered out" of these depictions of the brain: namely, that these are usually proportionately small differences amid many similarities (in size,

appearance, structure, and function). For instance, just a few of the regions of the brain showing no consistent sex differences are the occipi-
tal lobe, the temporal lobe, the locus coeruleus (part of the brain stem),
the striatum, which makes up a large part of the forebrain, and several
different components of the frontal lobe.[41] As Rebecca Jordan-Young
has put it, "Human brains, unlike genitals, cannot be 'sexed,' meaning that they cannot be sorted reliably into 'male-type' and 'female-
type' by observers who don't know the sex of the person they came
from." She further reminds us that "the identification of sex differences
in the brain is one of the longest-standing projects of neuroscience.
After more than two centuries of effort, surely any 'obvious' differences
would have emerged by now."[42]

In light of this, a more proportionate, valid portrait of sex differences in the brain would not allow for book titles such as *The Essential Difference* and *The Female Brain*.[43] If such differences can be established, it is only *parts* of the brain that are sex differentiated, not the
brain itself, and we should strive to maintain those differences in their
proper proportion to sex similarities in our minds. As I have argued
throughout, the most powerful feature of the filter metaphor is that
it specifically directs attention to these normally disattended similarities, challenging taken-for-granted assumptions about sex differences
and encouraging more proportionate conceptions of the relationship
between male and female bodies.

Conclusion: Excess, Continua, and the Flexible Mind

Sex difference is a "social fact" that performs "sociomental control."[1] The constraints imposed by social facts are invisible to us, as Émile Durkheim describes, unless we actively try to resist them.[2] Likewise, it is only once we try to imagine seeing bodies in other, or different, categories that we recognize how strongly the sex-difference filter constrains our imagination. As we have seen, the optical filters governing our visual perceptions are a powerful force: they make certain observations "obvious" to us and others "impossible" to imagine. My efforts to expose some of the sex similarities obscured by our normative ways of perceiving male and female bodies notwithstanding, the truth is that we have little sense of what human bodies would look like if we were somehow to step outside the filter of binary sex difference and into another optical paradigm. But it is certain that, seen through a different filter, different parts of the body would come into visual relief as "relevant," and other parts would recede into the "irrelevant" background, making us effectively blind to them.

When confronting something as profoundly reified as sex difference, it can be productive to identify *how* culture functions on a cognitive and perceptual level to create self-evidence. This has been the focus of my analysis for the last several chapters in presenting and applying the sociocognitive process of filtration and the conceptual system of filter analysis. Although the power dynamics that create the prevailing norms regarding sex differences may take the form of discursive power, in which dominant discourses—which no one controls, but which discipline all—synchronize and shape our perceptions (and our bodies) through ideas about normality, filter analysis can make us more aware of them and help us to identify how they work by highlighting practices of normative attention and disattention.[3] Perceiving sex requires that we anticipate, selectively seek out, and note sex differences. What filter analysis demonstrates is that, if we expected to see something else (e.g., sex similarity) sex differences might be as difficult for us to see as unsexed bodies are under our current sexpectations. Beginning at birth, we learn to ignore the similarity and overlap between the sexes, but thinking about sensory perception in terms of filtration may help cultivate the mental flexibility necessary to see more of the complexity and multiplicity of bodies, including both human commonalities *and* sex differences.

Emphasizing Excess

The most universally applicable insight of filter analysis is that empirical reality is always richer and more complex than what we perceive and thus experience. I have to this point limited my treatment of this disattended complexity to the case of sex attribution. However, a number of scholars have previously made the broader point that bodies are always excessive of the social categories through which we perceive and signify them. Elizabeth Grosz, for instance, argues that the body is always incomplete, open, and undetermined, exceeding all of the discourses through which it is understood.[4] Margaret Shildrick likewise highlights the ways that corporeality is inherently "leaky" and uncontainable.[5] Not only sex, then, but any categorical perception or experience of the body is based on the exclusion of noncategorical details.

By training our analytical lens on disattention, the body can become a powerful tool for social constructionist analysis, "talking back" through these spaces of excess. Joan Fujimura's work on the production of knowledge about genetic sex differences explicitly deals with this idea of bodily excess—which she evocatively calls "awkward surplus"— and the way it is filtered out during scientists' interpretive processes.[6] In Fujimura's words, "The concept of awkward surplus provides science studies with a way of talking about materiality that does not deny human mediation but also acknowledges material agency."[7] While my main objective has been precisely this—to explore how the metaphor of a filter and the concept of bodily excess can help advance our thinking about the social construction of the body by highlighting the ways the body seeps out of categories and interpretations—it is equally important to point out the generic sociological applicability of the concept of excessiveness and the analytical system of filter analysis.

For example, taking the idea of awkward surplus beyond the body, Fujimura argues that by adopting the perspectives of social science, gender studies, and the transgender and intersex social movements, one "literally can see differently when examining the work of geneticists and other scientists in the production of the science of sex," and in fact "new signals read through old frames are not seen."[8] In other words, the distinct filters of particular academic disciplines and social movements bring certain aspects of a given subject matter into relief and blind us to others. Edmund Leach actually begins the first chapter of *Culture and Communication* with a similar observation about the "filters" of social anthropologists: "All social anthropologists take as their subject matter the *variety* of human culture and society, and they all assume that their task is not only to describe what the varieties are but to explain why they exist."[9] If the subject matter of social anthropology is specifically the *differences* between cultures, this suggests that social anthropologists see their subject matter through a disciplinary filter that makes cultural commonalities irrelevant.

In a similar vein, I have already discussed a number of different ways that scientific research on sex differences is defined by a norm of disattending sex similarities. This has taken the form of highlighting relatively small differences in brain structure or genetics while leaving unmentioned the larger context of overwhelming similarities, as well as viewing as a "nonfinding" results that demonstrate no difference between the sexes; both are forms of bias in favor of finding differences. One question this raises is whether this privileging of difference over similarity is unique to research on sex, which is certainly possible given the prominence of cultural discourses that disproportionately fixate us on sex differences, or whether I am seeing one manifestation of a more generic feature of scientific research and social life. This question is a research project in its own right, but I will mention just a few examples of a similar privileging of differences and neglect of similarities in other contexts.

It would seem that with identity and labels in general that our selective attention is usually toward difference. The blind respondents illustrated this point in terms of disability and identity:

I think maybe blindness is researched too much. And I'll tell you why: Blindness is merely a loss of sight. Any other meanings we ascribe to blindness are probably cultural or limiting. For example, I'm going to go skydiving in about a month if the weather permits [. . .] and in September I'm going to go deer hunting. [. . .] Again, we limit ourselves as blind people. We're part of society also. [. . .] It's a very simple thing and with the right training we can be average Joe out there in society. [. . .] People ascribe a lot to blindness that simply isn't there. [. . .] We just can't see. And everything else [. . .] we're somewhere in the middle. (Matt, age 56, blind since birth)

Blind people can be kind of wary of studies because it makes us feel like guinea pigs, and people will come up with the outrageous ideas that say we're so different from everyone else. (Andrea, age 30, began losing vision at age 12)

When we define blind people as a group, we render invisible the many ways that they are similar to sighted people. That is to say, we are blind to the sameness between the sighted and the blind.

Historically this hyperattention to difference in defining identity categories is perhaps most spectacularly evident in the "one drop rule," the American genealogical convention according to which any trace of black blood makes a person black, a definition upheld by a Louisiana court as recently as 1983. The fact that we find it unproblematic when Barack Obama is referred to as the first black president even though his mother is white demonstrates that the fundamental logic of the "one drop rule" remains influential. This form of racial classification suppresses evidence of biological similarities between whites and blacks, while focusing on the single drop of blood that represents racial differences (e.g., even fifteen white ancestors are not sufficient to make a person white, whereas a single black ancestor is sufficient to make a person black).

Genetics research, which is consistently focused on finding group differences, is another particularly extreme case of inattention to sameness. "It is especially ironic that DNA has become a cultural resource for the construction of differences, for one of the insights of contemporary genomics research is the profound similarity, at least at the level of the DNA, among human beings and, indeed, between human beings and other species. . . . The cultural lesson of the Human Genome Project could be that we are all very much alike."[10] A final example of this asymmetrical attention to differences over similarities can be seen in the very concept of a "species," which from an evolutionary perspective requires ignoring the unbroken genealogical chain that

actually exists between these different groups, an evolutionary continuum that we mentally divide into distinct species by focusing on
differences rather than similarities. As Richard Dawkins has put it: "A
complete fossil record would make it very difficult to classify animals
into discrete nameable groups. If we had a complete fossil record, we
should have to give up discrete names and resort to some mathematical or graphical notation of sliding scales. The human mind far prefers
discrete names, so in one sense it is just as well that the fossil record
is poor."[11]

Regardless of whether this unbalanced attention to differences over
similarities actually constitutes a broader social pattern, there is great
epistemological value in analyzing *whatever* information is being disattended, whether in the scientific research process or elsewhere. For one
thing, it is interesting to consider whether there are arenas where the
reverse is true and we are selectively attentive to sameness and inatten-
tive to difference. For example, the emotional legitimacy of nationalism (or even nation-ness) is typically based on a notion of unity that ignores or eliminates differences, which John Hutchinson and Anthony
Smith have described as follows: "The people must be united; they
must dissolve all internal divisions; they must be gathered together in
a single historic territory, a homeland; and they must have legal equality and share a single public culture."[12] Similarly, from Benedict Anderson's *Imagined Communities*: "Regardless of the actual inequality and
exploitation that may prevail in each, the nation is always conceived as
a deep, horizontal comradeship."[13]

Beyond the question of attention to similarity versus difference, a
fantastic example of the insight that can be gained through studying
the disattended more generally is "junk" (or noncoding) DNA. Most
noncoding DNA lies *between* the genes on the chromosome, and until recently researchers ignored it, since its function was unknown,
and it was assumed to be essentially inert. Then in 2007 the news of
a study broke: these stretches of "junk" between the presumed much
more important genes are actually performing an array of important—
and previously invisible—functions. Not only that, genes are not even
as distinct from these stretches of "junk" as was previously assumed:
"The new work also overturns the conventional notion that genes
are discrete packets of information arranged like beads on a thread of
DNA. Instead, many genes overlap one another and share stretches of
molecular code."[14] There are numerous implications to this paradigm
shift; one is that many genetic diseases actually arise from errors in
the DNA *between* the genes, rather than in the genes themselves, so

scientists have been looking in the wrong place for the causes of these diseases as a result of their previous selective attention to genes.

In addition, Jerome Groopman, the author of *How Doctors Think*, has identified some of the most common cognitive conventions in medical research and diagnosis, many of which are based on some form of disattention, including anchoring, using prototypes, and confirmation biases.[15] As a further illustration of the prevalence of disattention, Groopman refers to a study in which one hundred radiologists were shown sixty chest x-rays, one of which was of a patient who was missing his left clavicle. "The study was meant to assess performance in noticing what was *not* on the film rather than merely searching for a positive finding—an exercise that points out our natural preference for focusing on positive data and ignoring the negative. . . . Remarkably, 60 percent of the radiologists failed to identify the missing clavicle."[16] While not necessarily specifically organized around similarity and difference, then, disattention is a central cognitive practice in medical research, diagnosis, and treatment.

Thinking even more broadly, an analytical focus on disattention highlights the exclusion practices that underlie all forms of categorization. As George Lakoff and Mark Johnson explain, categorization in general involves ignoring noncategorical "excess" information: "A categorization is a natural way of identifying a *kind* of object or experience by highlighting certain properties, downplaying others, and hiding still others. . . . To highlight certain properties is necessarily to downplay or hide others, which is what happens whenever we categorize something. Focusing on one set of properties shifts our attention away from others. When we give everyday descriptions, for example, we are using categorizations to focus on certain properties that fit our purposes. Every description will highlight, downplay, and hide."[17] What these processes of hiding and exclusion indicate is that categorical perceptions and experiences—which are arguably *all* perceptions—are significantly impoverished and limited in comparison with empirical reality. In a sense, categorization *is* filtration, based as it is on highlighting some features and ignoring others.

Further, some concept of excessiveness and disattention underlies a number of different theoretical positions, including phenomenology and deconstructionism. Maurice Merleau-Ponty, for example, writes that perception is "communicating with a world which is richer than what we know of it."[18] Compare this to what Mark Taylor identifies as "the guiding insight of deconstruction," which is that "every structure—be it literary, psychological, social, economic, political or religious—that organizes our experience is constituted and maintained through acts of exclusion. In the process of creating something, something else inevitably gets left out."[19] One of the most useful features of filter analysis is that it draws our analytical attention to this world of excluded properties.

The defining question of filter analysis is, what is being filtered out? By explicitly marking the disattended as a subject of investigation, filter analysis can help scholars to capture these processes of *not noticing* and thus to analyze the information that is normally ignored, in addition to what is known to be important and already receiving attention, significantly expanding the scope of our "epistemological lens."[20]

In generic terms, this disattended "perceptual residue" consists of all the features or details that would—if we did not exclude them—support alternate categorizations and meanings. As such, the perceptual residue actually contains the raw sensory data for the construction of different social worlds. I understand the concept of a *social world*, following Alfred Schutz, as the intersubjective meanings and processes of interpretation that are sociology's fundamental object of analysis.[21] Schutz further argues that an effective sociological analysis of meaning requires "reinterpretation" and "rearrangement of the meaning-structure" to clarify the researcher's understanding of people's behavior and perceptions.[22] This is precisely what filter analysis facilitates when it directs attention to the complexity and richness that is missing from any given filtered, categorical perception.

Like Betty Edwards in *Drawing on the Right Side of the Brain*, filter analysis encourages us to focus on the unmarked "negative space" *between* the distinct "forms" we are normally taught to see. Interestingly, Edwards describes this as a shift from seeing with the verbal, logical "left brain" to a different way of processing that is more intuitive and spatial ("right brain"), which she calls a "release from stereotypic expression."[23] I have similarly argued that part of what constrains our perceptions of bodies is language and categories, and that we should try to become more aware of the overall spatial proportion of sex dimorphism to human similarity. One of the anticipated results of learning to perceive the negative spaces of the body is, indeed, a release from stereotypic perception.

Another way to conceptualize the negative space between categories is to use the metaphor of a continuum. In the case of sex attribution, this negative space consists of all those elements of bodies that are similar between males and females. Accordingly, one may say that what filter analysis helps identify is the normally unseen *continuum* between male and female bodies. More broadly, the metaphor of a continuum is a useful way to think about the connective space between concepts normally assumed to be binary oppositions. It captures the way categorical distinctions must by definition exclude all details which are not categorical. More exactly, categorical distinctions exclude details that fall *between* social categories. As an illustration, in the next section I use the metaphor of a continuum to highlight the connective space between the concepts of *sex* and *gender*.

The Sex/Gender Continuum

The sex/gender distinction is one of the implicit targets of this research because it supports assumptions about the self-evidence of sex differences. While this conceptual distinction was a vital intervention, allowing feminists to make the critical argument that although biological differences (sex) might be inevitable, social differences and inequality (gender) are socially constructed and thus potentially changeable, it is organized around the idea that sex (but not gender) is a fixed natural binary, a self-evident fact.[24] Here I propose that one conceptual alternative to sex and gender that better accounts for the negative space of the distinction—the interaction of culture and biology in creating both sex and gender—is a continuum. Graphically speaking, when understood as a dichotomy, sex and gender are completely separate entities that can be represented, as in figure 21, as two different circles. All that we classify as "sex" is contained in the left circle and all that we classify as "gender" is contained in the right circle. There is nothing that is both sex and gender.

Along with those scholars writing in this area before me, I maintain that this clean separation of sex from gender is ultimately not viable. Any given expression or act of gender is experienced and performed in a body, and the body is "disciplined," or shaped, by gender (e.g.,

FIGURE 21 The sex/gender dichotomy.

through years of socialization into gendered social norms of bodily demeanor and grooming). In addition, our sex is a cultural phenomenon, rather than a purely biological category. Any experience we have of sex, whether our own or another person's, is shaped by social norms and expectations. As we have seen, the "social fact" of natural, binary sex difference organizes our perceptions—telling us what is relevant and what we can ignore—as well as structures our norms of grooming, adornment, and bodily demeanor so as to artificially polarize naturally similar human bodies.

Reconceptualizing sex and gender in light of the filter metaphor draws attention to the figurative "perceptual residue" or "excess" of the sex/gender distinction, the overlap and intersection between the two concepts that we must ignore in order to understand them as we normally do. In the image of a SexGender[25] continuum, represented in figure 22, the biological and cultural aspects located at opposite ends of the continuum are "ideal types,"[26] never realized as such, but always including at least some proportion of the other. The arrows are meant to indicate that the poles of the continuum are never actually reached. As such, the binary opposition ceases to exist; all that exists is the conceptual space between the two terms.

Most directly relevant for my analysis, the notion of a SexGender continuum suggests that it is not possible to distinguish what is materially true from what is culturally true about sex. There is no sex without gender, as Suzanne Kessler and Wendy McKenna so presciently argued in 1978: "The element of social construction is primary in *all aspects* of being male or female."[27] In the same vein, Judith Butler has described sexual difference as "the site where a question concerning the relation of the biological to the cultural is posed and reposed, where it must and can be posed, but where it cannot, strictly speaking, be answered. . . . Sexual difference has psychic, somatic and social dimensions that are never quite collapsible into one another but are not for that reason ul-

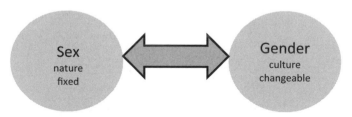

FIGURE 22 SexGender as a continuum.

timately distinct."[28] By recasting both sex and gender as socially constructed, what the SexGender continuum so effectively communicates is that "our understanding of what is natural about gender is itself a social and cultural formulation."[29]

While up to this point I have only addressed the implications of re-imagining the sex/gender distinction as a continuum, it bears mentioning that very similar questions come up in the sociology of the body more broadly: Where are the boundaries of social construction? Is there a point beyond which culture does not penetrate? Monica Casper and Lisa Jean Moore summarize the conceptual limitations of the nature/culture binary opposition for answering these questions well: "The nature/culture dualism forecloses the understanding of how 'nature' and 'culture' are formed, an understanding that is crucial to both feminist and scientific analyses. . . . The notion of 'formation' in no way denies the material reality of either 'nature' or 'culture.'"[30] My argument is that filter analysis provides a method to access the continuum between nature and culture and to conceptualize the cognitive processes by which this continuum—the complex compound of biology and culture these authors describe—is simplified and organized into the categorical distinctions we perceive and thus experience.

Cognitive Flexibility

When attempting to access the "perceptual residue" or the "unseen middle" of a continuum via filter analysis, however, it is important to recognize that the aim is a critique of dominant discourses, rather than access to "the Real." In the context of the sociology of the body, for instance, filter analysis is most useful as a device to identify bodily excess: those features or details of bodies that do not perfectly fit the available social categories. The idea of bodily excess is not intended as a way to access an extra-social body but as a strategy to critique the naturalness of social categories. This approach echoes Michel Foucault's argument that the hegemonic concept of sexuality cannot be resisted through sex (a categorical construction borne of the dominant discourse) but only through "bodies and pleasures."[31] Foucault's focus on bodies and pleasures is not a recourse to an extra-discursive body but a strategy to reveal and challenge currently dominant discourses on sex and sexuality. Filter analysis is likewise imagined as a tool to access alternate perceptions and experiences of the body that contest dominant categories and thus can ground social constructionism.

143

I have made a point of emphasizing that filter analysis cannot provide access to extra-social reality because I recognize that filters and continua, like all metaphors, constrain our thinking in some ways, creating new blind spots while clearing up earlier ones.[32] Indeed, there is no escape from metaphorical perception.[33] While new metaphors change our blind spots, and as such challenge previously taken-for-granted perceptions, they should not be understood to reveal "real" or "prediscursive" reality. However, in light of this, one final advantage of filter analysis must be emphasized: these epistemological insights are built into its conceptual structure. The epistemological standpoint that defines filter analysis suggests that every perception contains "perceptual residue"—blind spots, so to speak—and thus all facts, ideas, and perceptions ought to be understood from the outset to be challengeable and ultimately falsifiable.

Even so, metaphor development is a critical intellectual project—at least in so far as we use metaphors as a tool to proliferate cognitive and perceptual diversity, rather than to reveal "reality." Developing alternate metaphors is a fantastic opportunity to enrich our perceptions and cultivate "flexible mindedness."[34] Each new metaphor that enters the conceptual system shifts perceptions of reality: "New metaphors have the power to create a new reality. . . . If a new metaphor enters the conceptual system that we base our actions on, it will alter that conceptual system and the perceptions and actions that the system gives rise to. Much cultural change arises from the introduction of new metaphorical concepts and the loss of old ones."[35] Through the intellectual project of cultivating new metaphors, then, it is possible to encourage the perception of ambiguity and multiple realities, the acknowledgment of which can promote mental flexibility. Such flexibility is, as Eviatar Zerubavel argues, the best way to avoid the "epistemological pitfall of attributing objectivity to that which is only intersubjective."[36] The more different ways of perceiving something we can generate, that is, the less likely we are to make the mistaken assumption that any one way is the "real" or "correct" way.

In this project I have relied on the metaphor of a filter to identify and illustrate the blind spots of one particular view of human bodies—sex difference—by offering a different interpretation, a different arrangement of relevance and irrelevance, which is sex sameness. As opposed to adopting a different but equally rigid mindset, which would lead me to declare that sex sameness is, in fact, the correct view of the human body, I would like to argue for a "flexible-minded" approach and insist on the idea that there are multiple potential interpretations of the similarities and differences among human bodies. Given this dynamic potential, I must acknowledge that reversing the sex-difference filter and emphasizing sameness is an *alternate* interpretation, and one we never normally see because it is contrary to our social expectations and categories. It is not, however, the definitive interpretation. A flexible-minded view reminds us that entities need never have only one fixed meaning or appearance—even material, bodily entities.

While sex sameness is surely not the singular "truth" about bodies any more than sex difference is, using filter analysis to access some of the "perceptual residue" of sex attribution and to establish a continuum of bodies demonstrates that we *could* see "male" and "female" bodies as the same, and thus filter analysis functions to dislodge the hegemonic belief that sex difference is "self-evident" and "undeniable." In other words, these metaphors can help us to think critically about the dominant discourses that assume and proliferate the idea that sex difference is an obvious and purely biological truth about bodies.

More broadly, regardless of the specific content of our perceptions, by definition, the flexible mind is an open mind. It embraces complexity, acknowledges ambiguity, and questions oversimplification. For instance, applying the insights of mental flexibility to race, Zerubavel highlights the political importance of avoiding simple-minded, rigid categorizations in an editorial about then-candidate Barack Obama's March 18, 2008 speech on race in America.

One of the most remarkable things about Obama's Philadelphia address was the tremendous respect he paid to our intelligence by bringing nuance and complexity—something we sorely miss—into American politics. We have become used to simplification through either exaggerated contrast or explicit partisanship. Yet Obama chose to juxtapose rather than contrast black anger and white resentment, and refused to disown either his former black pastor or his own white grandmother despite the racist discourse they occasionally embraced. In so doing he asks us to grapple with the complexity of race in America. Rather than seeing the world in black and white, this "son of a black man from Kenya and a white woman from Kansas" opts for various shades of gray.[37]

Zerubavel goes on to examine the ways that President Obama embodies the complexities of racial categorization, specifically the norms of disattention involved in seeing him as "black" even though he—like so many other "black" people—has white ancestors. "The way we trace our descent essentially involves certain conventions of paying attention to some things and ignoring or denying others. Racial designations work this way. They presuppose particular patterns of genealogical denial where some of our ancestors are remembered while others are forgotten. It helps to be reminded of this denial by someone whose actual parents embodied the genealogical complexity often underlying 'racial' identity. After all, viewing Obama as 'black' requires ignoring the fact that one of his parents was 'white.'" When extracted from the context of race, Zerubavel's comments highlight the broad political agenda promoted by mental flexibility, which brings the focus away from identity categories to the sociocognitive practices through which distinctions get created and oversimplified, and by extension to the complexities that are too often "filtered out" of political discourse.

Arlene Stein has similarly argued for more attention to complexity in our understanding of sexual identity and identity politics, and her discussion makes explicit an additional factor, which is the connection between acknowledging complexity and attending to the *specificity* of individual experiences and identifications.[38] Highlighting this relationship between specificity, complexity, and categorical excessiveness, Shane Phelen writes that "specificity mandates conscious location of the self . . . and gestures to that in each of us which is irreducible to categories."[39] The complexities of President Obama's origin story, for instance, cannot be captured except through understanding the specific configuration of his genealogy. There is no identity *category* that can represent the specificity of his racial lineage.

The impulse to take apart identity categories and blur group boundaries through attention to complexity and specificity connects the cognitive sociological perspective I have been describing with other intellectual movements in feminist theory and poststructuralist philosophy. Perhaps most directly, in opening up the question of what is rendered invisible by the notion of sex difference, this study can serve as a case study in the damaging effects of binary exclusion, which in itself is a political act with a long history within feminism.[40] This is also one of queer theory's principle theoretical moves—to problematize binary sexual and gender categories, and identities in general.[41]

Joshua Gamson has written about the implications of queer theory's critique of identity categories for social movements: "If identities are indeed much more unstable, fluid, and constructed than movements have tended to assume . . . what happens to identity-based social movements such as gay and lesbian rights?"[42] By questioning categories like *white, black, lesbian, gay, male*, and *female* and examining the complexities they obscure, cognitive sociology also indirectly raises questions about the social movements that are organized by these categories. Certainly my argument that sex similarities are proportionately more dominant than sex differences begs the question of whether it is useful to continue to organize for "women's rights," for instance, which seems to require and naturalize precisely the distinction I have tried to bring into question.

In emphasizing the importance of cultivating mental flexibility vis-à-vis sex, this argument also speaks to the question of "strategic essentialism"—perhaps more fittingly called strategic rigidity in this context—a concept introduced by Gayatri Spivak to argue that there are times when it is both advantageous and necessary to operate provisionally as though the categories *sex* and *gender* are sound.[43] This self-conscious essentializing is designed to allow feminism to function politically and identity to function personally without relinquishing the idea that the category *woman* is a fictional unity. However, the category that strategic essentialism is most concerned with is *gender*, not *sex*. The "strategy" and "provisionality" refer largely to women's and men's social experiences (i.e., their gender). This strand of theory grew directly out of the critique of gender suggesting that whiteness, middle-class status, heterosexuality, and Western cultural values were operating as unmarked norms in the definition of gender. The "strategy" in question, then, is the self-conscious temporary bracketing of these critiques. Strategic essentialism refers only secondarily, if at all, to challenges to notions of binary biological sex. However, the concepts of perceptual filtration and cognitive flexibility are entirely compatible with the impulse of strategic essentialism. In light of this, the question that most interests me is how to draw attention to the fact that sex difference also reflects a strategy—a cognitive and cultural process—as opposed to a self-evident material reality. Given that biological sex differences remain the basis for most "folk theories" of inequality, what is most intellectually and politically pressing is to demonstrate that these differences are empirically small but are made significantly larger—physically, cognitively, and emotionally—through social processes.

One way to clarify this is to conduct research that shifts sex attribution from automatic to deliberate cognition. One of my key findings in chapter 4 was that blind sex attribution is slower and more deliberate, and in part as a result of this temporal difference, blind people have to contend with more ambiguity and complexity. Their rigid-minded assumptions about the obviousness of sex (which they acquire in the same manner as sighted people, by being socialized in a context of relentlessly emphasized sex differences) are frequently in tension with these deliberate processes of sex attribution. Sighted sex attribution, by contrast, is automatic, which is another word for "without conscious thought." Sighted people could benefit from slowing down at least occasionally and confronting the ambiguity and complexity that is erased through automatic sex attribution.

I am basing my thinking about the distinction between automatic and deliberate cognition on Paul DiMaggio's work summarizing cognitive psychological research relevant to the sociology of culture, where automatic cognition is defined as routine, everyday cognition that "relies heavily and uncritically upon culturally available schemata— knowledge structures that represent objects or events and provide default assumptions about their characteristics, relationships, and entailments under conditions of incomplete information."[44] Deliberate cognition, by contrast, is a slower, more critical, reflexive form of thought, which, while highly temporally inefficient, could be of great use in increasing awareness of the cognitive distortions underlying sex attribution.[45] The value of slowing down cognition and perception has been recognized previously in several different contexts, including medical diagnosis[46] and "sensuous" research methods.[47]

The psychological research suggests that there are at least three conditions that can induce deliberate cognition: attention, motivation, and schema failure.[48] In other words, people can switch from automatic to deliberate cognition when their attention is drawn to a problem, when inconsistencies disrupt a schema's unproblematic functioning, or when they are dissatisfied with the status quo. As an analytical device, filter analysis facilitates some of these same conditions, and thus may be a useful tool for promoting deliberate cognition about sex differences (as well as other taken-for-granted perceptions). The filter metaphor is explicitly conceived as a tool to draw attention to the anomalous information that is ignored in automatic cognition. By bringing this inconsistent evidence to the fore of our attention, filter analysis further demonstrates that our operative schemas cannot account for all of the available information, creating a kind of "schema failure." Finally, in highlighting all of the complexities that are normally disattended, filter analysis definitely stirs up disaffection with the oversimplifications of automatic sex attribution. Given this, at least analytically, perhaps the filter metaphor can help encourage more deliberate modes of cognition that address the specificities of the bodies we perceive, making us mindful of the simplification involved in categorization, and the blind spots we create when we disattend complexity.

In the most general terms, the sociological value of the filter metaphor is that it helps capture the complications and "things unseen" of everyday life, rendering them visible and therefore available for analysis. Further, filter analysis unsettles the taken-for-granted epistemology of sight by clarifying the relationship between what is seen and what is known. Whether that takes the form of challenging presumptions about the self-evidence of sex by bringing attention to the normally unacknowledged similarities between male and female bodies, highlighting the negative spaces of the conceptual distinction between sex and gender, foregrounding the complexities of biology and biography that are eclipsed by racial categories, or assembling the "irrelevant" data overlooked in scientific research for a detailed sociological analysis, the filter metaphor is a powerful analytical tool to take apart and examine the construction of self-evident social realities.

Appendix:
Methodological Notes

Early in my research I became interested in how the body has been conceptualized in sociology and gender studies. Both fields seemed to be struggling to integrate the fleshy materiality of the body with their defining commitments to ideas like the social construction of gender and reality more broadly. Several years later Eviatar Zerubavel introduced me to cognitive sociology, and it became instantly clear to me that the family of concepts he presented—in particular attention and disattention, polarization, lumping and splitting, and topological perception—provided an incredibly productive way to think about the social construction of the body that had not yet entered the ongoing discussion in either gender studies or the sociology of the body. As Wayne Brekhus has pointed out, cognitive sociology is translatable across nearly any subfield of sociological inquiry.[1] What I have tried to do in this book is to bring the insights of cognitive sociology to bear on the body, specifically the visual perception of differences between "male" and "female" bodies.

I mention the intellectual trajectory of the project because, for me, this theoretical argument that brings together cognitive sociology, the sociology of the body, and gender studies came first, and my ideas about what form of sociological data might empirically illustrate my claims came later. Distinct from more traditional "data-driven" sociological research methods, this sequencing is typical of formal cognitive sociology, which Zerubavel calls "social pattern analysis," in which researchers usually begin collecting data only after having committed themselves to a particular focus of scholarly attention.[2] Essentially conducting a form of "theoretical sampling," the researcher makes the decision about what data to collect on analytic grounds.[3] That is to say, the researcher firsts develops a set of "sensitizing" concepts that then provide guidance in approaching empirical instances.[4]

A second defining feature of social pattern analysis is that it often brings together substantively different groups, contexts, or levels of analysis to look for underlying social patterns.[5] These studies thus often lump together groups that may otherwise be regarded as too different to be related. Indeed, in any other context, blind people and transgender people would probably seem to have little in common. In fact, I imagine my blind respondents would be surprised to find themselves in the same study with transgender people—and vice versa. It is only by disregarding their obvious differences that the decision to bring these two groups together to analyze sex attribution can be understood.

In trying to capture the process of seeing sex, I had to address a methodological difficulty faced by any study of the taken-for-granted. Namely, how to make visible and analyze something that is largely automatic, and that most people believe is totally self-evident. Guided by the comparative approach of social pattern analysis, my eventual solution to this methodological challenge was to explore the perspectives of "outsiders," people who do not participate in visual sex attribution and "experts," people who are unusually self-conscious and deliberate about sex attribution. I chose to interview blind people because they literally cannot see sex, and as such their narratives provide access to a perceptual experience of sexed bodies that is totally different in sensory content from the typical sighted experience, reflecting rarely foregrounded nonvisual modes of perception. By highlighting their alternate perceptual reality of bodies, I sought to understand the extent to which the prevailing understanding of sex is specifically sex *seen* as opposed to sex *sensed* more broadly.

In light of the exceptional social prominence of visual perception, sociologists can gain great insight into the social construction of reality by bracketing the visual and attending instead to other modes of sensory perception. Perhaps most notably, in the spirit of Rod Michalko's argument that that blindness is not exceptional but can actually teach us about sight,[6] taking a multisensory approach to social research raises important epistemological questions about the seeming "self-evidence" of visual reality, and helps clarify the precise role of visual perception in the construction of taken-for-granted social realities.

I combined my interviews with blind people and interviews with transgender people, who I understand as "experts" on sex attribution. By viewing the body in light of the possibility of transitioning between sexes, transgender people often develop a deep awareness of the underlying similarities between male and female bodies as well as their most recalcitrant differences. Transgender people therefore offer an account of sexed bodies that is similar in its sensory content to the dominant perceptual experience (in that it is visual), but with a heightened awareness of sex cues that nontransgender people take for granted, and a unique point of view that brings some of the normally unseen similarities between male and female bodies into the foreground.

I use the term *transgender* as an umbrella term that encompasses transsexuals, cross-dressers, and anyone else who self-identifies as transgender or whose gender identity does not correspond normatively with his or her birth sex. In the interviews I asked all of my respondents to explain their understanding of the term *transgender* and whether they identified as transgender. This definition broadly reflects their responses. Under this very expansive definition, *transgender* can also include intersexuals—and I did interview several intersexuals who responded to my advertisements—but this remains a matter of debate in both intersex and transgender communities. When discussing specific respondents, I use the terminology they used to describe themselves to me as much as possible. I use the term *blind* because, on the whole, my respondents use the term rather than other labels such as *visually impaired*. In total, I interviewed forty-one transgender people and twenty-seven blind people.

Given their unique positions vis-à-vis sex attribution, one may question the extent to which insights from transgender and blind people can help us to understand the social construction of sex *in general*. In other words, these two groups are—in their own particular ways— substantially different from the average person. Richard Williams has written about how to approach theorizing from "extreme" cases, and his position is that we must assume that the findings obtained from such samples can provide insight into social behavior in general.[7] Brekhus has called this approach "universalizing from the marked," which involves looking for what is generic in categories that are normally understood only as group-specific.[8] It is in this spirit that I chose to study blind people and transgender people. I did not choose these groups because they can tell us something unique about blind people or transgender people. I studied them because I think they can tell us something about us all. Kristen Schilt has similarly argued that the experiences of transgender people can provide theoretical and empirical leverage on broader social processes; in her case, the social processes that uphold workplace inequality. She further explains that while highlighting transgender people's unique perspective on gender is not a new idea, in prior work the leverage provided by gender crossing remained theoretical, while her work gives these theories empirical weight.[9] This study furthers the empirical illustration of transgender people's insight into sex and gender, while also including a second group whose experiences provide a very different, but similarly unique, perspective on visual sex attribution.

In addition to comparing two very different populations, I further diversified my evidence—and thereby hopefully increased my argument's generalizability—by bringing in several additional, and equally eclectic, forms of data, including anthropometric measurements, figure drawing books, and photographs from anatomy textbooks. Throughout the analysis, I also interweave other snippets of popular culture, such as cartoons, works of art, and advertisements.[10]

My specific focus on the perceptual construction of sexed bodies dictated not only what forms of data I chose to include but what details I considered relevant within my data. With any empirical material, what we get out of it depends a great deal on what questions we put to it. It depends on which texts and passages we turn to for guidance in our interpretations, which ideas we think are important, and why. This is surely the case here. There is no doubt that my theoretical commitments—primarily to the role of cognition and perception in the social construction of sex and gender, the body, and reality more broadly—have shaped my interpretation and presentation of my respondents' narratives. This is not to say that I did not try to fairly represent their beliefs and experiences, or that I did not allow the things they said that I found surprising to shift and complicate my initial argument. The point is that my primary goal is not to characterize either group's experience but to explore a broader sociocognitive process, and I only use what my respondents have said in so far as it helps illustrate the normative cognitive and perceptual aspects of sex attribution.

In restricting my analytical focus in this way, I have undoubtedly ignored many other interesting aspects of my respondents' narratives. However, I do not view this analytic selectivity as a limitation. While the aim of more data-driven approaches is to represent one's empirical findings in all their detail, the only way to actually notice formal patterns is to confine one's attention to only certain aspects of actual situations.[11] In this light, deliberately viewing one's data selectively can be a methodological virtue. Brekhus has characterized the benefit of this approach as "thick analysis" (as opposed to "thick description"): "Thus rather than developing a thick and deep empirical description of a narrow slice of social life, s/he is interested in an analytically deep analysis."[12] It is in this spirit that I provide relatively "thin" descriptions of the details of my respondents' lives, using their words explicitly to reveal the analytic principles being studied—to provide a grounded means of conceptualizing the perceptual construction of sexed bodies *in general*.

My approach is also informed by questions about the limitations of the evidence of experience. In her well-known work challenging the uncritical use of first-hand accounts of experience as a transparent reflection of "reality" in historical scholarship, Joan Scott argues that it is always necessary to attend to the historical processes that *produce* our experiences. In her words, this means "insisting on the discursive nature of 'experience' and on the politics of its construction. Experience is at once always already an interpretation and something that needs to be interpreted."[13] Elizabeth Grosz makes the same point when she states that experience cannot be taken as an unproblematic given, since it is implicated in and produced by various social practices.[14] This critical view of the evidence of experience raises questions about methodological approaches in which there is very little theoretical intervention on the part of the researcher (e.g., thick description or some applications of grounded theory). The advantage of such approaches is a deep, nuanced account of people's beliefs and experiences, but the trade-off is that one risks uncritically reproducing hegemonic discourses. To avoid this, researchers need to do more than create a record of people's experience. We must analytically intervene from a theoretically informed position if we are to look beyond people's experiences to the social forces that *create* them. For this reason, I did not take my respondents' accounts strictly at face value all the time but viewed them as the products of (and therefore a productive site to mine for) broader cultural norms about sex and sex attribution.

In writing we always make choices about which aspects of our data will figure prominently in the final published work, and which will not be included at all—choices that have a direct and significant impact on the knowledge that is ultimately produced. These choices reflect our commitments and interests as researchers, yet, as Wendy Chapkis has described, it is still frowned upon to admit one's biases: "Despite several decades of feminist, antiracist, and poststructuralist insistence on situated knowledge, it can still be risky for a sociologist to admit to speaking from a specific location with a specific viewpoint rather than from a more 'objective' and unmarked space."[15] Nonetheless, biases and prejudgments are not only inevitable, they are a precondition of creating research—and more fundamentally of experience itself.[16] As such, they need not be viewed negatively, as long as one acknowledges the ways in which one's perspective is partial. As Donna Haraway has put it, "Feminist objectivity is about limited location and situated knowledge, not about transcendence and splitting of subject and object. It allows us to become answerable for what we learn how to see."[17] Openly acknowledging the interests and ideas that have shaped my decisions in this book is one of my main motivations in writing this appendix. Not to mention that the central metaphor of the book—the filter—was explicitly conceived to capture the cognitive and perceptual blind spots that make one's perspective always partial and selective.

———

To recruit my participants, I depended mostly on advertisements I posted in online forums and mailed to local and national blind and transgender organizations. The blind organizations included the National Foundation for the Blind, the New Jersey Foundation for the Blind, the Commission for the Blind and Visually Impaired, Lighthouse International, and the Commission for the Blind and Visually Handicapped. The transgender organizations included the Manhattan Lesbian, Gay, Bisexual & Transgender Community Center, Renaissance New Jersey, Monmouth Ocean Transgender, New Jersey TG Support Group, and Long Island Transgendered Expressions (LITE). I also requested referrals from each respondent at the time of his or her interview, and on several occasions I was able to generate a string of two or three contacts in this manner. In one case I interviewed a small concentration of participants affiliated with one particular organization, a cross-dressing club in New York City. They invited me to come to a group meeting where I met about ten members, seven of whom agreed to be interviewed. I returned to the club several times to conduct these interviews, and each time I also spent time observing and speaking casually with whoever was present that day.

My sample of forty-one transgender people included twenty-seven transsexuals (whether preoperative, postoperative, or nonoperative), seven people who prefer the term *transgender*, four self-identified cross-dressers, and three intersexuals. The vast majority of the transgender respondents were male-to-female (MTF); only five were female-to-male (FTM). They were located in twelve different states, but the sample was mostly concentrated in New York and New Jersey, and as a result, twenty-one of the interviews took place in person. Nine of the remaining interviews took place over the phone, and the remaining eleven interviews took place over e-mail or Internet chat. While diverse in age, ranging from approximately 19 to 71 years old, the transgender respondents were mostly white; only two were people of color (one was Asian, one Native American), and race/ethnicity information was not collected for five respondents.

The twenty-seven blind people I interviewed were located in sixteen different states within the United States, plus one person each from Guam and Kosovo. Due to their greater geographic dispersion, almost all of the interviews took the form of tape-recorded phone sessions or exchanges over e-mail or Internet chat. I had initially planned to conduct all of my interviews either in-person, or, when geographic distance precluded meeting face-to-face with a respondent, over the telephone. It therefore surprised me when over half of my blind respondents requested to be interviewed online rather than over the phone, but I learned very quickly that with the help of screen readers and voice recognition software, many blind people are avid computer users.

I did not observe any significant differences in content between the interviews I conducted online and those I conducted in-person or over the telephone. However, it was interesting from the standpoint of a researcher studying visual sex attribution to be unable to attribute the sex of my respondents. When they did not offer this information, I had to ask them outright whether they were male or female. The same thing was true of their age and race. Not surprisingly, given my focus, I never completed an interview without ultimately making a determination about the respondent's sex. However, in a few cases I did forget to ask for someone's age or race, which is why this information is occasionally not provided. (I am missing the age for two blind respondents and two transgender respondents, and the race for three blind respondents and five transgender respondents.)

The sample of blind people ranges in age from approximately 19 to 61, with about half over 30 and half under 30. Just over half of the

Table 11 Sample characteristics

Blind respondents		Transgender respondents	
Number of respondents	27	Number of respondents	41
Age range	19–61[a]	Age range	19–71[b]
Race	89 percent white[c]	Race	94 percent white[d]
Geographic location[e]	16 US states represented	Geographic location	12 US states represented
Sex	13 men	Sex/gender self-identification	27 transsexual
	14 women		7 transgender
			4 cross-dresser
			3 intersexual
			36 male to female
			5 female to male
Age of onset of blindness	Birth/infancy = 14		
	1–10 = 3		
	11–16 = 5		
	Over 16 = 5		

[a] Excludes missing data, N = 2.
[b] Excludes missing data, N = 2.
[c] Excludes missing data, N = 3.
[d] Excludes missing data, N = 5.
[e] Among the blind respondents, two locations outside of the United States were represented.

participants were born blind or lost their vision within their first year of life. An additional three respondents lost their vision between ages 1 and 10. Five went blind between age 10 and age 16. Though the sample was very evenly divided in terms of sex, with thirteen males and fourteen females, only three participants were people of color. (See table 11 for a summary of the sample characteristics.)

The research took the form of semistructured life-history interviews, which ranged in length from thirty minutes to approximately three hours. While I had a number of different questions in mind based on my interest in the sociocognitive and perceptual processes behind sex attribution, I also encouraged the respondents to direct the discussion in order to learn what was most salient to them about bodily sex and sex attribution. As a result, many of the interviews covered a huge variety of topics, and in my analysis I have bracketed and set aside all information that does not relate to bodies and sex attribution.

Some of the questions I arrived at the interviews planning to ask the blind respondents were the following:

What is the first thing you notice about people?
How do you tell if someone is male or female?
Have you ever assigned someone to the wrong sex category?

> Do you think that you would be able to feel (identify by touch) the difference be-
> tween a male arm and a female arm?

I often used the last question several times, substituting different body parts for *arm*. Among the questions I planned to ask the transgender respondents were the following:

> What was the first thing you changed about your appearance?
> Is there any part of your body that has not changed at all?
> What do you think is the single most powerful thing you/one can change in order
> to read successfully as the other sex?
> Thinking about your "old" body and your "new" body, what body parts did you
> have to de-emphasize? What did you have to emphasize?

Once the respondents told me how they identified (e.g., transsexual, cross-dresser, etc.), I adjusted these questions to be appropriate to their experience. For example, I would probably not ask a cross-dresser about his or her "old" and "new" body, because he or she may not have made any physical changes (although many MTF cross-dressers do wax their eyebrows and sometimes their legs, and some even get electrolysis to eliminate their facial hair). I tried to listen carefully to my respondents' self-descriptions and adjust my questions accordingly.

I used the qualitative data analysis software package Atlas.ti to thematically code and organize the interviews. The codes were generated both inductively and deductively. I had certain terms in mind at the outset, but I also noted themes that emerged as I was transcribing and reading the transcriptions. For instance, I knew based on my prior conceptual work that I was going to look for the following topics in the transgender narratives: selective attention, polarization, relevance, irrelevance, sameness, expectations, and evidence of expert knowledge. Additional themes that emerged inductively in the data included: pretransition androgyny, transdar, the notion that it is easy to pass, and genital similarities. Some of the themes that emerged as I was analyzing the interviews with blind people were a default position of obviousness, the idea of sex without polarization, and the temporality of sex attribution.

In addition to the interview questions, I asked most of the transgender respondents I met in person and a few of those I interviewed electronically to fill out a survey designed to rank the significance of different body parts (see fig. 23). I did not use the survey in phone interviews, although I usually covered the same topics verbally. In a

Indicate whether you have altered each body part and how important you feel it is for passing on a scale of 1-10. Please add any other body parts you feel I should have included in the extra space provided.

Body Part	Have you altered?	Importance for passing, 1-10 (10=high, 1=low)
Hair		
Lips		
Forehead		
Chest		
Elbows		
Buttocks		
Knees		
Ankles		
Eyebrows		
Chin		
Neck		
Abdomen		
Lower arms		
Genitals		
Calves		
Feet		
Ears		
Cheeks		
Shoulders		
Upper arms		
Hands		
Thighs		
Shins		

FIGURE 23 Survey instrument, transgender respondents.

small number of cases, I chose not to use the survey in a face-to-face interview that took place in a public setting when I sensed that the respondent was anxious about attracting attention. In the end, nineteen of my transgender respondents participated in the survey portion of the interview. I used the resulting data to compute some very simple quantitative measures, such as mean and median scores.

Like all studies, this one has limitations. One important question is whether I am capturing what my respondents say and believe about sex attribution or what they actually do—the cognitive and perceptual process. This is an unavoidable challenge of trying to analyze cognitive processes, since we largely have to infer what happens in the mind from what passes through to consciousness. There is a difference between accounts of a process and the process itself; the accounts are interesting and important, but they are not necessarily interchangeable. What people believe is involved in a process is often a reflection of cultural stories about what is relevant and how these distinctions *should* be made. Therefore, it may be that what I have presented are these cultural stories about sex and sex attribution. This is valuable information in and of itself, but it remains a question whether it tells us what people actually do. This disjuncture may also have been inadvertently increased by the way I structured some of the interview questions, particularly those questions that had to do with whether specific parts of the body are sex dimorphic or not. This isolated consideration of individual body parts may not be reflective of how most of the respondents actually determine people's sex in practice. Nonetheless, it generated a lot of interesting material on the nondichotomous body that may not otherwise have come out.

In the interest of analytic clarity, I discuss sex attribution mostly in isolation, but in reality there are always a number of different social filters in play simultaneously. Sexuality and norms of sexual attraction are particularly entangled in sex attribution because of the role of both sex difference and perception in attraction. This interrelatedness is further evidenced by the multiple meanings of the term *sex*, which can refer to a drive, an act, or an identity, in addition to a category of bodies. I explicitly told my respondents that I was studying how they distinguish male and female bodies, as opposed to what they find attractive. It was clear during the interviews that this separation was not always easy for the respondents to maintain, however, and comments about sexuality came up from time to time. But given that I explicitly directed the respondents away from these topics, I do not discuss sexuality and attraction in any real detail.

Another question is whether I am addressing the body proper, or just our perceptions of that fleshy materiality. This is a valid distinction to make for the purposes of analytic clarity, but I think it is fair to say that there is no other way we access bodies except through some form of sensory perception. As the gestalt psychologist Wolfgang Köhler put it, we can never make a direct statement about a physical event *as such*.[18] Our only contact with bodies is through what he calls direct experience (i.e., perception).[19] This is also David Armstrong's point, drawing on Michel Foucault, in the quotation that serves as one of the epigraphs of this book: "The body is what it is perceived to be; it could be otherwise if perception were different."[20] In light of this, an analysis of how the body is perceived through the senses may be the only analysis of the body's materiality that is possible.

It is also important to mention several potentially limiting features of my samples. The biggest concern about my sample of transgender respondents is that it is so heavily skewed toward MTF transgender people. When I became aware of it, I began to ask this question as part of the interview, asking my respondents for their opinions on why so few FTMs had contacted me. A number of people suggested to me that it is generally easier for FTMs to fully transition—"go stealth," as some of them put it—and that once they are living successfully as their sex of transition for a time they may not be interested in (or feel safe) discussing their experience as transgender.[21]

While I cannot be sure that this is the reason so few FTM transgender people volunteered for my study, it raises another factor that may bias my (and every other) sample of transgender people: the transgender identity is often not a permanent one. When their transition is complete, many transpeople would prefer that no one know that they ever identified as transgender. The result is that my sample does not include the experiences of those who have abandoned this identity label. By necessity, it only includes the voices of those who, in varying degrees, are currently "out" as transpeople.

One other potentially distorting factor is that a number of my transgender respondents view themselves as "leaders" or "experts" on trans identity. The respondents I have in mind are activists who run support groups, interface with politicians, or just routinely make themselves available to reporters, teachers, and researchers interested in learning about transgender identity. Having "experts" as informants has both advantages and disadvantages. One major disadvantage is that they typically have developed a series of "talking points" and pre-scripted answers. Since they have a tendency to revert to a script, these respondents sometimes seemed less willing to respond authentically to questions or to answer the exact questions posed. At the same time, people who are leaders in the transgender community often make excellent informants for some of the same reasons: they have thought a lot about transgender identity, are practiced at articulating their views, and have a level of comfort with themselves that can allow them to be wonderfully self-reflective and candid.

Even beyond this group of "expert" respondents, however, the vast majority of the transgender people I spoke with seemed very comfortable being interviewed, and some even made comments about the potential value of social research. This may reflect the fact that I was interviewing a self-selected group of transgender people who had agreed to speak with a researcher. On the whole, though, the respondents seemed to view the interview as a positive experience, and even as an opportunity to dispel some of the misinformation they perceive as circulating about transpeople in the media and the popular imagination. In this vein, there were three points my respondents made over and over, which they obviously felt were important for the general public to understand about being transgender. The first is a saying that a great many of the respondents used: "Gender is between the ears, not between the legs." I think their point is simply to explain how it is possible to be biologically male, for instance, but to be mentally and emotionally female. But this saying also relates to a second "message" the respondents seemed to want to be sure was communicated, which is that being transgender and attraction/sexuality are independent of one another. More specifically, being transgender is not the same as being gay, nor does changing one's gender necessarily change the direction of one's attraction (although it can). As one respondent explained it to me, the transgender population has basically the same distribution of heterosexuals, homosexuals, and bisexuals as the nontransgender population. The final point the respondents often emphasized in this context is that being transgender is not a choice. When considered in relation to the idea that "gender is between the ears," what this implies is that what is in the mind (gender) is not freely chosen, and in fact is more difficult to change than the body's sex. To put it another way, contrary to the meanings assigned by the sex/gender distinction, it may be that sex is actually *more* malleable than gender. This idea also interconnects in an interesting way with my argument that the a priori mental category of gender plays an enormous role in shaping our experience of the body's sex and reality more broadly. An additional implication of this family of ideas is that, contrary to the conventions of scientific and social scientific research, sex may be better understood as a *dependent* variable, and gender as an independent variable.

Overall, the blind respondents seemed far more skeptical of the value of social research than the transgender respondents, particularly studies that emphasize the ways blind people are different, and some of them had clearly agreed to talk with me despite great reservations. Questions about whether research on blindness limits assimilation grow out of larger debates about assimilation and difference in disability rights discourse. James highlighted this connection, framing his comments broadly in relation to people with disabilities:

I don't think it rude or offensive inherently to ask what it's like to be blind, retarded, polio survivor, quadriplegic, and on and on. However, after forty years of

163

the "educate the masses and they'll like us more and life will be better," either we ain't doin' very successful educating, or the masses ain't learning so good. Sooo . . . it is not very productive for folks to try to share their experience and often this just reinforces the able-bodied negative attitudes. In closing, there are a great many nuances in each person's life that affect their attitude, capabilities, limitations, beliefs, aspirations, experiences, and self-image, beyond the precise disability. (James, 54, legally blind since birth, totally blind since age 3)

When it seemed necessary and appropriate, I responded to these kinds of comments by assuring my respondents that I am at least as interested in the ways that they are similar to sighted people as I am in their differences. In fact, as I have stated throughout, I chose to interview blind people, not to understand their blindness, but to understand their sex perceptions and to explore the insight they provide for analytical statements about perceptions of sex more generally. In its very design, then, this study implicitly challenges the blindness to sameness between the blind and the sighted criticized by these respondents. This seemed to allay some of their anxieties, and my impression is that they usually felt more positive about the study by the end of the interview.

Aside from it being a self-selected group willing to speak with a researcher, the biggest potential limitation of my sample of blind people is that it includes only five people who became blind over the age of 16 (and only ten people who became blind over the age of 10). Over half of my sample was born blind or became blind during the first year of life. While I initially anticipated that I would find interesting differences between those respondents who never had vision or lost their vision at a very early age (and thus were never exposed to visual sex differences) and those who were sighted into late childhood or adulthood, I did not observe significant systematic differences in their descriptions of how they attribute sex. Even so, this question merits further investigation with a larger sample of people who became blind later in life.

Finally, given that both groups of respondents are predominantly white, it is possible that I inadvertently standardized my observations on white bodies. The cultural dynamics of gender and race are inextricable; in Jane Flax's words, "in contemporary America we never encounter an ungendered but raced person or a gendered but unraced one."[22] Further, the particular cues we use to determine sex can be racially variable and racially marked. For instance, one of the FTM transgender respondents, who is Asian, told me that he has observed that Asian males have an easier time transitioning from male to female because they tend to be shorter and have very little facial and body hair.

This interaction of sex and race cues is something that I was not able to fully explore, and it deserves much more explicit consideration.

However, I did ask the blind respondents to describe how they recognize another person's race in addition to how they recognize sex. Their near-unanimous response was that they almost never think about race, and many respondents shared stories about being surprised to learn—sometimes after several years of knowing someone—that he or she is not white. It is notable that these respondents seem to imagine race based on an unmarked white norm; that is, they assume people are white until something contests that view. Whether their strongly professed "color blindness" would hold up in a larger, more racially diverse sample of respondents requires further research. It certainly seems unlikely that a blind person of Afro-Caribbean descent, for example, would assume whiteness in the same way. Regardless, a study of blind people's phenomenal experiences of race could provide an interesting prism through which to examine the relationship between sex and race attribution as well as an instructive challenge to hegemonic sighted assumptions about the self-evidence of racial differences.

Taken as a whole, while the samples are definitely not representative of all transgender and blind people, I do not believe that my respondents are particularly unique. In any case, these potential limitations of my samples do not pose a significant analytical problem for me, since my primary goal is to explore a broader cognitive and perceptual process rather than to characterize blind or transgender people *as a group*, a task for which any concerns about the representativeness of my samples are highly relevant. Further, the analysis is meant to be provocative, rather than complete or representative in the strict methodological sense of the term. My explicit goal is to problematize the seeming perceptual "obviousness" of sex; to rearrange the taken-for-granted cognitive and perceptual map of the body, and to bring the nondichotomous body that is normally backgrounded into the foreground. I do not claim that this reorganized map of the body is necessarily a more valid representation of sex than perceptions that foreground sex differences, just that it is equally valid but much less often acknowledged. The point is not to establish that male and female bodies are similar or that they are different, but that we could see them either way, depending on what we focus on and what we ignore.

Notes

INTRODUCTION

1. Carol Barkalow, with Andrea Raab, *In the Men's House* (New York: Poseidon, 1990), p. 53. In the past, similar policies in the US Marine Corps required women to wear makeup and to take classes in hair care, makeup, poise, and etiquette, all as part of a deliberate policy of making them clearly distinguishable from male marines. See Judith Lorber, *Paradoxes of Gender* (New Haven: Yale University Press, 1994), p. 26.

2. Anne Fausto-Sterling, "The Five Sexes: Why Male and Female Are Not Enough," *The Sciences* (March/April 1993): 20–24.

3. See Sherry Ortner, "Is Male to Female as Nature Is to Culture?," in *Woman, Culture and Society*, ed. Michelle Rosaldo and Louise Lamphere (Stanford, CA: Stanford University Press, 1974), pp. 67–88.

4. Raymond Birdwhistell, *Kinesics and Context: Essays on Body Motion Communication* (Philadelphia: University of Pennsylvania Press, 1970), pp. 39–46. See also Cynthia Epstein, *Deceptive Distinctions: Sex, Gender, and the Social Order* (New Haven: Yale University Press, 1988).

5. Sarah Richardson, "Sexes, Species, and Genomes: Why Males and Females Are Not Like Humans and Chimpanzees," *Biology and Philosophy* 25, no. 5 (2010): 826.

6. Erving Goffman, *The Presentation of Self in Everyday Life* (New York: Anchor Books, 1959), pp. 3, 9, 79.

7. Phillip Vannini, Dennis Waskul, and Simon Gottschalk, *The Senses in Self, Society, and Culture: A Sociology of the Senses* (New York: Routledge, 2011), p. 15.

8. "Perceptual work" is similar to Waskul and Vannini's concept of "somatic work," which highlights the ways that to sense is

always to "make sense" of something. See Dennis Waskul and Phillip Vannini, "Smell, Odor, and Somatic Work: Sense-Making and Sensory Management," *Social Psychology Quarterly* 71, no. 1 (2008): 53, 63. See also Vannini, Waskul, and Gottschalk, *The Senses in Self, Society, and Culture*, p. 15.

9. See Arlie Hochschild, *The Managed Heart: The Commercialization of Human Feeling* (Berkeley: University of California Press, 1983), p. 198; David Snow and Leon Anderson, "Identity Work among the Homeless: The Verbal Construction and Avowal of Personal Identities," *American Journal of Sociology* 92 (1987): 1337–71; Arthur Frank, "Illness as Autobiographical Work: Dialogue as Narrative Destabilization." *Qualitative Sociology* 23 (2000): 135–56; Debra Gimlin, *Body Work: Beauty and Self-Image in American Culture* (Berkeley: University of California Press, 2002); Thomas DeGloma, "Awakenings: Autobiography, Memory, and the Social Logic of Personal Discovery," *Sociological Forum* 25, no. 3 (2010): 519–40.

10. Howard Becker, "Becoming a Marihuana User," *American Journal of Sociology* 59, no. 3 (1953): 242.

11. Charles Mills, "White Ignorance," in *Agnotology: The Making and Unmaking of Ignorance*, ed. Robert Proctor and Londa Schiebinger (Stanford, CA: Stanford University Press, 2008), p. 236. See also Martin Jay, *Downcast Eyes: The Denigration of Vision in Twentieth Century French Thought* (Berkeley: University of California Press, 1993).

12. Ann Beaulieu, "Brains, Maps and the New Territory of Psychology," *Theory and Psychology* 13 (2003): 565.

13. In some cases, the focus is on how innate brain capacities, such as pattern matching or mental rotation, may lead to and support certain cultural conventions of thought and perception. See, for example, David Gooding, "Cognition, Construction and Culture: Visual Theories in the Sciences," *Journal of Culture and Cognition* 4 (2004): 559.

14. Beaulieu, "Brains, Maps and the New Territory of Psychology"; Joseph Dumit, *Picturing Personhood: Brain Scans and Biomedical Identity* (Princeton, NJ: Princeton University Press, 2004); Kelly Joyce, "Appealing Images: Magnetic Resonance Imaging and the Production of Authoritative Knowledge," *Social Studies of Science* 35 (2005): 437–62; Joyce, "From Numbers to Pictures: The Development of Magnetic Resonance Imaging and the Visual Turn in Medicine," *Science as Culture* 15 (2006): 1–22; Morana Alac, "Working with Brain Scans: Digital Images and Gestural Interaction in fMRI laboratory," *Social Studies of Science* 38, no. 4 (2008): 483–508; Regula Valérie Burri, "Doing Distinctions: Boundary Work and Symbolic Capital in Radiology," *Social Studies of Science* 38, no. 1 (2008): 35–62.

15. Vannini, Waskul, and Gottschalk, *The Senses in Self, Society, and Culture*, p. 127.

16. Michael Smithson, *Ignorance and Uncertainty: Emerging Paradigms* (New York: Springer-Verlag, 1989); Smithson, "Ignorance and Science: Dilemmas, Perspectives, and Process," *Science Communication* 15, no. 2 (1993):

133–56; Susan Leigh Star, "The Sociology of the Invisible: The Primacy of Work in the Writings of Anselm Strauss," in *Social Organization and Social Process: Essays in Honor of Anselm Strauss*, ed. David Maines (Piscataway, NJ: Aldine Transaction, 1991), pp. 265–382; Susan Leigh Star and Anselm Strauss, "Layers of Silence, Arenas of Voice," *Computer Supported Cooperative Work* 8 (1999): 9–30; S. Holly Stocking and Lisa W. Holstein, "Constructing and Reconstructing Scientific Ignorance," *Knowledge: Creation, Diffusion, Utilization* 15 (1993): 186–210; Eviatar Zerubavel, *The Elephant in the Room: Silence and Denial in Everyday Life* (New York: Oxford University Press, 2006); Robert N. Proctor and Londa Schiebinger, eds., *Agnotology: The Making and Unmaking of Ignorance* (Stanford, CA: Stanford University Press, 2008); Monica Casper and Lisa Jean Moore, *Missing Bodies: The Politics of Visibility* (New York: New York University Press, 2009).

17. See, for example, Donald D. Hoffman and Manish Singh, "Salience of Visual Parts," *Cognition* 63 (1997): 29–78.

18. Casper and Moore, *Missing Bodies*, p. 4.

19. See, for instance, Judith Butler, *Gender Trouble: Feminism and the Subversion of Identity* (New York: Routledge, 1990); and Butler, *Bodies That Matter: On the Discursive Limits of "Sex"* (New York: Routledge, 1993).

20. Candace West and Don Zimmerman, "Doing Gender," *Gender & Society* 1, no. 2 (1987): 125–51.

21. On *transgender* as an umbrella term, see Susan Stryker, "(De)Subjugated Knowledges: An Introduction to Transgender Studies" in *The Transgender Studies Reader*, ed. Susan Stryker and Stephen Whittle (New York: Routledge, 2006), pp. 2, 4.

22. The definitions I provide here are based on a list of terms provided to me by one of my transgender respondents, which basically reflected the descriptions provided by my other respondents. On transmen going "stealth," see Kristen Schilt, *Just One of the Guys: Transgender Men and the Persistence of Gender Inequality* (Chicago: University of Chicago Press, 2010), p. 10. On defining the term *transgender*, see Stryker, "(De)Subjugated Knowledges," pp. 2–4.

23. Harold Garfinkel, *Studies in Ethnomethodology* (Englewood Cliffs, NJ: Prentice Hall, [1964] 1967), p. 38.

24. See Schilt, *Just One of the Guys*, p. 8.

25. Stryker, "(De)Subjugated Knowledges," pp. 3–4.

26. Lennard Davis, *Enforcing Normalcy: Disability, Deafness, and the Body* (London: Verso, 1995), p. 4.

27. Stephen Kuusisto, *Planet of the Blind* (New York: Dell Publishing, Bantam Doubleday Dell Publishing Group, 1998), p. 148; Rod Michalko, *The Mystery of the Eye and the Shadow of Blindness* (Toronto: University of Toronto Press, 1998), pp. 156–57.

28. See, for example, Butler, *Gender Trouble*; Anne Fausto-Sterling, *Sexing the Body: Gender Politics and the Construction of Sexuality* (New York: Basic

Books, 2000); Joan Fujimura, "Sex Genes: A Critical Sociomaterial Approach to the Politics and Molecular Genetics of Sex Determination," *Signs* 32, no. 1 (2006): 49–82; Suzanne Kessler, *Lessons from the Intersexed* (New Brunswick, NJ: Rutgers University Press, 1998); Suzanne Kessler and Wendy McKenna, *Gender: An Ethnomethodological Approach* (Hoboken, NJ: John Wiley & Sons, 1978); Thomas Laqueur, *Making Sex: Body and Gender from the Greeks to Freud* (Cambridge, MA: Harvard University Press, 1990); Emily Martin, "The Egg and the Sperm: How Science Has Constructed a Romance Based on Stereotypical Male-Female Roles," *Signs* 16, no. 3 (1991): 485–501; Lisa Jean Moore, *Sperm Counts: Overcome by Man's Most Precious Fluid* (New York: New York University Press, 2007).

29. For example, Alice Dreger, *Hermaphrodites and the Medical Invention of Sex* (Cambridge, MA: Harvard University Press, 1998); Fausto-Sterling, *Sexing the Body*; Kessler, *Lessons from the Intersexed*; Sharon Preves, *Intersex and Identity: The Contested Self* (New Brunswick, NJ: Rutgers University Press, 2003).

30. For example, see Laqueur, *Making Sex*.

31. See Fausto-Sterling, *Sexing the Body*; Fujimura, "Sex Genes"; Martin, "The Egg and the Sperm"; Moore, *Sperm Counts*; Nelly Oudshoorn, *Beyond the Natural Body: An Archaeology of Sex Hormones* (London: Routledge, 1994).

32. Mary Hawkesworth, "Confounding Gender," *Signs* 22, no. 3 (1997): 31.

33. See Erving Goffman, *Frame Analysis: An Essay on the Organization of Experience* (Boston: Northeastern University Press, [1974] 1986), pp. 201–46; Eviatar Zerubavel, *Social Mindscapes: An Invitation to Cognitive Sociology* (Cambridge, MA: Harvard University Press, 1997), p. 37; Karen Cerulo, *Culture in Mind: Toward a Sociology of Culture and Cognition* (New York: Routledge, 2002), pp. 17–18; Wayne Brekhus, "The Rutgers School: A Zerubavelian Culturalist Cognitive Sociology," *European Journal of Social Theory* 10, no. 3 (2007): 458.

34. Casper and Moore, *Missing Bodies*, p. 5.

35. Émile Durkheim, *The Rules of Sociological Method* (New York: The Free Press, [1895] 1982), p. 2.

36. Zerubavel, *Elephant in the Room*, p. 16.

37. See Edgar Rubin, *Visuell wahrgenommene Figuren* (Copenhagen: Gyldendal, [1915] 1921).

38. Zerubavel, *Elephant in the Room*, p. 65.

CHAPTER ONE

1. Bronislaw Malinowski, *The Sexual Life of Savages in North Western Melanesia* (New York: Halcyon House, 1929).

2. See James Bagby, "A Cross-Cultural Study of Perceptual Predominance in Binocular Rivalry," *Journal of Abnormal and Social Psychology* 54 (1957): 331–34.

3. See Margaret Steffensen, Chitra Joag-Dev, and Richard C. Anderson, "A Cross-Cultural Perspective on Reading Comprehension," *Reading Research Quarterly* 15, no. 1 (1979): 10–29; Richard Nisbett and Takahiko Masuda, "Culture and Point of View," *Proceedings of the National Academy of Sciences of the United States of America* 100, no. 19 (2003): 11163.

4. Zerubavel, *Social Mindscapes*, p. 33.

5. Ludwik Fleck, *Genesis and Development of a Scientific Fact* (Chicago: University of Chicago Press, [1935] 1981).

6. Thomas Kuhn, *The Structure of Scientific Revolutions* (Chicago: University of Chicago Press, [1962] 1996), p. 117. Eviatar Zerubavel observes similar historical transformations in perception in his analysis of the shifting cartographic representations of the "new world" in the several hundred years after Columbus's initial encounter. See Zerubavel, *Terra Cognita: The Mental Discovery of America* (New Brunswick, NJ: Transaction Publishers, 1992 [2003]). On historical differences in sensory perception, see also Yi-Fu Tuan, *Segmented Worlds and Self* (Minneapolis: University of Minnesota Press, 1982), pp. 120–32; Donald Lowe, *History of Bourgeois Perception* (Chicago: University of Chicago Press, 1982), p. 85; Laqueur, *Making Sex*; Ruth Simpson, "The Germ Culture: Metaphor, Modernity, and Epidemic Disease," (PhD dissertation, Department of Sociology, Rutgers University, 2006).

7. Peter Powers, Joyce Andriks, and Elizabeth Loftus, "The Eyewitness Accounts of Males and Females," *Journal of Applied Psychology* 64 (1979): 339–47.

8. Christian Meissner and John Brigham, "Thirty Years of Investigating the Own-Race Bias in Memory for Faces: A Meta-Analytic Review," *Psychology, Public Policy, & Law* 7 (2001): 3–35.

9. Charles Goodwin, "Professional Vision," *American Anthropologist* 96, no. 3 (1994): 606–33.

10. Fleck, *Genesis and Development of a Scientific Fact*, p. 92.

11. Norwood Russell Hanson, *Patterns of Discovery: An Inquiry into the Conceptual Foundations of Science* (Cambridge: Cambridge University Press, 1965), p. 17.

12. Jerome Groopman, *How Doctors Think* (Boston: Houghton Mifflin, 2007), p. 200. Groopman also points out that, although at the beginning of their training there are differences among doctors in their visual-spatial abilities, through optical socialization they can all achieve the professional expertise required: "This ability can be enhanced to the expert level by repeated practice and regular feedback about success and error in technique" (p. 142). On professional optical socialization in radiology, see also Joyce, "From Numbers to Pictures," p. 15.

13. C. Wright Mills, *People, Power, and Politics: The Collected Essays of C. Wright Mills* (New York: Ballantine Books, 1963), p. 460.

14. Gary Alan Fine, *Morel Tales: The Culture of Mushrooming* (Cambridge, MA: Harvard University Press, 1998), pp. 102, 113.

15. Pierre Bourdieu, *Distinction: A Social Critique of the Judgment of Taste* (Cambridge, MA: Harvard University Press, 1984), p. 44.

16. On the sociocultural dimension of perception, see Zerubavel, *Social Mindscapes*, pp. 23–34.

17. See Susan Fiske and Shelley Taylor, *Social Cognition*, 2nd ed. (New York: McGraw Hill, 1991), p. 99; Ron Burnett, *How Images Think* (Cambridge, MA: MIT Press, 2004), pp. 32–34; Michalko, *Mystery of the Eye*, p. 142; Georgina Kleege, *Sight Unseen* (New Haven, CT: Yale University Press, 1999), p. 96; Maurice Merleau-Ponty, *Phenomenology of Perception* (London: Routledge & Kegan Paul, [1945] 1962), p. 7. See also Jay, *Downcast Eyes*, p. 62.

18. While we often use the term *mirror image* to convey that two things are totally identical, it is important to remember that reflections in a mirror are actually distorted copies, since they are reversed. Thanks to Eviatar Zerubavel for reminding me of this fact. Even the metaphor for totally un-distorted perception involves some distortion, reinforcing my fundamental position that there is no such thing as "perfect" or "pure" perception.

19. Kleege, *Sight Unseen*, p. 22; See also George Lakoff and Mark Johnson, *Metaphors We Live By* (Chicago: University of Chicago Press, 1980), p. 48; Jay, *Downcast Eyes*, pp. 2, 587.

20. Peter Berger and Thomas Luckmann, *The Social Construction of Reality: A Treatise in the Sociology of Knowledge* (Garden City, NJ: Doubleday Anchor, [1966] 1967), p. 140.

21. Berger and Luckmann, *Social Construction of Reality*, p. 23.

22. Zerubavel, *Social Mindscapes*, p. 23.

23. Notable previous attempts to explicitly develop a sociology of perception include an article by Arthur Child ("The Sociology of Perception" [1950]), Mary Douglas's edited volume, *Essays in the Sociology of Perception* (1982), and "Social Optics" and "The Social Gates of Consciousness," the second and third chapters of Zerubavel's *Social Mindscapes* (1997). Most recently, see Vannini, Waskul, and Gottschalk, *The Senses in Self, Society, and Culture.*

24. Georg Simmel, "Sociology of the Senses: Visual Interaction," in *Introduction to the Science of Sociology*, ed. Robert Park and Ernest Burgess (New York: Greenwood Press, [1908] 1924), p. 358.

25. See Erving Goffman, *Behavior in Public Places* (New York: Free Press, 1963).

26. Garfinkel, *Studies in Ethnomethodology*, pp. 35–75.

27. Arthur Child, "The Sociology of Perception," *Journal of Genetic Psychology* 77 (1950): 293–303.

28. Lowe, *History of Bourgeois Perception.*

29. Vannini, Waskul, and Gottschalk, *The Senses in Self, Society, and Culture*, p. 15.

30. See Émile Durkheim, *The Elementary Forms of Religious Life* (New York: Free Press, [1912] 1995); Durkheim, *Suicide* (New York: Free Press, [1897] 1966).

31. Karl Marx, *The Marx-Engels Reader*, 2nd ed., ed. R. C. Tucker (New York: W. W. Norton, 1978).

32. Charles Horton Cooley, *Social Organization: A Larger Study of the Mind* (New York: Schocken, [1909] 1962).

33. See, for instance, Jay, *Downcast Eyes*; Lowe, *History of Bourgeois Perception*; and Yi-Fu Tuan, "Sight and Pictures," *Geographical Review* 69, no. 4 (1979): 413–422.

34. Vannini, Waskul, and Gottschalk, *The Senses in Self, Society, and Culture*, pp. 61–80.

35. For one account of these debates in the context of visual perception, see Zenon Pylyshyn, *Seeing and Visualizing: It's Not What You Think* (Cambridge, MA: MIT Press, 2003), pp. 50–53, 62–67, 72–73. See also Pierre Jacob and Marc Jeannerod, *Ways of Seeing: The Scope and Limits of Visual Cognition* (Oxford: Oxford University Press, 2003), p. 140; Jay, *Downcast Eyes*, p. 9; Eviatar Zerubavel, *The Fine Line: Making Distinctions in Everyday Life* (New York: Free Press, 1991), p. 6; Zerubavel, *Social Mindscapes*, pp. 23–24.

36. Harry Lawless, "Olfactory Psychophysics," in *Tasting and Smelling*, ed. Gary Beauchamp and Linda Bartoshuk (San Diego, CA: Academic Press, 1997), p. 168.

37. On the importance of maintaining a distinction between sensory stimuli and what we consciously perceive, see Wolfgang Köhler, *Gestalt Psychology* (New York: Liveright Publishing Group,1929), pp. 71–85; Kuhn, *Structure of Scientific Revolutions*, pp. 192–93; Mohan Matthen, *Seeing, Doing, and Knowing: A Philosophical Theory of Sense Perception* (Oxford: Clarendon Press, 2005), p. 2.

38. Kuhn, *Structure of Scientific Revolutions*.

39. Karl Mannheim, *Ideology and Utopia: An Introduction to the Sociology of Knowledge* (New York: Harvest, 1936), p. 266; Tamotsu Shibutani, "Reference Groups as Perspectives," *American Journal of Sociology* 60 (1955): p. 564.

40. Fleck, *Genesis and Development of a Scientific Fact*, p. 39; Mannheim, *Ideology and Utopia*, p. 3.

41. Mannheim, *Ideology and Utopia*, p. 275.

42. Frederic Bartlett, *Remembering: A Study in Experimental and Social Psychology* (Cambridge: Cambridge University Press, 1932); Kessler and McKenna, *Gender*, p. 158.

43. Mary Chayko, *Connecting: How We Form Social Bonds and Communities in the Internet Age* (Albany: State University of New York Press, 2002), pp. 35–36.

44. Bourdieu, *Distinction*, p. 101.

45. Gregory Bateson, "A Theory of Play and Fantasy," in *Steps to an Ecology of Mind* (New York: Ballantine Press, [1955] 1972); Goffman, *Frame Analysis*.

46. Murray Davis, *Smut: Erotic Reality/Obscene Ideology* (Chicago: University of Chicago Press, 1983), p. 285n17; Alfred Schutz and Thomas Luckmann, *The Structures of the Life World* (Evanston, IL: Northwestern University Press, 1973), p. 250; Zerubavel, *Social Mindscapes*, p. 24.

47. Deborah Tannen, *Framing in Discourse* (New York: Oxford University Press, 1993), pp. 14–16.

48. Edward E. Jones, *Interpersonal Perception* (New York: W. H. Freeman, 1990), pp. 82, 84; Shelley Taylor, Letitia Peplau, and David Sears, *Social Psychology*, 10th ed. (Englewood Cliffs, NJ: Prentice Hall, 2000), pp. 56–57.

49. Jerome S. Bruner and Leo Postman, "On the Perception of Incongruity: A Paradigm," *Journal of Personality* 18 (1949): 206–23. See also Kuhn, *Structure of Scientific Revolutions*, pp. 112–13.

50. Merleau-Ponty, *Phenomenology of Perception*, p. 28. See also Burnett, *How Images Think*, pp. 32–34.

51. Kuhn, *Structure of Scientific Revolutions*, p. 116. See also Zerubavel, *Social Mindscapes*, pp. 45–46.

52. Simpson, "Germ Culture," p. 86.

53. This focus follows Garfinkel's concept of *background expectancies*, or "expectancies that lend commonplace scenes their familiar, life-as-usual character," which emerge from and reproduce "the stable social structures of everyday activities" (*Studies in Ethnomethodology*, p. 37). Zerubavel likewise highlights expectations as powerful clues that reveal the social order (see, for instance, *Fine Line*, p. 23).

54. Jerome Bruner, "Social Psychology and Perception," in *Readings in Social Psychology*, ed. Eleanor E. Macoby, Theodore M. Newcomb, and Eugene L. Hartley (New York: Henry Holt, 1958), p. 85.

55. Taylor, Peplau, and Sears, *Social Psychology*, p. 53.

56. See Goffman, *Frame Analysis*, pp. 201–46; Zerubavel, *Social Mindscapes*, p. 37; Brekhus, "Rutgers School," p. 458. On *rules of irrelevance*, see also Goffman, "Fun in Games," in *Encounters: Two Studies in the Sociology of Interaction* (Indianapolis, IN: Bobbs-Merrill, 1961). On *civil inattention*, see Goffman, *Behavior in Public Places*.

57. See, for example, A. H. C. van der Heijden, *Attention in Vision: Perception, Communication and Action* (New York: Taylor and Francis, 2004).

58. Zerubavel, *Elephant in the Room*, p. 23.

59. Benjamin Lee Whorf, "Science and Linguistics," in *Language, Thought, and Reality*, ed. John Carroll (Cambridge, MA: MIT Press, [1940] 1956), pp. 213–14.

60. Schutz and Luckmann, *Structures of the Life World*, p. 250, emphasis added.

61. John Carroll and Joseph Casagrande, "The Function of Language Classifications in Behavior," in *Readings in Social Psychology*, ed. Eleanor Macoby, Theodore Newcomb, and Eugene Hartley (New York: Henry Holt, 1958). See also John Lucy, *Grammatical Categories and Cognition: A Case Study of the Linguistic Relativity Hypothesis* (Cambridge: Cambridge University Press, 1992), which compares English speakers to Yucatec speakers, and in which he similarly finds that differences in number-marking patterns correlate with memory and classification preferences.

62. Ruth Hubbard, Barbara Fried, and Mary Henifin, *Biological Woman: The Convenient Myth* (Rochester, NY: Schenkman Books, 1982), pp. 11–12.

63. On face work, see Erving Goffman, "On Face-work: An Analysis of Ritual Elements of Social Interaction," *Psychiatry* 18, no. 3 (1955): 213–31; and Goffman, *Interaction Ritual: Essays on Face-to-Face Behavior* (New York: Pantheon Books, 1967). On framing, see Goffman, *Frame Analysis*.

64. Fiske and Taylor, *Social Cognition*, p. 15.

65. David Morgan and Michael Schwalbe, "Mind and Self in Society: Linking Social Structure and Social Cognition," *Social Psychology Quarterly* 53, no. 2 (1990): 156.

66. Cerulo, *Culture in Mind*, p 8.

67. Bourdieu, *Distinction*, pp. 50, 86, emphasis added.

68. Ibid., pp. 2, 28, 44. See also Bourdieu, *The Rules of Art: Genesis and Structure of the Artistic Field* (Stanford, CA: Stanford University Press, [1992] 1996), p. 318.

69. Shibutani, "Reference Groups as Perspectives," p. 131, emphasis added.

70. Fleck, *Genesis and Development of a Scientific Fact*, p. 93. On restricted attention, see also p. 84.

71. Kuhn, *Structure of Scientific Revolutions*, p. 111.

72. Goffman, *Frame Analysis*, pp. 343, 146.

73. On "rules of irrelevance," see Goffman, "Fun in Games," pp. 19–26. See also Berger and Luckmann, *Social Construction of Reality*, pp. 44–45, on "relevance structures." On the definition of the situation, see William I. Thomas, *The Unadjusted Girl: With Cases and Standpoint for Behavior Analysis* (Montclair, NJ: Patterson Smith, [1923] 1969); and Goffman, *Presentation of Self in Everyday Life*.

74. Joan Emerson, "Behavior in Private Places: Sustaining Definitions of Reality in Gynecological Examinations," in *Recent Sociology No. 2*, ed. Hans Dreitzel (London: Macmillan, 1970), p. 76.

75. Mary Douglas, *Purity and Danger: An Analysis of Concepts of Pollution and Taboo* (New York: Routledge and Keegan Paul, 1966), p. 163. See also Else Frenkel-Brunswik, "Intolerance of Ambiguity as an Emotional and Perceptual Personality Variable," *Journal of Personality* 18 (1949): 108–43.

76. William James, "The Types of Philosophic Thinking," in *A Pluralistic Universe: Hibbert Lectures at Manchester College on the Present Situation in Philosophy* (Rockville, MD: Arc Manor, 2008), p. 9.

77. Tuan, *Segmented Worlds and Self*, p. 133.

78. Ibid., p. 133. See also p. 120.

79. Edmund Leach, *Culture and Communication: The Logic by Which Symbols Are Connected. An Introduction to the Use of Structuralist Analysis in Social Anthropology* (Cambridge: Cambridge University Press, 1976), p. 32. See also pp. 33–34.

80. Douglas, *Purity and Danger*, p. 5. See also Frenkel-Brunswick, "Intolerance of Ambiguity," p. 119.

81. Casper and Moore make a similar argument about social patterns of invisibility. See *Missing Bodies*, p. 4.

82. Bourdieu, *Distinction*, pp. 2, 28, 44, 50; Bourdieu, *Rules of Art*, p. 318.

83. Alfred Schutz, *The Phenomenology of the Social World* (Evanston, IL: Northwestern University Press, [1932] 1967), p. 9.

84. Emerson, "Behavior in Private Places," p. 76.

85. See Sandra Bem, *The Lenses of Gender: Transforming the Debate on Sexual Inequality* (New Haven, CT: Yale University Press, 1993), p. 2.

86. *Merriam-Webster Online Dictionary*, s.v. "filter," accessed September 22, 2008, http://www.merriam-webster.com/dictionary/filter; *The American Heritage Dictionary of the English Language, New College Edition* (Boston: Houghton Mifflin, 1978 [1969]), p. 492, s.v. "filter."

87. Thomas DeGloma and Asia Friedman, "Thinking with Socio-Mental Filters: Exploring the Social Structuring of Attention and Significance" (paper presented at the Annual Meeting of the American Sociological Association, Philadelphia, PA, 2005).

88. See Donald Broadbent, *Perception and Communication* (London: Pergamon,1958); Janine Mendola, "Contextual Shape Processing in Human Visual Cortex: Beginning to Fill-In the Blanks," in *Filling In: From Perceptual Completion to Cortical Reorganization*, ed. Luiz Pessoa and Peter De Weerd (Oxford: Oxford University Press, 2003), p. 40.

89. Jun Wang, Brett A. Clementz, and Andreas Keil, "The Neural Correlates of Feature-Based Selective Attention When Viewing Spatially and Temporally Overlapping Images," *Neuropsychologia* 45, no. 7 (2007): 1393–99.

90. Claudia Mello-Thoms, Calvin F. Nodine, Harold L. Kundel, "What Attracts the Eye to the Location of Missed and Reported Breast Cancers?" *ETRA* (2002): 111–17.

91. Mark D. Lescroart, Irving Biederman, Xiaomin Yue, and Jules Davidoff, "A Cross-Cultural Study of the Representation of Shape: Sensitivity to Generalized Cone Dimensions," *Visual Cognition* 18, no. 1 (2010): 50–66.

92. See Karen Cerulo, *Never Saw It Coming: Cultural Challenges to Envisioning the Worst* (Chicago: University of Chicago Press, 2006), p. 236.

93. Broadbent, *Perception and Communication*, p. 174.

94. Ibid., p. 298. For a discussion of drive as a biological concept, see Steven Epstein, "A Queer Encounter: Sociology and the Study of Sexuality," in *Sexuality and Gender*, ed. Christine Williams and Arlene Stein (Malden, MA: Blackwell, 2002), p. 46.

95. Nikolai Trubetzkoy, *Principles of Phonology* (Berkeley: University of California Press, [1939] 1969), pp. 51–52.

96. Davis, *Smut*, p. 285n17.

97. Ibid., p. 216.

98. Zerubavel directly references Davis when he employs the term, writing that "what we experience through our senses is normally 'filtered' through various interpretive frameworks" (Zerubavel, *Social Mindscapes*, p. 24).

99. Vannini, Waskul, and Gottschalk, *The Senses in Self, Society, and Culture*, p. 20.

100. Ibid., p. 87, emphasis added.

101. See ibid., p. 35, for one discussion of attention.

102. Schutz and Luckmann, *Structures of the Life World*, p. 250. See also Jeffrey Alexander, "Toward a Theory of Cultural Trauma," in *Cultural Trauma and Collective Identity*, ed. Jeffrey C. Alexander, Ron Eyerman, Bernhard Giesen, Neil J. Smelser, and Piotr Sztompka (Berkeley: University of California Press, 2004); and Ron Eyerman, "Cultural Trauma: Slavery and the Formation of African American Identity," in Alexander et al., *Cultural Trauma and Collective Identity*.

CHAPTER TWO

1. On the assumption that visual perception is complete and undistorted, see Michalko, *Mystery of the Eye*, pp. 18, 42. On perceptual selectivity, see Kuhn, *Structure of Scientific Revolutions*, pp. 112–13, 151; Bruner, "Social Psychology and Perception," pp. 85, 92–93; and Zerubavel, *Social Mindscapes*, p. 24.

2. Casper and Moore, *Missing Bodies*, p. 3.

3. Bracketed ellipses indicate omissions in quotes from interviews conducted in my study. They are used to differentiate omitted material from faltering or fragmented speech, which is marked by suspension points without brackets.

4. Kessler and McKenna, *Gender*, pp. 4–6. See also Garfinkel, *Studies in Ethnomethodology*.

5. Karin Martin, "Becoming a Gendered Body: Practices of Preschools," *American Sociological Review* 63 (August 1998): 494–511.

6. Bruner, "Social Psychology and Perception," pp. 92–93, 85.

7. See, for example, Kessler and McKenna, *Gender*.

8. Fausto-Sterling, *Sexing the Body*, pp. 126–232.

9. Carol Tavris, *The Mismeasure of Woman* (New York: Touchstone, 1992), pp. 336–37.

10. Anelis Kaiser, Sven Haller, Sigrid Schmitz, and Cordula Nitsch, "On Sex/Gender Related Similarities and Differences in fMRI Language Research," *Brain Research Reviews* 61, no. 2 (2009): 49.

11. See also Epstein, *Deceptive Distinctions*, p. 39; Lorber, *Paradoxes of Gender*, p. 39; Wendy Cealy Harrison and John Hood-Williams, *Beyond Sex and Gender* (London: Sage Publications, 2002), p. 111; Roger Lancaster, *The Trouble with Nature: Sex and Science in Popular Culture* (Los Angeles: University of California Press, 2003), p. 20; Judith Lorber and Lisa Jean Moore, *Gendered Bodies, Feminist Perspectives* (Los Angeles: Roxbury, 2007), p. 15; Paula Caplan and Jeremy Caplan, *Thinking Critically about Research on Sex and Gender* (New York: HarperCollins, 1994).

12. C. Jacob Hale, "Tracing a Ghostly Memory in My Throat: Reflections on FTM Feminist Voice and Agency," in *Men Doing Feminism*, ed. Tom Digby (New York: Routledge, 1998), p. 107.

13. Patrick Hopkins, "How Feminism Made a Man out of Me: The Proper Subject of Feminism and the Problem of Men," in Digby, *Men Doing Feminism*, p. 33. See also Susan Bordo, *The Male Body: A New Look at Men in Public and in Private* (New York: Farrar, Strauss and Giroux, 1999), p. 29.

14. See Dreger, *Hermaphrodites and the Medical Invention of Sex*, pp. 127–28.

15. Sigmund Freud first used the term *overdetermined* to describe the idea that there were multiple causes of the psychological phenomena that interested him, such as dreams and hysteria, and that no psychological symptom could be cleared up without taking each of these multiple causes into account. See, for instance, Freud, *The Interpretation of Dreams*, ed. A. A. Brill (New York: Modern Library, [1911] 1950). The concept of *overdetermination* was later adopted by Louis Althusser in a positive sense to describe the fundamental complexity of every meaning and form of identity. On Althusser's use of the concept, see J. K. Gibson-Graham, *The End of Capitalism (as We Knew It)* (Minneapolis: University of Minnesota Press, [1996] 2006), pp. 26–28. The term also refers to the deconstructionist position that any textual "reading" is unconsciously shaped by various assumptions, presuppositions, and institutionalized interpretative strategies.

16. Lancaster, *The Trouble with Nature*, p. 76.

17. On discursive power, see Michel Foucault, *The History of Sexuality, Volume 1* (New York: Vintage Books, 1978).

18. See Butler, *Gender Trouble*; Butler, *Bodies that Matter*; and Butler, *Undoing Gender* (New York: Routledge, 2004).

19. Zerubavel, *Social Mindscapes*, p. 51. See also Bruner, "Social Psychology and Perception," p. 94.

20. See Tuan, *Segmented Worlds and Self*, p. 117; John Berger, *Ways of Seeing* (London: British Broadcasting Corporation and Penguin Books, [1972] 1977), pp. 8–9; Michalko, *Mystery of the Eye*, p. 82.

21. Zerubavel, *Fine Line*, p. 71.

22. Tuan, *Segmented Worlds and Self*, p. 132.

23. See Kessler and McKenna, *Gender*, p. 3.

24. Shulamith Firestone, *The Dialectic of Sex: The Case for Feminist Revolution* (New York: William Morrow, 1970).

25. On "excessive sex-distinction," see Charlotte Perkins Gilman, *Women and Economics: A Study of the Economic Relation between Men and Women as a Factor in Social Evolution* (Boston: Small, Maynard, 1898), pp. 29–32; Simone de Beauvoir, *The Second Sex* (New York: Knopf, [1949] 1973), pp. xxiv–xxv; and Ortner, "Is Male to Female as Nature Is to Culture?"

26. See Zerubavel, *Fine Line*, p. 46–47.

27. Ibid., p. 35.

28. Ibid., p. 119.

29. For another statement that it is impossible to be blind to sex, see Epstein, *Deceptive Distinctions*, p. 39.
30. Butler, *Undoing Gender*, p. 176.
31. Lorber, *Paradoxes of Gender*, p. 26.
32. Kessler and McKenna, *Gender*, p. 164.
33. Raewyn Connell, *Gender and Power: Society, the Person, and Sexual Politics* (Stanford, CA: Stanford University Press, 1987), p. 66.
34. See Berger and Luckmann, *Social Construction of Reality*, p. 60.
35. Fleck, *Genesis and Development of a Scientific Fact*, p. 144.
36. Merleau-Ponty, *Phenomenology of Perception*, p. 67.
37. Garfinkel, *Studies in Ethnomethodology*, p. 38.
38. Kessler and McKenna, *Gender*, p. 164.
39. Butler, *Undoing Gender*, p. 42.
40. Linda Nicholson, "Interpreting Gender," *Signs* 20, no. 1 (1994): 98.
41. Kessler and McKenna, *Gender*, p. 157.
42. Ibid., p. 156.
43. Hale, "Consuming the Living, Dis(Re)Membering the Dead in the Butch/FTM Borderlands," *GLQ* 4, no. 2 (1998): 336.
44. Ibid., p. 336.
45. Chris Shilling, *The Body and Social Theory*, 2nd ed. (London: Sage Publications, 2003), p. 60 (see also p. 10).
46. See Fine, *Morel Tales*.
47. See Durkheim, *Elementary Forms of Religious Life*.
48. For a longer discussion of foundational and contextual mental filters, see Degloma and Friedman, "Thinking With Socio-Mental Filters."
49. See the discussion of the essence/accident distinction in Book Z of Aristotle's *Metaphysics*. See also Diana Fuss, *Essentially Speaking: Feminism, Nature, and Difference* (New York: Routledge, 1989), pp. 2–3.
50. See Jamie Mullaney, "Making it 'Count': Mental Weighing and Identity Attribution," *Symbolic Interaction* 22, no. 3 (1999): 269–83.
51. Emerson, "Behavior in Private Places," p. 78.
52. Bryan Turner, *The Body and Society* (Oxford: Blackwell, 1984). See also Alexandra Howson, *Embodying Gender* (London: Sage Publications, 2005), p. 1; as well as Shilling's notion of the "absent-present" body in sociology (Shilling, *Body and Social Theory*, p. 17).
53. See Asia Friedman, "Unintended Consequences of the Feminist Sex/Gender Distinction," *Genders* 43 (2006).
54. For examples of this position, see Bordo, *Male Body*, p. 263; Connell, *Gender and Power*, pp. 137, 191; Moira Gatens, *Imaginary Bodies: Ethics, Power, and Corporeality* (London: Routledge, 1996), pp. 8–10; Lorber, *Paradoxes of Gender*, p. 22; Toril Moi, *What Is a Woman? And Other Essays* (Oxford: Oxford University Press, 1999), pp. 112–14; West and Zimmerman, "Doing Gender," p. 127; Iris Marion Young, *On Female Bodily Experience: "Throwing Like a Girl" and Other Essays* (New York: Oxford University Press, 2005), pp. 32–36.

55. See Bordo, *Male Body*, p. 37; Connell, *Gender and Power*, p. 66; Lorber, *Paradoxes of Gender*, pp. 17–18.
56. Connell, *Gender and Power*, p. 91.
57. On exceptions to binary sex, see Dreger, *Hermaphrodites and the Medical Invention of Sex*; Kessler, *Lessons from the Intersexed*; and Preves, *Intersex and Identity*. On historical changes in perceptions of sex, see Dreger, *Hermaphrodites and the Medical Invention of Sex*; Laqueur, *Making Sex*; Marian Lowe, "Social Bodies: The Interaction of Culture and Women's Biology," in *Biological Woman: The Convenient Myth*, ed. Ruth Hubbard, Barbara Fried, and Mary Henifin (Rochester, NY: Schenkman Books, 1982), p. 109; and Joan Meyerowitz, *How Sex Changed: A History of Transsexuality in the United States* (Cambridge, MA: Harvard University Press, 2004). On gendered constructions of sex in scientific research, see Melanie Blackless et al., "How Sexually Dimorphic Are We? Review and Synthesis," *American Journal of Human Biology* 12 (2000): 151–66; Fausto-Sterling, *Sexing the Body*, p. 3; Cordelia Fine, *Delusions of Gender: How Our Minds, Society, and Neurosexism Create Difference* (New York: W. W. Norton, 2010); Barbara Fried, "Boys Will Be Boys: The Language of Sex and Gender," in Hubbard, Fried, and Henifin, *Biological Woman: The Convenient Myth*, pp. 62–63; Fujimura, "Sex Genes," p. 50; Martin, "The Egg and the Sperm," p. 486; Moore, *Sperm Counts*; Oudshoorn *Beyond the Natural Body*, p. 39; Rebecca Young and Evan Balaban, "Psychoneuroindoctrinology," *Nature* 443, no. 12 (2006): 634; Rebecca Jordan-Young, *Brain Storm: The Flaws in the Science of Sex Differences* (Cambridge, MA: Harvard University Press, 2010).
58. Hawkesworth, "Confounding Gender," p. 31.
59. Kessler and McKenna, *Gender*, p. xi.
60. Ibid., p. 137.
61. Ibid., p. viii.
62. Ibid., p. 154. Kessler and McKenna adopted this term from Garfinkel, *Studies in Ethnomethodology*, p. 157.
63. Kessler and McKenna, *Gender*, 18.
64. The discussion of the overlay experiment appears in Kessler and McKenna, *Gender*, pp. 145–53.
65. Ibid., p. 158.
66. Donna Haraway is one possible exception here. See her article "Situated Knowledges: The Science Question in Feminism and the Privilege of Partial Perspective," *Feminist Studies* 14, no. 3 (1988): 575–99, in which she writes: "I want a feminist writing of the body that metaphorically emphasizes vision" (p. 582). While Haraway's writing on situated knowledge and partial perspective is an important piece of the intellectual backdrop of the book, they are fundamentally works of theory and philosophy rather than empirical illustrations of the specific mechanisms of partial perspective and the visual construction of the body.
67. Butler, *Gender Trouble*, p. 25.

68. Butler, *Undoing Gender,* p. 198. See also Butler, *Bodies that Matter,* p. ix.

69. See Jay Prosser, *Second Skins: The Body Narratives of Transsexuality* (New York: Columbia University Press, 1998), p. 41; Epstein, "A Queer Encounter," pp. 49–52. On queer theory's critique of the sex categories (and binary oppositions more broadly), see also Arlene Stein and Ken Plummer, "'I Can't Even Think Straight': 'Queer' Theory and the Missing Sexual Revolution in Sociology," *Sociological Theory* 12 (1994): 181–82.

70. On the idea that the body is always sensed, see Howson, *Embodying Gender,* p. 2. On the central role of the audience in the construction of reality more generally, see Goffman, *Presentation of Self in Everyday Life,* particularly the concepts of *inference* (p. 3), *performance teams* (p. 79), and *working consensus* (p. 10).

71. Vannini, Waskul, and Gottschalk, *The Senses in Self, Society, and Culture,* p. 30.

72. Casper and Moore, *Missing Bodies,* p. 2.

73. Elizabeth Grosz, *Volatile Bodies: Toward a Corporeal Feminism* (Bloomington: University of Indiana Press, 1994), p. 94.

74. See Garfinkel, *Studies in Ethnomethodology,* pp. 146–47; Les Feinberg, *Transgender Warriors: Making History from Joan of Arc to Dennis Rodman* (Boston: Beacon Press, 1996); Jennifer Finney-Boylan, *She's Not There: A Life in Two Genders* (New York: Broadway Books, 2003); Noelle Howey, *Dress Codes of Three Girlhoods—My Mother's, My Father's, and Mine* (New York: Picador, 2003); Leila J. Rupp and Verta Taylor, *Drag Queens at the 801 Cabaret* (Chicago: University of Chicago Press, 2003).

75. Dreger, *Hermaphrodites and the Medical Invention of Sex,* p. 9, emphasis added.

76. See Bryan Turner, *Regulating Bodies: Essays in Medical Sociology* (London: Routledge, 1992), pp. 118, 254–56. See also Shilling, *Body and Social Theory,* pp. ix, 182; and Nicholson, "Interpreting Gender," pp. 82–83.

77. Oudshoorn, *Beyond the Natural Body,* p. 39; Blackless, "How Sexually Dimorphic Are We?," p. 151. See also Londa Schiebinger, *Nature's Body: Gender in the Making of Modern Science* (Boston: Beacon Press, 1993).

78. Laqueur, *Making Sex,* p. 10.

CHAPTER THREE

1. Garfinkel, *Studies in Ethnomethodology,* pp. 146–47.

2. Kessler and McKenna, *Gender,* pp. 6, 158.

3. See Mullaney, "Making it 'Count.'"

4. Kessler and McKenna, *Gender,* p. 17.

5. See Tuan, *Segmented Worlds and Self,* p. 117; Berger, *Ways of Seeing,* pp. 8–9; Michalko, *Mystery of the Eye,* p. 82.

6. Tuan, *Segmented Worlds and Self,* p. 117.

7. On the emic/etic distinction, see Kenneth Pike, *Language in Relation to a Unified Theory of the Structure of Human Behavior*, 2nd edition (The Hague, Neth.: Mouton, 1967).
8. Goffman, *Presentation of Self in Everyday Life*, p. 24.
9. Osagie K. Obasogie, "Do Blind People See Race? Social, Legal, and Theoretical Considerations," *Law & Society Review* 44, nos. 3/4 (2010): 585–616.
10. Judith Gerson, "There Is No Sex without Gender," *Sociological Forum* 20, no. 1 (2005): 180.
11. Kessler and McKenna, *Gender*, pp. 8–9. See also Gerson, "There Is No Sex without Gender," p. 180.
12. Butler, *Gender Trouble*, p. 7.
13. Ferdinand de Saussure, *A Course in General Linguistics* (Peru, IL: Open Court Publishing, 1986), p. 66.
14. Saussure, *Course in General Linguistics*, p. 117.
15. Betsy Lucal, "What It Means to Be Gendered Me: Life on the Boundaries of a Dichotomous Gender System," *Gender and Society* 13, no. 6 (1999): 789.
16. Nora Vincent, *Self-Made Man: One Woman's Journey into Manhood and Back* (New York: Penguin, 2006), p. 51.
17. Schilt, *Just One of the Guys*, pp. 65–66.
18. Zerubavel, *Fine Line*, p. 24.
19. Ibid., p. 16.
20. On "tertiary" sex characteristics, see Birdwhistell, *Kinesics and Context*, p. 42.
21. It is necessary to emphasize the cultural specificity of these statements. It is well known that different cultures have different social norms of physical presentation. Here I base my analysis on hegemonic US norms. Whether the grooming practices in other cultures share the formal features of dominant US practices requires further research.
22. Kessler and McKenna, *Gender*, pp. 161, 164; West and Zimmerman, "Doing Gender," p. 137; Connell, *Gender and Power*, pp. 80–81. See also Bordo, *Male Body*, pp. 26, 39; Lorber, *Paradoxes of Gender*, pp. 18–19, 22–24.
23. Caitlin Killian, "The Other Side of the Veil: North African Women in France Respond to the Headscarf Affair," *Gender & Society* 17, no. 4 (2003): 570; Nancy Lindisfarne, "Starting from Below: Fieldwork, Gender, and Imperialism Now," *Critique of Anthropology* 22, no. 4 (2002): 417; Gül Aldikaçti Marshall, "Ideology, Progress, and Dialogue: A Comparison of Feminist and Islamist Women's Approaches to the Issues of Head Covering and Work in Turkey," *Gender & Society* 19, no. 1 (2005): 110–11; Fatima Mernissi, *Women and Islam: An Historical and Theological Enquiry*, trans. Mary Jo Lokeland (Oxford: Basil Blackwell, 1991), p. 93.
24. Marshall, "Ideology, Progress, and Dialogue," p. 110.
25. Lucal, "What It Means to be Gendered Me," p. 785.
26. See Barkalow, with Raab, *In the Men's House*, photo insert. One of the photographs is of a group of students in a math class. The caption states

that the author is the only woman in the room and asks the reader to try to pick her out.

27. Arnold Van Gennep, *The Rites of Passage* (Chicago: University of Chicago Press, [1909] 1960), p. 11. See also, Zerubavel, *Fine Line*, pp. 18–24; On the creation and maintenance of gender boundaries, see also Judith Gerson and Kathy Peiss, "Boundaries, Negotiation, Consciousness: Reconceptualizing Gender Relations," *Social Problems* 32, no. 4 (1985): 319–20.

28. Zerubavel, *Fine Line*, p.18.

29. Epstein, *Deceptive Distinctions*, p. 229; Sandra Bartky, "Foucault, Femininity, and the Modernization of Patriarchal Power," in *Feminism and Foucault: Reflections on Resistance*, ed. Irene Diamond and Lee Quinby (Boston: Northeastern University Press, 1988).

30. Kessler and McKenna, *Gender*, pp. 6, 157; West and Zimmerman "Doing Gender," pp. 126, 130, 133, 140.

31. Kessler and McKenna, *Gender*, p. 157.

32. Jerome M. Levine and Gardner Murphy, "The Learning and Forgetting of Controversial Material," in *Readings in Social Psychology*, ed. Eleanor E. Macoby, Theodore M. Newcomb, and Eugene L. Hartley (New York: Henry Holt, 1958), p. 40; Lancaster, *Trouble with Nature*, p. 76.

33. Lancaster, *Trouble with Nature*, p. 76.

CHAPTER FOUR

1. Laqueur, *Making Sex*, p. 10.

2. Michael Messner, *Taking the Field: Women, Men, and Sports* (Minneapolis: University of Minnesota Press, 2002), pp. 67–68.

3. Daniel Goleman, *Vital Lies, Simple Truths* (New York: Simon & Schuster, 1985), p. 107.

4. Jason Cromwell, *Transmen and FTMs: Identities, Bodies, Genders, and Sexualities* (Urbana: University of Illinois Press, 1999), p. 104.

5. Ibid., p. 105.

6. For one critique, see Ibid., p. 105.

7. For a useful discussion of this terminology, see also Schilt, *Just One of the Guys*, p. 15.

8. In other contexts (e.g., on the telephone) other sensory information is more relevant than visual information. Whenever visual information is available to us, however, we heavily emphasize and privilege it.

9. Hans Jonas, "The Nobility of Sight: A Study in the Phenomenology of the Senses," in *The Phenomenon of Life: Toward a Philosophical Biology* (Chicago: University of Chicago Press, 1982). See also Jay, *Downcast Eyes*, p. 24.

10. Grosz, *Volatile Bodies*, p. 98.

11. West and Zimmerman, "Doing Gender."

12. Erving Goffman, *Interaction Ritual*, p. 133.

13. See, for example, Stryker, "(De)Subjugated Knowledges," pp. 8–9; Kate Bornstein, *Gender Outlaw: On Men, Women, and the Rest of Us* (New York: Routledge, 1994); Les Feinberg, *Trans Liberation: Beyond Pink or Blue* (Boston: Beacon Press, 1999); Lucal, "What It Means to Be Gendered Me;" Steven Seidman, introduction to *Queer Theory/Sociology* (Cambridge: Blackwell, 1996), p. 12; Arlene Stein and Ken Plummer, "'I Can't Even Think Straight,'" pp. 181–82.
14. Zerubavel, *Social Mindscapes*, p. 51. See also Bruner, "Social Psychology and Perception," p. 94.
15. Mullaney, "Making It 'Count,'" p. 271.
16. Karen Danna-Lynch, "Switching Roles: The Process of Mental Weighing," *Poetics* 38 (2010): 166.
17. Zerubavel, *Fine Line*, p. 122.
18. Lancaster, *Trouble with Nature*, p. 72.

CHAPTER FIVE

1. Zerubavel, *Fine Line*, pp. 80, 115.
2. Robin Meadows, "Sex and the Spotted Hyena," *Smithsonian Zoogoer* 24, no. 3 (1995).
3. Cynthia Eller, *Am I a Woman? A Skeptic's Guide to Gender* (Boston: Beacon Press, 2003), pp. 1–2.
4. Lee Ellis et al., *Sex Differences: Summarizing More Than a Century of Scientific Research* (New York: Taylor and Francis, 2008), p. 18.
5. Birdwhistell, *Kinesics and Context*, pp. 39–46; Gary Taylor, *Castratation: An Abbreviated History of Western Manhood* (New York: Taylor and Francis, 2000), pp. 150–51.
6. Barkalow, *In the Men's House*, photo insert.
7. Kate Zernike, "Sizing Up America: Signs of Expansion from Head to Toe," *New York Times*, March 1, 2004.
8. Ibid., A1.
9. Ibid., A18. "Eleven percent of men overall had a 'prominent seat,' but that ranged from 24 percent among black men to 9 percent among whites, 8 percent among Hispanics, and 6 percent among 'others.'"
10. Annemarie Mol, *The Body Multiple: Ontology in Medical Practice* (Durham: Duke University Press, 2002), p. 148.
11. Thomas Szarl, a transplant surgeon, as quoted in Renee Fox, "Through the Lenses of Biology and Sociology: Organ Replacement," in *Debating Biology: Sociological Reflections on Health, Medicine, and Society*, ed. Simon Williams, Lynda Birke, and Gillian Bendelow (London: Routledge, 2003), p. 237.
12. Fox, "Through the Lenses of Biology and Sociology," p. 237.
13. For one account, see Tavris, *Mismeasure of Woman*. See also Lisa Jean Moore and Adele E. Clarke, "Clitoral Conventions and Transgressions:

Graphic Representations in Anatomy Texts, c. 1900–1991," *Feminist Studies* 21, no. 2 (1995): 255–301.

14. See Wayne Brekhus, "A Sociology of the Unmarked: Redirecting Our Focus," *Sociological Theory* 16, no. 1 (1998): 35.

15. Society for the Study of Manga Techniques, *How to Draw Manga Bodies and Anatomy* (Tokyo: Graphic-sha, 1996), pp. 14, 26–30, 82, 84; Jack Hamm, *Drawing the Head and Figure* (New York: Perigree, 1963), pp. 2, 7, 15–16, 39, 62, 97; Lee Hammond, *Draw Real People!* (Cincinnati: North Light Books, 1996), pp. 32, 37, 42.

16. Hammond, *Draw Real People!*, p. 31.

17. Hamm, *Drawing the Head and Figure*, p. 39.

18. Ibid., p. 29.

19. Ibid., p. 34.

20. Ibid., p. 4.

21. Hammond, *Draw Real People!*, p. 28.

22. Ibid., p. 41.

23. Hamm, *Drawing the Head and Figure*, p. 4.

24. Hammond, *Draw Real People!*, p. 49.

25. Hamm, *Drawing the Head and Figure*, p. 92.

26. Ibid., p. 104.

27. Ibid., p. 16.

28. Eller, *Am I a Woman?*, p. 113.

29. For one account, see de Beauvoir, *Second Sex*, pp. 10, 14–16. See also Fausto-Sterling, *Sexing the Body*, pp. 49–50; John Money and Anke Ehrhardt, *Man and Woman, Boy and Girl: Differentiation and Dimorphism of Gender Identity from Conception to Maturity* (Baltimore, MD: Johns Hopkins University Press, 1972).

30. Cealy Harrison and Hood-Williams, *Beyond Sex and Gender*, p. 120.

31. Richardson's critique is primarily directed at Laura Carrel and Huntington F. Willard's 2005 article in *Nature* claiming that genetic differences between men and women are significantly greater than previously thought (Carrel and Willard, "X-Inactivation Profile Reveals Extensive Variability in X-Linked Gene Expression in Females," *Nature* 434, no. 7031 (2005): 400–404), and the subsequent reporting of these findings in *Newsweek*, the *Los Angeles Times*, and the *New York Times*, which claimed that men and women differ almost as much as humans differ from chimpanzees (Fred Guterl, "The Truth about Gender," *Newsweek*, March 27, 2005) and that males and females are essentially the equivalent of two different species (Maureen Dowd, "X-celling Over Men," *New York Times*, March 20, 2005).

32. Richardson, "Sexes, Species, and Genomes," p. 828.

33. Ibid., p. 826.

34. See Kate Millett, "Sexual Politics: A Manifesto for Revolution," in *Radical Feminism*, ed. Anne Koedt, Ellen Levine, and Anita Rapone (New York: Quadrangle Books, 1973), pp. 366–67; Nancy Topping Bazin and Alma

Freeman, "The Androgynous Vision," *Women's Studies* 2, no. 2 (1974): 185–215; and Ann Ferguson, "Androgyny as an Ideal for Human Development," in *Feminism and Philosophy*, ed. Mary Vetterling-Bragin, Frederick Elliston, and Jane English (Totowa, NJ: Littlefield, Adams, 1977). Sandra Bem's well-known "Sex Role Inventory" (see Bem, "The Measurement of Psychological Androgyny," *Journal of Consulting and Clinical Psychology* 42 [1974]: 155–62) is another example of a similar conceptualization of androgyny. Bem classifies people as having one of four gender-role orientations (masculine, feminine, androgynous, undifferentiated). The androgynous individual is a female or male who has a high degree of both feminine and masculine traits.

35. Alison Jaggar, *Feminist Politics and Human Nature* (Totowa, NJ: Rowman and Allenheld, 1983), p. 87. See also Carolyn Heilbrun, *Toward a Recognition of Androgyny* (New York: W. W. Norton, [1964] 1993), p. xii, for an explicit statement that her use of androgyny should not be confused with physiological androgyny.

36. Jaggar, *Feminist Politics and Human Nature*, pp. 87–88.

37. See, for example, Janice Raymond, "The Illusion of Androgyny," *Quest* (Summer 1975): 61–64; Catherine Stimpson, "The Androgyne and the Homosexual," *Women's Studies* 2, no. 2 (1974): 242.

38. For example, Raymond, "Illusion of Androgyny," pp. 61–64. Such critiques of androcentric formulations were one of the important motors for sexual-difference feminism, the argument that difference ought to be the basis for equality, not sameness (e.g., Lorber, *Paradoxes of Gender*, pp. 52–53; Tavris, *Mismeasure of Woman*). However, I maintain it is possible and useful to revisit notions of sex sameness and quite deliberately disentangle them from androcentric meanings and assumptions, rather than to retreat and focus on sex differences.

39. Monique Wittig, "One Is Not Born a Woman," *Feminist Issues* 1, no. 2 (1981): 48. See also Andrea Dworkin, *Woman Hating* (New York: Dutton, 1974), p. 183; Jaggar, *Feminist Politics and Human Nature*, p. 100.

40. See, for example, Louann Brizendine, *The Female Brain* (New York: Morgan Road Books, 2006); Brizendine, *The Male Brain* (New York: Random House, 2010); Simon Baron-Cohen, *The Essential Difference: The Truth about the Male and Female Brain* (New York: Basic Books, 2003).

41. Ellis et al., *Sex Differences*, pp. 58–65.

42. Rebecca Jordan-Young, *Brain Storm*, pp. 50–51.

43. See Baron-Cohen, *Essential Difference*; Brizendine, *Female Brain*; and Brizendine, *Male Brain*.

CONCLUSION

1. Zerubavel, *Fine Line*, p. 51; Zerubavel, *Social Mindscapes*, p. 17. See also Bruner, "Social Psychology and Perception," p. 94.

2. Durkheim, *Rules of Sociological Method*, p. 2.
3. See Foucault, *History of Sexuality.*
4. Grosz, *Volatile Bodies*, p. xi.
5. Margaret Shildrick, *Leaky Bodies and Boundaries: Feminism, Postmodernism and, (Bio)ethics* (New York: Routledge, 1997). See also Howson, *Embodying Gender*, p. 117; Hale, "Tracing a Ghostly Memory in my Throat," p. 115; Shilling, *Body and Social Theory*, p. 10.
6. Fujimura, "Sex Genes," p. 51.
7. Ibid., p. 52.
8. Ibid., pp. 52, 69.
9. Leach, *Culture and Communication*, p. 3.
10. Dorothy Nelkin and M. Susan Lindee, *The DNA Mystique: The Gene as a Cultural Icon* (Ann Arbor: University of Michigan Press, 2004), p. 126.
11. Richard Dawkins, *The Blind Watchmaker: Why the Evidence of Evolution Reveals a Universe without Design* (New York: W. W. Norton, [1986] 2006), p. 373.
12. John Hutchinson and Anthony Smith, eds., *Nationalism*, Oxford Readers (Oxford: Oxford University Press, 1995), pp. 4–5.
13. Benedict Anderson, *Imagined Communities: Reflections on the Origin and Spread of Nationalism* (London: Verso, 1991 [1983]), p. 7.
14. Rick Weiss, "Intricate Toiling Found in Nooks of DNA Once Believed to Stand Idle," *Washington Post*, June 14, 2007.
15. Groopman, *How Doctors Think*, pp. 65, 126.
16. Ibid., p. 179.
17. Lakoff and Johnson, *Metaphors We Live By*, p. 163.
18. Merleau-Ponty, *Phenomenology of Perception*, p. 186.
19. Mark Taylor, "What Derrida Really Meant," *New York Times*, October 14, 2004, A29.
20. On "reverse marking" as a sociological research strategy, see Brekhus, "Sociology of the Unmarked," pp. 43, 49.
21. Schutz, *Phenomenology of the Social World*, pp. 9–11.
22. Ibid., p. 10.
23. Betty Edwards, *Drawing on the Right Side of the Brain* (Los Angeles: J. P. Tarcher, 1979), pp. vii, 20.
24. See, for instance, Ortner, "Is Male to Female as Nature Is to Culture?"; Gayle Rubin, "The Traffic in Women: Notes on the 'Political Economy' of Sex," in *Toward an Anthropology of Women*, ed. Rayna Reiter (New York: Monthly Review Press, 1975). See also, Fausto-Sterling, *Sexing the Body*, pp. 3–4.
25. I use the term *SexGender* here to evoke both the original distinction between the terms *sex* and *gender* as well as the refusal of their separation.
26. On the concept of an "ideal type," see Max Weber, "Objectivity in Social Science and Social Policy," in *The Methodology of the Social Sciences*, ed. and trans. E. A. Shils and H. A. Finch (New York: Free Press, [1904] 1949), p. 90.
27. Kessler and McKenna, *Gender*, p. 7, emphasis added.

28. Butler, *Undoing Gender*, p. 186.
29. Gerson, "There Is No Sex without Gender," p. 179.
30. Casper and Moore, *Missing Bodies*, p. 828.
31. Foucault, *History of Sexuality*, p. 157.
32. Humberto Maturana and Francisco Varela, *The Tree of Knowledge: The Biological Roots of Human Understanding* (Boston: Shambhala Publications, 1987), p. 242.
33. Lakoff and Johnson, *Metaphors We Live By*, p. 239.
34. Zerubavel, *Fine Line*, p. 120–122; Zerubavel, *Social Mindscapes*, p. 57.
35. Lakoff and Johnson, *Metaphors We Live By*, p. 145.
36. Zerubavel, *Social Mindscapes*, pp. 10–11.
37. Zerubavel, "Presidential Race," editorial, *Philadelphia Inquirer*, March 23, 2008.
38. Arlene Stein, "The Incredible Shrinking Lesbian World and Other Queer Conundra," *Sexualities* 13, no. 1 (2010): 10.
39. Shane Phelen, *Getting Specific: Postmodern Lesbian Politics* (Minneapolis: University of Minnesota Press, 1994), p. 11.
40. See, for instance, Epstein, *Deceptive Distinctions*, pp. 17–45; Ludmilla Jordanova, "Natural Facts: A Historical Perspective on Science and Sexuality," in *Nature, Culture, and Gender*, ed. Carol MacCormack and Marilyn Strathern (Cambridge: Cambridge University Press, 1980); Lorber, *Paradoxes of Gender*, pp. 323–324; Ortner, "Is Male to Female as Nature Is to Culture?"; Michelle Zimbalist Rosaldo and Louise Lamphere, introduction to *Woman, Culture, and Society* (Stanford, CA: Stanford University Press, 1974).
41. Stein and Plummer, " 'I Can't Even Think Straight,' " pp. 181–82.
42. Joshua Gamson, "Must Identity Movements Self-Destruct? A Queer Dilemma," *Social Problems* 42, no. 3 (1995): 391.
43. See Gayatri Chakravorty Spivak, *The Postcolonial Critic: Interviews, Strategies, Dialogues* (New York: Routledge, 1990).
44. Paul DiMaggio, "Culture and Cognition," *Annual Review of Sociology* 23 (1997): 269.
45. Ibid., p. 271.
46. See Groopman, *How Doctors Think*, pp. 66, 185.
47. On "sensuous scholarship," see Vannini, Waskul, and Gottschalk, *The Senses in Self, Society, and Culture*, p. 69. Their argument regarding temporality is that part of what we gain by attending to the senses during data collection, particularly those other than vision, is that we slow down and therefore we notice things we wouldn't normally perceive.
48. DiMaggio, "Culture and Cognition," pp. 271–72.

APPENDIX

1. Brekhus, "Rutgers School," p. 454.
2. Eviatar Zerubavel, "Generally Speaking: The Logic and Mechanics of Social Pattern Analysis," *Sociological Forum* 22, no. 2 (2007): 9–10. See also

Zerubavel, "If Simmel Were a Fieldworker: On Formal Sociological Theory and Analytic Field Research," *Symbolic Interaction* 3, no. 2 (1980): 30.

3. On theoretical sampling, see Barney Glaser and Anselm Strauss, *The Discovery of Grounded Theory: Strategies for Qualitative Research* (Chicago: Aldine, 1967); Anselm Strauss, *Qualitative Analysis for Social Scientists* (Cambridge: Cambridge University Press, 1987), p. 38.

4. On sensitizing concepts, see Harold Blumer, "What Is Wrong with Social Theory?" *American Sociological Review* 19 (1954): 7. See also Zerubavel, "If Simmel Were a Fieldworker," p. 31.

5. Zerubavel, "Generally Speaking," p. 6.

6. Michalko, *Mystery of the Eye*, pp. 32, 123, 156–57.

7. Richard Williams, "Introduction: Challenges to the Homogenization of 'African-American,'" *Sociological Forum* 10 (1995): 545.

8. Wayne Brekhus, "A Mundane Manifesto," *Journal of Mundane Behavior* 1, no. 1 (2000): 100.

9. Schilt, *Just One of the Guys*, p. 8.

10. See Zerubavel, "Generally Speaking," p. 4, on generalizability in social pattern analysis.

11. Ibid., p. 10. See also Zerubavel, "If Simmel Were a Fieldworker," p. 29.

12. Brekhus, "Rutgers School," p. 463. See also Zerubavel, *Social Mindscapes*, p. 10; Zerubavel, "If Simmel Were a Fieldworker," pp. 28, 30.

13. Joan Scott, "The Evidence of Experience," *Critical Inquiry* 17 (1991): 797.

14. Grosz, *Volatile Bodies*, p. 94.

15. Wendy Chapkis, "Productive Tensions: Ethnographic Engagement, Complexity, and Contradiction," *Journal of Contemporary Ethnography* 39, no. 5 (2010): 484.

16. Hans-Georg Gadamer, *Philosophical Hermeneutics* (Berkeley: University of California Press, 1976), p. 9. "Prejudgments," in Gadamer's words, "constitute the initial directedness of our whole ability to experience. Prejudices are biases of our openness to the world. They are simply conditions whereby we experience something—whereby what we encounter says something to us."

17. Haraway, "Situated Knowledges," p. 583.

18. Köhler, *Gestalt Psychology*, p. 27.

19. See also Howson, *Embodying Gender*, p. 2.

20. David Armstrong, "Bodies of Knowledge: Foucault and the Problem of Human Anatomy," in *Sociological Theory and Medical Sociology*, ed. Graham Scambler (London: Tavistock, 1987), p. 66.

21. On transmen "going stealth," see also Schilt, *Just One of the Guys*, p. 10.

22. Jane Flax, "Race/Gender and the Ethics of Difference," in *Ethics: The Big Questions*, ed. James Sterba (Malden, MA: Blackwell, 1998), p. 439.

Bibliography

Ainsworth, William, and Steven Greenberg. "Auditory Processing of Speech." In *Listening to Speech: An Auditory Perspective,* edited by Steven Greenberg and William Ainsworth, 3–17. Mahwah, NJ: Lawrence Erlbaum Associates, 2006.

Alac, Morana. "Working with Brain Scans: Digital Images and Gestural Interaction in fMRI laboratory." *Social Studies of Science* 38, no. 4 (2008): 483–508.

Alers-Hankey, Victoria, and Joanna Chisholm, eds. *Photographic Atlas of the Body.* Buffalo, NY: Firefly Books, 2004.

Alexander, Jeffrey C. "Toward a Theory of Cultural Trauma." In *Cultural Trauma and Collective Identity,* edited by Jeffrey C. Alexander, Ron Eyerman, Bernhard Giesen, Neil J. Smelser, and Piotr Sztompka, 1–30. Berkeley: University of California Press, 2004.

Anderson, Benedict. *Imagined Communities: Reflections on the Origin and Spread of Nationalism.* London: Verso, 1991 [1983].

Aristotle. *Metaphysics.* Translated by W. D. Ross. Oxford: Clarendon Press, 1908.

Armstrong, David. "Bodies of Knowledge: Foucault and the Problem of Human Anatomy." In *Sociological Theory and Medical Sociology,* edited by Graham Scambler, 59–75. London: Tavistock, 1987.

Ayabe-Kanamura, Saho, Inna Schicker, Matthias Laska, Robyn Hudson, Hans Distel, Tatsu Kobayakawa, and Sachiko Saito. "Differences in Perception of Everyday Odors: A Japanese-German Cross-Cultural Study." *Chemical Senses* 23, no. 1 (1998): 31–38.

Bagby, James. "A Cross-Cultural Study of Perceptual Predominance in Binocular Rivalry." *Journal of Abnormal and Social Psychology* 54 (1957): 331–34.

Barkalow, Carol, with Andrea Raab. *In the Men's House*. New York: Poseidon Press, 1990.

Baron-Cohen, Simon. *The Essential Difference: The Truth about the Male and Female Brain*. New York: Basic Books, 2003.

Bartky, Sandra. "Foucault, Femininity, and the Modernization of Patriarchal Power." In *Feminism and Foucault: Reflections on Resistance*, edited by Irene Diamond and Lee Quinby, 61–85. Boston: Northeastern University Press, 1998.

Bartlett, Frederic. *Remembering: A Study in Experimental and Social Psychology*. Cambridge: Cambridge University Press, 1932.

Bateson, Gregory. "A Theory of Play and Fantasy." In *Steps to an Ecology of Mind*, 177–93. New York: Ballantine Press, 1972 [1955].

Bazin, Nancy Topping, and Alma Freeman. "The Androgynous Vision." *Women's Studies* 2, no. 2 (1974): 185–215.

Beaulieu, Ann. "Brains, Maps and the New Territory of Psychology." *Theory and Psychology* 13 (2003): 561–68.

Becker, Howard. "Becoming a Marihuana User." *American Journal of Sociology* 59, no. 3 (1953): 235–42.

Bem, Sandra. *The Lenses of Gender: Transforming the Debate on Sexual Inequality*. New Haven, CT: Yale University Press, 1993.

———. "The Measurement of Psychological Androgyny." *Journal of Consulting and Clinical Psychology* 42 (1974): 155–62.

Berger, John. *Ways of Seeing*. London: Penguin Books, 1977 [1972].

Berger, Peter L., and Thomas Luckmann. *The Social Construction of Reality: A Treatise in the Sociology of Knowledge*. Garden City, NJ: Doubleday Anchor, 1967 [1966].

Birdwhistell, Ray L. *Kinesics and Context: Essays on Body Motion Communication*. Philadelphia: University of Pennsylvania Press, 1970.

Blackless, Melanie, Anthony Charuvastra, Amanda Derryck, Anne Fausto-Sterling, Karl Lauzanne, and Ellen Lee. "How Sexually Dimorphic Are We? Review and Synthesis." *American Journal of Human Biology* 12 (2000): 151–66.

Blumer, Herbert. "What Is Wrong with Social Theory?"*American Sociological Review* 19 (1954): 3–10.

Bordo, Susan. *The Male Body: A New Look at Men in Public and in Private*. New York: Farrar, Strauss and Giroux, 1999.

———. *Unbearable Weight: Feminism, Western Culture, and the Body*. Berkeley: University of California Press, 1993.

Bornstein, Kate. *Gender Outlaw: On Men, Women, and the Rest of Us*. New York: Routledge, 1994.

Bourdieu, Pierre. *Distinction: A Social Critique of the Judgment of Taste*. Cambridge, MA: Harvard University Press, 1984.

———. *The Rules of Art: Genesis and Structure of the Artistic Field*. Stanford, CA: Stanford University Press, 1996 [1992].

Brekhus, Wayne. "A Mundane Manifesto." *Journal of Mundane Behavior* 1, no. 1 (2000): 89–106.

———. "The Rutgers School: A Zerubavelian Culturalist Cognitive Sociology." *European Journal of Social Theory* 10, no. 3 (2007): 453–70.

———. "A Sociology of the Unmarked: Redirecting Our Focus." *Sociological Theory* 16, no. 1 (1998): 34–51.

Brizendine, Louann. *The Female Brain*. New York: Morgan Road Books, 2006.

———. *The Male Brain*. New York: Random House, 2010.

Broadbent, Donald. *Perception and Communication*. London: Pergamon, 1958.

Bruner, Jerome. "Social Psychology and Perception." In *Readings in Social Psychology*, edited by Eleanor E. Macoby, Theodore M. Newcomb, and Eugene L. Hartley, 85–94. New York: Henry Holt, 1958.

Bruner, Jerome, and Leo Postman. "On the Perception of Incongruity: A Paradigm." *Journal of Personality* 18 (1949): 206–23.

Burnett, Ron. *How Images Think*. Cambridge, MA: MIT Press, 2004.

Burri, Regula Valérie. "Doing Distinctions : Boundary Work and Symbolic Capital in Radiology." *Social Studies of Science* 38, no. 1 (2008): 35–62.

Butler, Judith. *Bodies That Matter: On the Discursive Limits of "Sex."* New York: Routledge, 1993.

———. *Gender Trouble: Feminism and the Subversion of Identity*. New York: Routledge, 1990.

———. *Undoing Gender*. New York: Routledge, 2004.

Caplan, Paula, and Jeremy Caplan. *Thinking Critically about Research on Sex and Gender*. New York: HarperCollins, 1994.

Carrel, Laura, and Huntington F. Willard. "X-Inactivation Profile Reveals Extensive Variability in X-Linked Gene Expression in Females." *Nature* 434, no. 7031 (2005): 400–404.

Carroll, John B., and Joseph B. Casagrande. "The Function of Language Classifications in Behavior." In *Readings in Social Psychology*, edited by Eleanor E. Macoby, Theodore M. Newcomb, and Eugene L. Hartley, 18–31. New York: Henry Holt, 1958.

Casper, Monica, and Lisa Jean Moore. *Missing Bodies: The Politics of Visibility*. New York: New York University Press, 2009.

Cealy Harrison, Wendy, and John Hood-Williams. *Beyond Sex and Gender*. London: Sage Publications, 2002.

Cerulo, Karen. *Culture in Mind: Toward a Sociology of Culture and Cognition*. New York: Routledge, 2002.

———. *Never Saw It Coming: Cultural Challenges to Envisioning the Worst*. Chicago: University of Chicago Press, 2006.

Chapkis, Wendy. "Productive Tensions: Ethnographic Engagement, Complexity, and Contradiction." *Journal of Contemporary Ethnography* 39, no. 5 (2010): 483–97.

Chayko, Mary. *Connecting: How We Form Social Bonds and Communities in the Internet Age*. Albany: State University of New York Press, 2002.

Child, Arthur. "The Sociology of Perception." *Journal of Genetic Psychology* 77 (1950): 293–303.

Colapinto, John. *As Nature Made Him: The Boy Who Was Raised As a Girl*. New York: HarperCollins, 2000.

Connell, Raewyn. *Gender and Power: Society, the Person, and Sexual Politics*. Stanford, CA: Stanford University Press, 1987.

———. *Masculinities*. Berkeley: University of California Press, 1995.

Cooley, Charles Horton. *Social Organization: A Larger Study of the Mind*. New York: Schocken, 1962 [1909].

Cromwell, Jason. *Transmen and FTMs: Identities, Bodies, Genders, and Sexualities*. Urbana: University of Illinois Press, 1999.

Danna-Lynch, Karen. "Switching Roles: The Process of Mental Weighing." *Poetics* 38 (2010): 165–83.

Davis, Lennard. *Enforcing Normalcy: Disability, Deafness, and the Body*. London: Verso, 1995.

Davis, Murray S. *Smut: Erotic Reality/Obscene Ideology*. Chicago: University of Chicago Press, 1983.

Dawkins, Richard. *The Blind Watchmaker: Why the Evidence of Evolution Reveals a Universe without Design*. New York: W. W. Norton, 2006 [1986].

de Beauvoir, Simone. *The Second Sex*. New York: Knopf, 1975 [1952].

DeGloma, Thomas. "Awakenings: Autobiography, Memory, and the Social Logic of Personal Discovery." *Sociological Forum* 25, no. 3 (2010): 519–40.

DeGloma, Thomas, and Asia Friedman. "Thinking with Socio-Mental Filters: Exploring the Social Structuring of Attention and Significance." Paper presented at the Annual Meeting of the American Sociological Association, Philadelphia, PA, 2005.

DiMaggio, Paul. "Culture and Cognition." *Annual Review of Sociology* 23 (1997): 263–87.

Douglas, Mary. Introduction to *Essays in the Sociology of Perception*, edited by Mary Douglas, 11–13. New York: Routledge, 1982.

———. *Purity and Danger: An Analysis of Concepts of Pollution and Taboo*. New York: Routledge and Keegan Paul, 1966.

Dowd, Maureen. "X-celling Over Men." *New York Times*, March 20, 2005.

Dreger, Alice Domurat. *Hermaphrodites and the Medical Invention of Sex*. Cambridge, MA: Harvard University Press, 1998.

Dumit, Joseph. *Picturing Personhood: Brain Scans and Biomedical Identity*. Princeton, NJ: Princeton University Press, 2004.

Durkheim, Émile. *The Elementary Forms of Religious Life*. New York: Free Press, 1995 [1912].

———. *The Rules of Sociological Method*. New York: Free Press, 1982 [1895].

———. *Suicide*. New York: Free Press, 1966 [1897].

Dworkin, Andrea. *Woman Hating*. New York: Dutton, 1974.

Edwards, Betty. *Drawing on the Right Side of the Brain*. Los Angeles: J. P. Tarcher, 1979.

Efron, David. "Gesture, Race and Culture: A Tentative Study of Some of the Spatio-temporal and 'Linguistic' Aspects of the Gestural Behaviour of Eastern Jews and Southern Italians in New York City, Living Under Similar as Well as Different Environmental Conditions." In *The Body Reader: Social Aspects of the Human Body*, edited by Ted Polhemus, 68–72. New York: Pantheon Books, 1973 [1941].

Eller, Cynthia. *Am I a Woman? A Skeptic's Guide to Gender*. Boston: Beacon Press, 2003.

Ellis, Lee, Scott Hershberger, Evelyn Field, Scott Wersinger, Sergio Pellis, David Geary, Craig Palmer, Katherine Hoyenga, Amir Hetsroni, and Kazmer Karadi. *Sex Differences: Summarizing More Than a Century of Scientific Research*. New York: Taylor and Francis, 2008.

Emerson, Joan P. "Behavior in Private Places: Sustaining Definitions of Reality in Gynecological Examinations." In *Recent Sociology No. 2*, edited by Hans P. Dreitzel, 74–97. London: Macmillan, 1970.

Epstein, Cynthia. *Deceptive Distinctions: Sex, Gender, and the Social Order*. New Haven, CT: Yale University Press, 1988.

Epstein, Steven. "A Queer Encounter: Sociology and the Study of Sexuality." In *Sexuality and Gender*, edited by Christine Williams and Arlene Stein, 44–59. Malden, MA: Blackwell, 2002.

Eugenides, Jeffrey. *Middlesex: A Novel*. New York: Picador, 2002.

Eyerman, Ron. "Cultural Trauma: Slavery and the Formation of African American Identity." In *Cultural Trauma and Collective Identity*, edited by Jeffrey C. Alexander, Ron Eyerman, Bernhard Giesen, Neil J. Smelser, and Piotr Sztompka, 60–111. Berkeley: University of California Press, 2004.

Fausto-Sterling, Anne. "The Bare Bones of Sex: Part 1-Sex and Gender." *Signs* 30, no. 2 (2005): 1491–1527.

———. "The Five Sexes: Why Male and Female Are Not Enough." *The Sciences*, March/April 1993, 20–24.

———. *Sexing the Body: Gender Politics and the Construction of Sexuality*. New York: Basic Books, 2000.

Featherstone, Mike. "The Body in Consumer Culture." *Theory, Culture and Society* 1, no. 1 (1982): 18–33.

Feinberg, Les. *Transgender Warriors: Making History from Joan of Arc to Dennis Rodman*. Boston: Beacon Press, 1996.

———. *Trans Liberation: Beyond Pink or Blue*. Boston: Beacon Press, 1999.

Ferguson, Ann. "Androgyny as an Ideal for Human Development." In *Feminism and Philosophy*, edited by Mary Vetterling-Bragin, Frederick Elliston, and Jane English, 45–69. Totowa, NJ: Littlefield, Adams, 1977.

Fine, Cordelia. *Delusions of Gender: How Our Minds, Society, and Neurosexism Create Difference*. New York: W. W. Norton, 2010.

Fine, Gary Alan. *Morel Tales: The Culture of Mushrooming*. Cambridge, MA: Harvard University Press, 1998.

Finney-Boylan, Jennifer. *She's Not There: A Life in Two Genders*. New York: Broadway Books, 1993.

Firestone, Shulamith. *The Dialectic of Sex: The Case for Feminist Revolution*. New York: William Morrow, 1970.

Firth, Raymond. "Postures and Gestures of Respect." In *The Body Reader: Social Aspects of the Human Body*, edited by Ted Polhemus, 88–108. New York: Pantheon Books, 1978 [1970].

Fiske, Susan, and Shelley Taylor. *Social Cognition*, 2nd ed. New York: McGraw Hill, 1991.

Flax, Jane. "Race/Gender and the Ethics of Difference." In *Ethics: The Big Questions*, edited by James P. Sterba, 435–41. Malden, MA: Blackwell, 1998.

Fleck, Ludwik. *Genesis and Development of a Scientific Fact*. Chicago: University of Chicago Press, 1981 [1935].

Foucault, Michel. *The History of Sexuality, Volume 1: An Intoduction*. New York: Vintage Books, 1978.

Fox, Renee. "Through the Lenses of Biology and Sociology: Organ Replacement." In *Debating Biology: Sociological Reflections on Health, Medicine, and Society*, edited by Simon J. Williams, Lynda Birke, and Gillian A. Bendelow, 235–44. London: Routledge, 2003.

Frank, Arthur. "Illness as Autobiographical Work: Dialogue as Narrative Destabilization." *Qualitative Sociology* 23 (2000): 135–56.

Frenkel-Brunswik, Else. "Intolerance of Ambiguity as an Emotional and Perceptual Personality Variable." *Journal of Personality* 18 (1949): 108–43.

Freud, Sigmund. *The Interpretation of Dreams*. Edited by A. A. Brill. New York: Modern Library, 1950 [1911].

———. *Three Essays on the Theory of Sexuality*. Translated by James Strachey. New York: Basic Books, 1962 [1905].

Fried, Barbara. "Boys Will Be Boys: The Language of Sex and Gender." In *Biological Woman: The Convenient Myth*, edited by Ruth Hubbard, Barbara Fried, and Mary Henifin, 47–70. Rochester, NY: Schenkman Books, 1982.

Friedman, Asia. "Unintended Consequences of the Feminist Sex/Gender Distinction." *Genders* 43 (2006). http://www.genders.org/g43/g43_friedman.html.

Fujimura, Joan. "Sex Genes: A Critical Sociomaterial Approach to the Politics and Molecular Genetics of Sex Determination." *Signs* 32, no. 1 (2006): 49–82.

Fuss, Diana. *Essentially Speaking: Feminism, Nature, and Difference*. New York: Routledge, 1989.

Gadamer, Hans-Georg. *Philosophical Hermeneutics*. Berkeley: University of California Press, 1976.

Gamson, Joshua. "Must Identity Movements Self-Destruct?: A Queer Dilemma." *Social Problems* 42, no. 3 (1995): 390–407.

Garfinkel, Harold. *Studies in Ethnomethodology*. Englewood Cliffs, NJ: Prentice Hall, 1967 [1964].

Gatens, Moira. *Imaginary Bodies: Ethics, Power, and Corporeality.* London: Routledge, 1996.

Gendernauts. DVD. Directed by Monika Treut. Hamburg, Ger.: Hyena Films, 1999.

Gerson, Judith. "There Is No Sex without Gender." *Sociological Forum* 20, no. 1 (2005): 179–81.

Gerson, Judith, and Kathy Peiss. "Boundaries, Negotiation, Consciousness: Reconceptualizing Gender Relations." *Social Problems* 32, no. 4 (1985): 317–29.

Gibson-Graham, J. K. *The End of Capitalism (as We Knew It).* Minneapolis: University of Minnesota Press, 2006 [1996].

Gilman, Charlotte Perkins. *Women and Economics: A Study of the Economic Relation between Men and Women as a Factor in Social Evolution.* Boston: Small, Maynard, and Co, 1898.

Gimlin, Debra L. *Body Work: Beauty and Self-Image in American Culture.* Berkeley: University of California Press, 2002.

Glaser, Barney, and Anselm Strauss. *The Discovery of Grounded Theory: Strategies for Qualitative Research.* Chicago: Aldine, 1967.

Goffman, Erving. *Behavior in Public Places.* New York: Free Press, 1963.

———. *Frame Analysis: An Essay on the Organization of Experience.* Boston: Northeastern University Press, 1986 [1974].

———. "Fun in Games." In *Encounters: Two Studies in the Sociology of Interaction,* 17–81. Indianapolis, IN: Bobbs-Merrill, 1961.

———. *Interaction Ritual: Essays on Face-to-Face Behavior.* New York: Pantheon Books, 1967.

———. "On Face-Work: An Analysis of Ritual Elements of Social Interaction." *Psychiatry* 18, no. 3 (1955): 213–31.

———. *The Presentation of Self in Everyday Life.* New York: Anchor, Doubleday, 1959.

Goleman, Daniel. *Vital Lies, Simple Truths.* New York: Simon & Schuster, 1985.

Gooding, David. "Cognition, Construction, and Culture: Visual Theories in the Sciences." *Journal of Culture and Cognition* 4 (2004): 551–93.

Goodwin, Charles. "Professional Vision." *American Anthropologist* 96, no. 3 (1994): 606–33.

Groopman, Jerome. *How Doctors Think.* Boston: Houghton Mifflin, 2007.

Grosz, Elizabeth. *Volatile Bodies: Toward a Corporeal Feminism.* Bloomington: University of Indiana Press, 1994.

Guterl, Fred. "The Truth about Gender." *Newsweek,* March 27, 2005.

Hale, C. Jacob. "Consuming the Living, Dis(Re)Membering the Dead in the Butch/FTM Borderlands." *GLQ* 4, no. 2 (1998): 311–48.

———. "Tracing a Ghostly Memory in My Throat: Reflections on FTM Feminist Voice and Agency." In *Men Doing Feminism,* edited by Tom Digby, 99–129. New York: Routledge, 1998.

Hamm, Jack. *Drawing the Head and Figure.* New York: Perigree, 1963.

Hammond, Lee. *Draw Real People!* Cincinnati, OH: North Light Books, 1996.

Hanson, Norwood Russell. *Patterns of Discovery: An Inquiry into the Conceptual Foundations of Science.* Cambridge: Cambridge University Press, 1965.

Haraway, Donna. "Situated Knowledges: The Science Question in Feminism and the Privilege of Partial Perspective." *Feminist Studies* 14, no. 3 (1988): 575–99.

Hawkesworth, Mary. "Confounding Gender." *Signs* 22, no. 3 (1997): 649–85.

Heilbrun, Carolyn. *Toward a Recognition of Androgyny.* New York: W.W. Norton, 1993 [1964].

Hochschild, Arlie. *The Managed Heart: The Commercialization of Human Feeling.* Berkeley: University of California Press, 1983.

Hoffman, Donald D., and Manish Singh. "Salience of Visual Parts." *Cognition* 63 (1997): 29–78.

Hopkins, Patrick. "How Feminism Made a Man out of Me: The Proper Subject of Feminism and the Problem of Men." In *Men Doing Feminism*, edited by Tom Digby, 33–56. New York: Routledge, 1998.

Howey, Noelle. *Dress Codes of Three Girlhoods—My Mother's, My Father's, and Mine.* New York: Picador, 2002.

Howson, Alexandra. *Embodying Gender.* London: Sage Publications, 2005.

Howson, Alexandra, and David Inglis. "The Body in Sociology: Tensions Inside and Outside Sociological Thought." *Sociological Review* 49, no. 3 (2001): 297–317.

Hubbard, Ruth, Barbara Fried, and Mary Henifin, eds. *Biological Woman: The Convenient Myth.* Rochester, NY: Schenkman Books, 1982.

Hutchinson, John, and Anthony Smith, eds. *Nationalism.* Oxford Readers. Oxford: Oxford University Press, 1995.

Jacob, Pierre, and Marc Jeannerod. *Ways of Seeing: The Scope and Limits of Visual Cognition.* Oxford: Oxford University Press, 2003.

Jaggar, Alison. *Feminist Politics and Human Nature.* Totowa, NJ: Rowman and Allenheld, 1983.

James, William. *A Pluralistic Universe: Hibbert Lectures at Manchester College on the Present Situation in Philosophy.* Rockville, MD: Arc Manor, 2008.

Jay, Martin. *Downcast Eyes: The Denigration of Vision in Twentieth Century French Thought.* Berkeley: University of California Press, 1993.

Jonas, Hans. *The Phenomenon of Life: Toward a Philosophical Biology.* Chicago: University of Chicago Press, 1982.

Jones, Edward E. *Interpersonal Perception.* New York: W. H. Freeman, 1990.

Jordanova, Ludmilla. "Natural Facts: A Historical Perspective on Science and Sexuality." In *Nature, Culture, and Gender*, edited by Carol MacCormack and Marilyn Strathern, 42–69. Cambridge: Cambridge University Press, 1980.

Jordan-Young, Rebecca. *Brain Storm: The Flaws in the Science of Sex Differences.* Cambridge, MA: Harvard University Press, 2010.

Joyce, Kelly. "Appealing Images: Magnetic Resonance Imaging and the Production of Authoritative Knowledge." *Social Studies of Science* 35 (2005): 437–62.

———. "From Numbers to Pictures: The Development of Magnetic Resonance Imaging and the Visual Turn in Medicine." *Science as Culture* 15 (2006): 1–22.

Kaiser, Anelis, Sven Haller, Sigrid Schmitz, and Cordula Nitsch. "On Sex/ Gender Related Similarities and Differences in fMRI Language Research." *Brain Research Reviews* 61, no. 2 (2009): 49–59.

Kessler, Suzanne. *Lessons from the Intersexed.* New Brunswick, NJ: Rutgers University Press, 1998.

Kessler, Suzanne, and Wendy McKenna. *Gender: An Ethnomethodological Approach.* Hoboken, NJ: John Wiley & Sons, 1978.

Killian, Caitlin. "The Other Side of the Veil: North African Women in France Respond to the Headscarf Affair." *Gender & Society* 17, no. 4 (2003): 567–90.

Kleege, Georgina. *Sight Unseen.* New Haven, CT: Yale University Press, 1999.

Köhler, Wolfgang. *Gestalt Psychology.* New York: Liveright Publishing Group, 1929.

Kuhn, Thomas. *The Structure of Scientific Revolutions.* Chicago: University of Chicago Press, 1996 [1962].

Kuusisto, Stephen. *Planet of the Blind.* New York: Dell Publishing, Bantam Doubleday Dell Publishing Group, 1998.

Lakoff, George, and Mark Johnson. *Metaphors We Live By.* Chicago: University of Chicago Press, 1980.

Lancaster, Roger N. *The Trouble with Nature: Sex and Science in Popular Culture.* Los Angeles: University of California Press, 2003.

Laqueur, Thomas. *Making Sex: Body and Gender from the Greeks to Freud.* Cambridge, MA: Harvard University Press, 1990.

Largey, Gale Peter, and Watson, David Rodney. "The Sociology of Odors." *American Journal of Sociology* 7, no. 6 (1972): 1021–34.

Lawless, Harry. "Olfactory Psychophysics." In *Tasting and Smelling,* edited by Gary K. Beauchamp and Linda Bartoshuk, 125–74. San Diego, CA: Academic Press, 1997.

Leach, Edmund. *Culture and Communication: The Logic by Which Symbols Are Connected. An Introduction to the Use of Structuralist Analysis in Social Anthropology.* Cambridge: Cambridge University Press, 1976.

Lescroart, Mark D., Irving Biederman, Xiaomin Yue, and Jules Davidoff. "A Cross-Cultural Study of the Representation of Shape: Sensitivity to Generalized Cone Dimensions." *Visual Cognition* 18, no. 1 (2010): 50–66.

Levine, Jerome M., and Gardner Murphy. "The Learning and Forgetting of Controversial Material." In *Readings in Social Psychology,* edited by Eleanor E. Macoby, Theodore M. Newcomb, and Eugene L. Hartley, 94–101. New York: Henry Holt, 1958.

Lindisfarne, Nancy. "Starting from Below: Fieldwork, Gender, and Imperialism Now." *Critique of Anthropology* 22, no. 4 (2002): 403–23.

Lorber, Judith. *Paradoxes of Gender.* New Haven, CT: Yale University Press, 1994.

Lorber, Judith, and Lisa Jean Moore. *Gendered Bodies, Feminist Perspectives*. Los Angeles: Roxbury, 2007.

Lowe, Donald. *History of Bourgeois Perception*. Chicago: University of Chicago Press, 1982.

Lowe, Marian. "Social Bodies: The Interaction of Culture and Women's Biology." In *Biological Woman: The Convenient Myth*, edited by Ruth Hubbard, Barbara Fried, and Mary Henifin, 91–116. Rochester, NY: Schenkman Books, 1982.

Lucal, Betsy. "What It Means to Be Gendered Me: Life on the Boundaries of a Dichotomous Gender System." *Gender and Society* 13, no. 6 (1999): 781–89.

Lucy, John. *Grammatical Categories and Cognition: A Case Study of the Linguistic Relativity Hypothesis*. Cambridge: Cambridge University Press, 1992.

Lueptow, Lloyd, Lori Garovich-Szabo, and Margaret Lueptow. "Social Change and the Persistence of Sex Typing: 1974–1997." *Social Forces* 80, no. 1 (2001): 1–36.

Malinowski, Bronislaw. *The Sexual Life of Savages in North Western Melanesia*. New York: Halcyon House, 1929.

Mannheim, Karl. *Ideology and Utopia: An Introduction to the Sociology of Knowledge*. New York: Harvest, 1936.

Marshall, Gül Aldikaçti. "Ideology, Progress, and Dialogue: A Comparison of Feminist and Islamist Women's Approaches to the Issues of Head Covering and Work in Turkey." *Gender & Society* 19, no. 1 (2005): 104–20.

Martin, Emily. "The Egg and the Sperm: How Science Has Constructed a Romance Based on Stereotypical Male-Female Roles." *Signs* 16, no. 3 (1991): 485–501.

Martin, Karin. "Becoming a Gendered Body: Practices of Preschools." *American Sociological Review* 63, no. 4 (1998): 494–511.

Marx, Karl. *The Marx-Engels Reader*. 2nd ed. Edited by R. C. Tucker. New York: W.W. Norton, 1978.

Matthen, Mohan. *Seeing, Doing, and Knowing: A Philosophical Theory of Sense Perception*. Oxford: Clarendon Press, 2005.

Maturana, Humberto, and Francisco Varela. *The Tree of Knowledge: The Biological Roots of Human Understanding*. Boston: Shambhala Publications, 1987.

McMinn, Robert Matthew Hay, Ralph T. Hutchings, and Bari M. Logan. *Picture Tests in Human Anatomy*. Chicago: Year Book Medical Publishers, 1986.

Meadows, Robin. "Sex and the Spotted Hyena" *Smithsonian Zoogoer* 24, no. 3 (1995). http://nationalzoo.si.edu/Publications/ZooGoer/1995/3/sexand thespottedhyena.cfm.

Meissner, Christian, and John Brigham. "Thirty Years of Investigating the Own-Race Bias in Memory for Faces: A Meta-Analytic Review." *Psychology, Public Policy, & Law* 7 (2001): 3–35.

Mello-Thoms, Claudia, Calvin F. Nodine, and Harold L. Kundel. "What Attracts the Eye to the Location of Missed and Reported Breast Cancers?" *ETRA* (2002): 111–17.

Mendola, Janine. "Contextual Shape Processing in Human Visual Cortex:

Beginning to Fill-In the Blanks." In *Filling In: From Perceptual Completion to Cortical Reorganization*, edited by Luiz Pessoa and Peter De Weerd, 38–58. Oxford: Oxford University Press, 2003.

Merleau-Ponty, Maurice. *Phenomenology of Perception*. London: Routledge & Kegan Paul, 1962 [1945].

Mernissi, Fatima. *Women and Islam: An Historical and Theological Enquiry*. Translated by Mary Jo Lokeland. Oxford: Basil Blackwell, 1991.

Messner, Michael. *Taking the Field: Women, Men, and Sports*. Minneapolis: University of Minnesota Press, 2002.

Meyerowitz, Joanne. *How Sex Changed: A History of Transsexuality in the United States*. Cambridge, MA: Harvard University Press, 2002.

Michalko, Rod. *The Mystery of the Eye and the Shadow of Blindness*. Toronto: University of Toronto Press, 1998.

Millett, Kate. "Sexual Politics: A Manifesto for Revolution." In *Radical Feminism*, edited by Anne Koedt, Ellen Levine, and Anita Rapone, 365–67. New York: Quadrangle Books, 1973.

Mills, Charles. "White Ignorance." In *Agnotology: The Making and Unmaking of Ignorance*, edited by Robert Proctor and Londa Schiebinger, 230–49. Stanford, CA: Stanford University Press, 2008.

Mills, C. Wright. *People, Power, and Politics: The Collected Essays of C. Wright Mills*. New York: Ballantine Books, 1963.

Moi, Toril. *What Is a Woman? And Other Essays*. Oxford: Oxford University Press, 1999.

Mol, Annemarie. *The Body Multiple: Ontology in Medical Practice*. Durham, NC: Duke University Press, 2002.

Money, John, and Anke Ehrhardt. *Man and Woman, Boy and Girl: Differentiation and Dimorphism of Gender Identity from Conception to Maturity*. Baltimore, MD: Johns Hopkins University Press, 1972.

Moore, Lisa Jean. *Sperm Counts: Overcome by Man's Most Precious Fluid*. New York: New York University Press, 2007.

Moore, Lisa Jean, and Adele E. Clarke. "Clitoral Conventions and Transgressions: Graphic Representations in Anatomy Texts, c. 1900–1991." *Feminist Studies* 21, no. 2 (1995): 255–301.

Morgan, David, and Michael Schwalbe. "Mind and Self in Society: Linking Social Structure and Social Cognition." *Social Psychology Quarterly* 53, no. 2 (1990): 148–64.

Mullaney, Jamie. "Making it 'Count': Mental Weighing and Identity Attribution." *Symbolic Interaction* 22, no. 3 (1999): 269–83.

Nelkin, Dorothy, and M. Susan Lindee. *The DNA Mystique: The Gene as a Cultural Icon*. Ann Arbor: University of Michigan Press, 2004.

Nicholson, Linda. "Interpreting Gender." *Signs* 20, no. 1 (1994): 79–105.

Nisbett, Richard, and Takahiko Masuda. "Culture and Point of View." *Proceedings of the National Academy of Sciences of the United States of America* 100, no. 19 (2003): 11163–70.

Obasogie, Osagie K. "Do Blind People See Race? Social, Legal, and Theoretical Considerations." *Law & Society Review* 44, nos. 3/4 (2010): 585–616.

Ortner, Sherry. "Is Male to Female as Nature Is to Culture?" In *Woman, Culture, and Society*, edited by Michelle Rosaldo and Louise Lamphere, 67–88. Stanford, CA: Stanford University Press, 1974.

Oudshoorn, Nelly. *Beyond the Natural Body: An Archaeology of Sex Hormones.* London: Routledge, 1994.

Phelen, Shane. *Getting Specific: Postmodern Lesbian Politics.* Minneapolis: University of Minnesota Press, 1994.

Pike, Kenneth, *Language in Relation to a Unified Theory of the Structure of Human Behavior*, 2nd ed. The Hague, Neth.: Mouton, 1967.

Powers, Peter, Joyce Andriks, and Elizabeth Loftus. "The Eyewitness Accounts of Males and Females." *Journal of Applied Psychology* 64 (1979): 339–47.

Preves, Sharon E. *Intersex and Identity: The Contested Self.* New Brunswick, NJ: Rutgers University Press, 2003.

Proctor, Robert N., and Londa Schiebinger, eds. *Agnotology: The Making and Unmaking of Ignorance.* Stanford, CA: Stanford University Press, 2008.

Prosser, Jay. *Second Skins: The Body Narratives of Transsexuality.* New York: Columbia University Press, 1998.

Pylyshyn, Zenon W. *Seeing and Visualizing: It's Not What You Think.* Cambridge, MA: MIT Press, 2003.

Raymond, Janice. "The Illusion of Androgyny." *Quest* (Summer 1975): 57–66.

Richardson, Sarah. "Sexes, Species, and Genomes: Why Males and Females are not like Humans and Chimpanzees." *Biology and Philosophy* 25, no. 5 (2010): 823–41.

Rosaldo, Michelle Zimbalist, and Louise Lamphere. Introduction to *Woman, Culture, and Society*, edited by Michelle Rosaldo and Louise Lamphere, 1–15. Stanford, CA: Stanford University Press, 1974.

Rubin, Edgar. *Visuell wahrgenommene Figuren.* Copenhagen: Gyldendal, 1921 [1915].

Rubin, Gayle. "The Traffic in Women: Notes on the 'Political Economy' of Sex." In *Toward an Anthropology of Women*, edited by Rayna Reiter, 157–210. New York: Monthly Review Press, 1975.

Rupp, Leila J., and Verta Taylor. *Drag Queens at the 801 Cabaret.* Chicago: University of Chicago Press, 2003.

Saussure, Ferdinand de. *A Course in General Linguistics.* Peru, IL: Open Court Publishing, 1986.

Schiebinger, Londa. *Nature's Body: Gender in the Making of Modern Science.* Boston: Beacon Press, 1993.

Schilt, Kristen. *Just One of the Guys: Transgender Men and the Persistence of Gender Inequality.* Chicago: University of Chicago Press, 2010.

Schutz, Alfred. "Making Music Together: A Study in Social Relationship." *Social Research* 18 (1951): 76–97.

———. *The Phenomenology of the Social World*. Evanston, IL: Northwestern University Press, 1967 [1932].

Schutz, Alfred, and Thomas Luckmann. *The Structures of the Life World*. Evanston, IL: Northwestern University Press, 1973.

Scott, Joan. "The Evidence of Experience." *Critical Inquiry* 17 (1991): 773–97.

Seidman, Steven. Introduction to *Queer Theory/Sociology*, edited by Steven Seidman, 1–30. Cambridge: Blackwell, 1996.

Shibutani, Tamotsu. "Reference Groups and Social Control." In *Human Behavior and Social Processes*, edited by Arnold Rose, 128–45. Boston: Houghton Mifflin, 1962.

———. "Reference Groups as Perspectives." *American Journal of Sociology* 60 (1955): 562–69.

Shildrick, Margaret. *Leaky Bodies and Boundaries: Feminism, Postmodernism, and (Bio)ethics*. New York: Routledge, 1997.

Shilling, Chris. *The Body and Social Theory*. 2nd ed. London: Sage Publications, 2003.

Simmel, Georg. "Sociology of the Senses: Visual Interaction." In *Introduction to the Science of Sociology*, edited by Robert Park and Ernest Burgess, 356–61. New York: Greenwood Press, 1924 [1908].

Simpson, Ruth. "The Germ Culture. Metaphor, Modernity, and Epidemic Disease." PhD diss., Department of Sociology, Rutgers University, 1996.

Smithson, Michael. "Ignorance and Science: Dilemmas, Perspectives, and Process." *Science Communication* 15, no. 2 (1993): 133–56.

———. *Ignorance and Uncertainty: Emerging Paradigms*. New York: Springer-Verlag, 1989.

Snow, David, and Leon Anderson. "Identity Work among the Homeless: The Verbal Construction and Avowal of Personal Identities." *American Journal of Sociology* 92 (1987): 1337–71.

Society for the Study of Manga Techniques. *How to Draw Manga Bodies and Anatomy*. Tokyo: Graphic-sha, 1996.

Spivak, Gayatri Chakravorty. *The Postcolonial Critic: Interviews, Strategies, Dialogues*. New York: Routledge, 1990.

Star, Susan Leigh. "The Sociology of the Invisible: The Primacy of Work in the Writings of Anselm Strauss." In *Social Organization and Social Process: Essays in Honor of Anselm Strauss*, edited by David Maines, 265–382. Piscataway, NJ: Aldine Transaction, 1991.

Star, Susan Leigh, and Anselm Strauss. "Layers of Silence, Arenas of Voice." *Computer Supported Cooperative Work* 8 (1999): 9–30.

Steffensen, Margaret, Chitra Joag-Dev, and Richard C. Anderson. "A Cross-Cultural Perspective on Reading Comprehension." *Reading Research Quarterly* 15, no. 1 (1979): 10–29.

Stein, Arlene. "The Incredible Shrinking Lesbian World and Other Queer Conundra." *Sexualities* 13, no. 1 (2010): 1–12.

Stein, Arlene, and Ken Plummer. "'I Can't Even Think Straight': 'Queer' Theory and the Missing Sexual Revolution in Sociology." *Sociological Theory* 12 (1994): 178–87.

Stimpson, Catherine. "The Androgyne and the Homosexual." *Women's Studies* 2, no. 2 (1974): 237–47.

Stocking, S. Holly, and Lisa W. Holstein. "Constructing and Reconstructing Scientific Ignorance." *Knowledge* 15 (1993): 186–210.

Strauss, Anselm. *Qualitative Analysis for Social Scientists*. Cambridge: Cambridge University Press, 1987.

Stryker, Susan. "(De)Subjugated Knowledges: An Introduction to Transgender Studies." In *The Transgender Studies Reader*, edited by Susan Stryker and Stephen Whittle, 1–17. New York: Routledge, 2006.

Tannen, Deborah. *Framing in Discourse*. New York: Oxford University Press, 1993.

Tavris, Carol. *The Mismeasure of Woman*. New York: Touchstone, 1992.

Taylor, Gary. *Castration: An Abbreviated History of Western Manhood*. New York: Taylor and Francis, 2000.

Taylor, Mark. "What Derrida Really Meant." *New York Times*, October 14, 2004, A29.

Taylor, Shelley E., Letitia Anne Peplau, and David O. Sears. *Social Psychology*, 10th ed. Englewood Cliffs, NJ: Prentice Hall, 2000.

Thomas, William I. *The Unadjusted Girl: With Cases and Standpoint for Behavior Analysis*. Montclair, NJ: Patterson Smith, 1969 [1923].

Trubetzkoy, Nikolai. *Principles of Phonology*. Berkeley: University of California Press, 1969 [1939].

Tuan, Yi-Fu. *Segmented Worlds and Self*. Minneapolis: University of Minnesota Press, 1982.

———. "Sight and Pictures." *Geographical Review* 69, no. 4 (1979): 413–22.

Turner, Bryan. *The Body and Society*. Oxford: Blackwell, 1984.

———. *Regulating Bodies: Essays in Medical Sociology*. London: Routledge, 1992.

Udry, Richard. "Biological Limits of Gender Construction." *American Sociological Review* 65, no. 3 (2000): 443–57.

van der Heijden, A. H. C. *Attention in Vision: Perception, Communication, and Action*. New York: Taylor and Francis, 2004.

Van Gennep, Arnold. *The Rites of Passage*. Chicago: University of Chicago Press, 1909 [1960].

Vannini, Phillip, Dennis Waskul, and Simon Gottschalk. *The Senses in Self, Society, and Culture: A Sociology of the Senses*. New York: Routledge, 2011.

Vincent, Nora. *Self-Made Man: One Woman's Journey into Manhood and Back*. New York: Penguin, 2006.

Wakefield, Claire E., Judi Homewood, and Alan Taylor. "Cognitive Compensations for Blindness in Children: An Investigation Using Odour Naming." *Perception* 33 (2004): 429–42.

Wang, Jun, Brett A. Clementz, and Andreas Keil. "The Neural Correlates of

Feature-Based Selective Attention When Viewing Spatially and Temporally Overlapping Images." *Neuropsychologia* 45, no. 7 (2007): 1393–99.

Waskul, Dennis, and Phillip Vannini. "Smell, Odor, and Somatic Work: Sense-Making and Sensory Management." *Social Psychology Quarterly* 71, no. 1 (2008): 53–71.

Weber, Max. "Objectivity in Social Science and Social Policy." In *The Methodology of the Social Sciences*, edited and translated by Edward A. Shils and Harry A. Finch, 49–112. New York: Free Press, 1949 [1904].

Weiss, Rick. "Intricate Toiling Found in Nooks of DNA Once Believed to Stand Idle." *Washington Post*, June 14, 2007.

West, Candace, and Don H. Zimmerman. "Doing Gender." *Gender & Society* 1, no. 2 (1987): 125–51.

Whorf, Benjamin Lee. "Science and Linguistics." In *Language, Thought, and Reality*, edited by John B. Carroll, 207–19. Cambridge, MA: MIT Press, 1956 [1940].

Williams, Richard. "Introduction: Challenges to the Homogenization of 'African-American.'" *Sociological Forum* 10 (1995): 535–46.

Williams, Simon J., and Gillian Bendelow. *The Lived Body: Sociological Themes, Embodied Issues.* Oxford: Taylor and Francis, 1998.

Wittig, Monique. "One Is Not Born a Woman." *Feminist Issues* 1, no. 2 (1981): 47–54.

Young, Iris Marion. *On Female Bodily Experience: "Throwing Like a Girl" and Other Essays.* New York: Oxford University Press, 2005.

Young, Rebecca, and Evan Balaban. "Psychoneuroindoctrinology." *Nature* 443, no. 12 (2006): 634.

Zernike, Kate. "Sizing Up America: Signs of Expansion from Head to Toe." *New York Times*, March 1, 2004.

Zerubavel, Eviatar. *The Elephant in the Room: Silence and Denial in Everyday Life.* New York: Oxford University Press, 2006.

———. *The Fine Line: Making Distinctions in Everyday Life.* New York: Free Press, 1991.

———. "Generally Speaking: The Logic and Mechanics of Social Pattern Analysis." *Sociological Forum* 22, no. 2 (2007): 1–15.

———. *Hidden Rhythms: Schedules and Calendars in Social Life.* Berkeley: University of California Press, 1981.

———. "If Simmel Were a Fieldworker: On Formal Sociological Theory and Analytic Field Research." *Symbolic Interaction* 3, no. 2 (1980): 25–34.

———. "Presidential Race." Editorial. *Philadelphia Inquirer*, March 23, 2008.

———. *Social Mindscapes: An Invitation to Cognitive Sociology.* Cambridge, MA: Harvard University Press, 1997.

———. *Terra Cognita: The Mental Discovery of America.* New Brunswick, NJ: Transaction Publishers, 2003 [1992].

Index

Adam's apple, 59, 68, 77
ambiguity, 26, 44; ignored, 2, 26,
    44, 47, 74; sex, 43, 73, 100–102,
    147
Anderson, Benedict, 138
androcentrism, 119–20
appearance, 68–70
Armstrong, David, 161
attention, 148; collective, 20; to
    difference, 2–3, 11, 36, 43–45,
    77–80, 85, 136–38; scholarly,
    155; selective, 13, 22–25, 85,
    136, 138

babies, 115–16
background, 14; relegation to, 14,
    23, 33, 45, 88, 90, 111; visibil-
    ity of, 15, 90, 95, 110–11, 165
Bagby, James, 16
Balaban, Evan, 52, 180n57
balance, of male and female
    features, 91
Barkalow, Carol, 82, 116
Baron-Cohen, Simon, 132, 186n40
Becker, Howard, 5
Bem, Sandra, 28, 176n85
Berger, Peter, 19, 45
binary classification, 3, 35
biological explanations for neces-
    sity of sex attribution, 44
Birdwhistell, Raymond, 4
Blackless, Melanie, 52, 57, 180n57
blind respondents, 7–8, 41, 55,
    64–73, 99–109, 136–37, 157;
    and lack of polarization, 101–2;
    and ocularcentrism, 70–71;

and sex cues, 64–69; and sex
    similarities, 106–8; suspicious
    of social research, 11, 163–64;
    temporality of blind percep-
    tion, 99–100
blind spots, 89, 144
body, social construction of,
    13–14, 33, 51–52, 56–57,
    135–36
body parts: sex-ambiguous,
    74, 95–99, 106–7, 116–18;
    sex-marked and unmarked,
    80; sex-specificity of, 11, 53,
    59–63, 104–5. See also specific
    body parts
body size, and gender, 39, 108–9,
    116–18
Bourdieu, Pierre, 17, 24–25, 28
brain, sex differences in, 132–33.
    See also neuroscience
breasts, 77, 89, 117, 129
Brekhus, Wayne, 151, 153, 155
Brizendine, Louann, 132, 186n40
Broadbent, Donald, 13, 30
Bruner, Jerome S., 21
Butler, Judith, 6, 12, 41, 46, 54, 74,
    142, 169n28
buttocks, 118

Casper, Monica, 13, 143
Cerulo, Karen, 13, 24, 170n33,
    175n66
Chapkis, Wendy, 156
Child, Arthur, 19
children, 34–37, 88, 115–16
clothing, 1, 39, 65, 81